CW00403342

Dear Islandman

compiled by

R. M. Lockley

Edited by Ann Mark
Sketches by Doris Lockley

GOMER

First Impression—June 1996

ISBN 1 85902 296 0

Printed in Wales at
Gomer Press, Llandysul, Dyfed

Contents

Foreword

This is a selection of letters exchanged between Ronald Lockley and his fiancée, Doris Shellard, during the year before their marriage in 1928. During that time, Ronald Lockley lived on the Welsh island of Skokholm, restoring its derelict farmhouse and preparing a living for himself and his future wife.

Some excerpts from Ronald Lockley's diaries and letters from other members of their families also appear.

I would like to thank my sister-in-law Jess Graves for her kind help with typing, my husband for his patience and criticism, and David Saunders of The Dyfed Wildlife Trust for his assistance. I must also congratulate my father, who, for all his life, has been such an assiduous diarist and preserver of letters.

A.M.

Introduction

The idea of publishing the letters exchanged by my parents during the time they were engaged had long been in my father's mind. A few years ago he was asked to come back to Wales to make a film for television about his early life, entitled *The Islandman*. The making of this inspired Father to get down to reassembling the letters into some sort of order which would make an acceptable book. This was no easy task, for many were undated, indecipherable from being immersed in sea water, written in pencil, thrust into gardening bags or simply lost! Fortunately Father has always kept a diary, so he has been able to draw on these for missing information.

Today, as Father will be the first to tell you, extreme old age has few compensations, except an excuse that the memory is willing to supply the information, but pen and typewriter are not. He might also add that his only daughter will, under his instruction, carry out any necessary paper work. Briefly, this is how I came to write this introduction. The hard work had all been done because the manuscript had reached the typescript stage, which made cutting and editing much easier. Father tells me his children have always been his severest critics; we poke fun at him for his rather pedantic flowery style and author's license, and though we respect him for his very great ability, we know too much! This has been a fascinating exercise for me, because, although this story has been told before in his earliest books, this version is rather special, the most sincere and honest, spoken from the heart before worldly matters and sophistication had laid a hand upon his experience.

The scene opens in the village of St Mellons, today almost joined to the city of Cardiff by urban sprawl, wider roads dotted with petrol pumps and commuter traffic. In 1927 it was a quiet little hamlet, where my grandparents lived on an attractive estate known as Tŷ'r Bont (The House by the Bridge), containing about a dozen acres of fields and woodland bordering the Rhymney River which separates the Welsh shire of Glamorgan from what was then the English shire of Monmouth (now known as Gwent).

Here my grandfather, Harry Shellard (known as 'Papa' to his

daughters, 'Pop Shell'd' to the younger set, and always 'Mr. S.' to my father), lived with his wife Edith Shellard ('Mama' and 'Mrs. S.'). My mother, their younger daughter Doris Shellard (born 1893 and always referred to as 'Do', pronounced doe), lived with them to assist with the smallholding and large kitchen garden. The elder daughter Violet Thomas (Vi) had been married for some while, and lived on a farm in North Pembrokeshire called Rhyd-y-gath (Cat's Ford). She had met her husband Martin Thomas at Cardiff University. They had two children, Mary and Brian.

My mother had attended art school in London but she never completed the course; she hated the disciplines the lessons put on her work, and begged to come home to the country. After this her father arranged for a colleague of his, the flamboyant Cardiff artist Edgar Thomas, to teach her privately; she blossomed under his tutelage. Grandpa Shellard was the complete extrovert; artistic, eccentric, gregarious and well known in Cardiff for his dental practice. He was reputed to be ahead of his time in the modelling of natural looking false teeth! He was also a successful amateur artist, recognized locally for his landscapes and portraits in oils. The waiting room at his surgery in Cardiff High Street was full of lovely antique furniture, paintings and objets d'art—a joy to his patients! Going to a sale or an exhibition with Grandpa was a real education, for he would stand in front of some great master and enthuse (or otherwise) on colour and technique in such an infectious way. Grandmama Shellard, perhaps fortunately for the family budget, was as careful with money as her husband was careless, totally conventional, loved shopping and pretty clothes and kept an immaculate household, so much so that she quite put her daughters off domesticity!

My paternal Grandmother Emily Lockley, had run a private school in Whitchurch, Cardiff though she was retired by the time the letters were written. She had brought up a large family almost single handed. Her husband, Harry Lockley, who lived and worked in London, only paid infrequent visits, due to his tendency to gamble the already scarce funds in the Lockley household! Grannie Lockley was religious, conventional, autocratic, very conscious of her place in life, almost to the point of snobbishness. There were four daughters, and two sons, the eldest Enid (housekeeping for Ronald), Kenneth (working for an export firm in Burma), Kathleen (teacher and international lacrosse player), Aline (also teaching) and the youngest Marjorie. My father, Ronald Mathias Lockley (born 8th November 1903) was the fifth child and spoiled darling of the family. Perhaps because of a year's convalescence after acute appendicitis at the age of thirteen, he stayed at home longer than his sisters, who went away to boarding school.

On leaving Cardiff High School, Father had taken up a small holding near Whitchurch. In 1922, he removed to ten acres of land a few fields upriver from Tŷ'r-Bont, on which his mother had built a small bungalow for him to begin a poultry farm. In the same year Enid resigned from the staff of her mother's school, and took the post of unpaid housekeeper for her very beloved younger brother. They did not make a fortune but formed an efficient and happy partnership there for five years.

Inevitably the Lockleys and the Shellards, having many interests in common, became friends. Tŷ'r-Bont had a fine tennis court and all the Lockleys were keen tennis players so Pop Shellard was in his element, for he loved to have hordes of young people around who would join with him in any kind of sport, as well as hikes and picnics in the Black Mountains. My mother was introduced to the game of lacrosse by the Lockley sisters, and my father played hockey.

The friendship of my parents ripened slowly during those five years as near neighbours. Both of them were passionately interested in natural history. Father had become an expert on birds, from studying them and taking notes since childhood, but more especially through Harry Shellard. Both men liked to escape into the wilder country on camping trips. In Harry's car they ranged westward to the farthest islands of the Pembrokeshire coast. During Whitsun 1927 they visited the uninhabited island of Skokholm, one hundred hectares, its farm buildings abandoned and roofless, its Norman-founded dwelling house tumbling down. Because it had no safe harbour no one lived there any more. Both men were wildly excited by all they saw and the beauty of this island. It was the sort of place my father had dreamed of owning for years. On making enquiries they discovered Skokholm could be leased at a low rent from the hereditary landlord who lived in Dale Castle on the mainland opposite. After some ticklish negotiations Father found himself tenant of the island for twenty-one years at £25-0-0 per annum.

When he returned in triumph to his farm, and told Do of his good fortune, she unaccountably burst into tears. When he asked her the reason, she said she had always longed to live on a remote and beautiful island. Whereupon—he says, being the perfect gentleman—he took pity on her, and said she could come along and help to develop it. She immediately dried her eyes and accepted the offer! He was obliged to dampen her ardour by saying she could not come for at least a year for there was no roof on the island house. That night, tossing in his bed, he realised he had proposed marriage. Next day Father accused her of falling in love with an island rather than the new tenant. My mother replied: 'It is all yours and Papa's fault for painting such a marvellous picture of all the island's attractions. Please remember I have not seen it myself. The least you could do is to take the future chatelaine to inspect it'.

But both believed they were in love now, with the island and each other. His diary of July 12th 1927, has but one sentence: 'This day Doris and I discovered our love for each other.' They spent the following day climbing in the lovely Brecon Beacons. There are no more entries in the diary until 5th August, when he records the ups and downs of the final negotiations to secure the successful lease of Skokholm. On 6th August quite a cavalcade of both families assembled at Martinshaven, the little mainland harbour nearest to Skokholm. Grannie Lockley, Pop Shellard, Enid, Do and her uncle. Father had arranged to take them out to see the island on a sailing boat, *The Foxtrot*, manned by the fisherman who had ferried Father and Harry out on their previous visit. It was a fine day and they caught a pollack on the way over. On arrival the womenfolk were horrified by the state of the house except Do, who set about cleaning up an old fisherman's frying pan of its layers of grease and gulls' eggs, in which to cook the fish. Revived by this meal, eaten outside with a grand view of the seacoast and surrounding islands, even Grannie Lockley decided to spend the night; she was made as comfortable as possible in the lighthouse store-shed near the island landing stage. The others cat-napped in the heather and wandered about most of the night enjoying the nocturnal arrival of thousands of shearwaters and storm petrels. The next day with a rising wind from the south, the fishermen were anxious to return. There were some tense moments when everyone had to leap into the boat at the right moment as the southerly waves dashed against the landing steps. The visitors were troubled with seasickness as the *Foxtrot,* true to her name, danced wildly back to Martinshaven.

This is the background of the letters exchanged between the engaged couple, who had agreed to be married one year after discovering their love on July 12th, 1927. Neither wavered in their determination to live their dreams on Skokholm Island, although everyone else tried to dissuade them from embarking on this Robinson Crusoe existence. Both incurable romantics, they believed a living could be made off the land, and nothing would change their minds. The time of engagement was particularly difficult for my mother, for there was tension at home, pressure from both sides of the family to abandon this island idea, as well as a certain amount of disapproval from both mothers. In a more permissive society, it is likely that they would not have endured living apart so long. My mother often declared that she and father were born sixty years too soon!

And yet, without the enforced separation, there would have been a different story and we might never have had this collection of love-letters. As it is, we can share the tale of the Islandman and his sweetheart, my father and mother, and their love for the beautiful island of Skokholm.

Doris Lockley née Shellard

Ronald Lockley

Part 1

July to October 1927

Engagement and Departure

Chaffinches

Ronald's diary, 12 July, 1927:

This day Doris and I discovered our love for each other.

Letter to Doris from Ronald's mother:

Hurlingham, London
1 August, 1927

My dearest Doris,

As I am not able to give you a good big hug, I can only write and tell you how pleased we all are that you and Ron love each other.

There is nothing like true love in the whole world. It makes straight many a rugged road, and beautifies and purifies life at all times. God bless and keep you both is my true prayer.

I am coming down to Ron's farm in less than a fortnight's time, and shall be able to have a long talk over everything, and give you in person the love that I send with this letter. All my family send their love with mine.

Yours affectionately,
Emilie Lockley

P.S. I suppose Ron must have his little joke—he writes quite solemnly about living on a desert island!

Letter to Doris from her sister, Vi:

Rhydygath, Llanfyrnach, Pembs
30 July

Dearest Do,

Mama's letter this morning has put my mind all in a dither, so that I am wandering inefficiently about, not knowing whether I have saucepans or loaves in my hands, or which it is I want. Although I am thinking you and Ronald don't seem yet to have thought enough to say anything wise. But straightway I was awfully glad and happy that I had to let out my feelings on the nearest suitable object, which was young Brian, and in my joy, give him a big hug.

Loving Ron, and Ron you, you will be mostly, always perhaps, tremendously happy. I'm terribly happy for you, for I think you are well suited to each other, and that is the most important thing—but, if you will believe a woman buried in the heart of these Welsh hills, the other items are very nice trimmings!

Mama's letter as far as this big event is concerned is most unsatisfactory. She simply writes that Ron has asked you to marry him, that you seem fond of each other and, although it is a great surprise to her, she thinks you may well be suited to each other. Now, is that enough information for a loving sister? Do you think of being married this year, next year, or sometime? Can you come, if only for a weekend, and tell me all? Down here I feel thoroughly away from everything. . .

I am sorry this won't be a decent long letter. We are having the first real busy day threshing the oats. The maid has been out all day, so I have had my hands full. I must now finish this letter, put the cream in the can, tie and label it, and drop a line to Mama all in twenty minutes. Then bath and feed Brian, and be out in the hayguard as soon as poss. to lead the horse working the straw pitcher.

How did your hay crop turn out? And how does your mare, Bright, behave?

Martin sends his love and says something to the effect that 'he must ask me what I thought of marriage before he congratulated you!' Then he added that Ron seemed to him to be one of the very best . . . So there you are. Do write soon all that you can.

Fondest love,

Vi

Letter to Doris from Dorothy Davies, an old and loving friend of both Vi and Do, and a teacher at Llandovery school:

Llandovery
August 1927

My darling Do,

Because I know it is the most wonderful thing in the world I am so very glad for you. Your letter had a wonderful pulse of life in it, and made me sure how utterly happy you were. Can you tell Ron from me that he is a very lucky young man? I met him once, and liked him awfully . . .

The fairies blessed you with eternal youth when you were born, I always *thought* they had, and now I *know* it's true. And they'll never take back their gift because you are going to live as you have always lived, so near the things they love, flowers and birds and wild creatures, under the sun and moon and stars. Why it's all a most wonderful dream to think of you two planning to live happily on a deserted island! Yes, almost too unreal. But please write and tell me more about your island, to help my present faith in your dream and its accomplishment. It's very hard to picture it in my situation at the moment—end of term and harassed pupils rushing into exams. I am terribly busy and utterly tired . . . I wish you happiness always. Goodnight my dear.

Yours ever lovingly,
Dorothy

Letter to Doris from Vi, after some marriage plans were announced:

Llanfyrnach
September

My dear Do,

Thank you for your letter. Of course it's the most gorgeous idea imaginable. Yet I can understand the wise shaking their heads over it. Mama will be dead against it. Doesn't she believe that I am hopelessly out of everything here? You'll be worse situated, except that you'll have peace and quiet on your lonely island—no tiresome hawkers and tramps knocking at your door. I can understand your and Ron's enthusiasm for your plan. I wonder if the house is derelict, where you will live—at first? You know our bitter experience here with masons and carpenters, and everywhere in the country it's the same difficulty, so it's certain you won't get them to help on an island unless you double their wages?

Martin says that if the owner is asking one thousand pounds for the island, he'll probably take much less—it seems to be the rule here that you must bargain for hours over any purchase—even a pig for bacon—and begin by asking double what you expect to get. Martin also wants to know if R. wants a partner—a tactless offer I say, at the moment, when the greatest desire of you two is a paradise *a deux.*

Can you harvest chinchillas whatever the weather? I think we are almost bankrupt here by the inability to harvest the crops which have at last been induced to grow on these rainwashed hills.

The constant rain is enough to make you weep. We've had wet days ever since we cut the first hay, it's now been turned three times, and got wet each time, maybe we'll get it in today. . .

Liz and I help when we aren't getting meals—washing is a nightmare . . .

Let me hear more of your island plans, I'd wish to hear whether they mature or not!

Best of love,
Vi

Ronald's diary, 12 August, 1927:

. . . excited and worried over great changes imminent, selling the poultry farm and going to live on Skokholm. Decided to sell farm stock and business as going concern for 500 pounds to tenant L . . . and I am to go down to the island to see if chinchilla farming is possible by getting rid of the wild rabbits before spring breeding—Mr. S. to be my partner in this enterprise of course . . . tension and friction in both families.

Ronald's diary, 11 October, 1927:

. . . called at Tyr Bont to say goodbye to Do . . . went off with piles of fruit for myself and my hosts the Codd family of Trehill and Hook Farms near Martynshaven . . .

First letter from Doris:

Tyr Bont
12 October

Dearest Ron,

I hope you don't expect a diary of today because I've done nothing—absolutely. We all felt a bit dazed—at least I did—to think that you had said goodbye, and started off on the island adventure so casually like that! I don't want to realise it either, or if I do I'll just fling down everything, hang convention and rush after you.

After you had gone I don't remember what happened, I felt quite numb. But at last woke up to the routine of feeding the farm stock, first of all the fowls . . . forgot to deliver the milk until 11.30 so I was late for the promised lunch with Muriel. She is always interesting, she hates the thought of killing and skinning the chinchillas—won't bear thinking about it. She suggested bulb raising, like the Scilly Isles. Skokholm should be perfect, its light soil just right for bulbs—witness how bluebells thrive. She gave me a vegetarian lunch, a salad of red cabbage and small chopped onions; so I am pleased you are far away!

Raced home just in time to feed the fowls, and catch the bus to meet your Mother in Cardiff. We changed the opal engagement ring for a silver and amethyst one. I hope you'll like it—it has a very pretty setting. It was ten shillings cheaper than the other one! Your Mother seemed a bit shocked when I told her I had not wanted you to buy an engagement ring, as we were saving up for living on the island. It seems she is superstitious about opals being unlucky, but believes amethysts bring good fortune! We had tea at Café Dorothy. We talked about you—lots, and I found your Mother a bit miserable—I was also miserable, so that was two of us! It was dark when I got home, to find the fowls in bed without their supper, not even shut against foxes. Discovered Tom had sold the pigs for 25s each when I had expressly told him to bring them home if they did not fetch 30s. However, glad they are gone, though I don't know what Papa will say—he likes to loll over the sty door and admire the way they grow, but of course never dreams of feeding or mucking them out. So you see I have done nothing all day of any interest, saving of course that rather lugubrious talk and tea with your doting Mother.

But thinking the bulb farming idea over, now I am in bed, I am rather taken with it. Do think about it seriously, and I'll get a book about it from the library—at present my ignorance about bulbs is abysmal.

I wonder where you are sleeping tonight? I'm ready for sleep myself,

So with all my love as ever,

D.

Oh why, why, why, why, why, why, didn't I come with you?

PART 2

October to November 1927

The arrival of Storm Petrel

Storm-petrels

Trehill Farm, Marloes
15 October, 1927

Dearest Doris,

Your letter was food for a starving mate in a strange world—it was a reminder of you at your round of life at home. Please write daily and post to me, as I hope to do for your benefit (conceit!)

I am scribbling this in my bedroom at Trehill, with the added pleasure that the room has memories of you—I believe you and Mother used this very room when you were here on your visit of approval—but all the others were shocked at the mess of the ruined house, and 'the hopeless lack of the amenities that count in civilisation today'—the criticism I heard from your uncle later, talking to Mother, who agreed with his view, adding that the bare loneliness appalled her.

Well, this pad you gave me looks good enough for all the letters I intend to write in the busy days ahead—it's a huge block, so that my wrist is bent over it awkwardly, making my writing all wobbly (Ass! Take the top sheet off and write on it flat on the table, did I hear you say? Of course—that's better!).

Seems hardly possible that we were rowing together on Llangorse Lake only a few days ago, watching grebes and coots, discussing our hopes and plans. But a lot of water has run through Jack Sound since. Farm sold, and all my worldly possessions of any use packed up and following me down to Pembrokeshire in that crazy lorry which I hired so cheaply. It went better than my old Talbot 8, which had two punctures on the way.

I called briefly on agent Lucas at H'west, a most excellent friendly man but for whom, I am sure, we should not have got the island on lease so favourably. Of course this long lease was the simplest way out of the money difficulty. Lucas told me the landlord Colonel R.V.L-P. is one of the best, and has never turned a tenant out in his life. So I said light heartedly that I will be certain of a renewal of my present lease of 21 years when it expires. He replied quite seriously 'Of course, if the dear Colonel is still alive!'

The Trehill folk Jim Codd and his sister Polly have stowed all my stuff in the corner of their big barn, nor can I get them to accept anything for their trouble or my keep. But they were delighted to share in that crate of fruit you sent.

Ever since I arrived I have been searching for a suitable boat, but 'tis as difficult as it was in Cardiff—especially as I know so little about sea boats, having been an inland creature all my life so far. Wednesday at Milford Haven, I examined all sorts of boats offered for sale, chiefly too large or too small, and not one to equal the *Lizzie* of Penarth—I don't know why your father persisted in condemning it as too cranky with that reversing propeller—but he knows more about boats than I do. Of all the villages visited in the last two days, Solva was the prettiest, with its long sandy harbour curving inland through cottages. It contained the only boat I considered suitable, though it may be a bit small—measures about 16'6" x 5'9" beam—and the owner wants too much for it—fifty pounds. It does have a handy size inboard motor. Just now I am pretty sick of noisy motor-boats, and begin to think more pleasantly of a suitable sailing boat.

Rabbits are fetching 4½d. a lb., which is on average 10d. each, at Marloes. It seems stupid to sell them at this price when the skin itself properly dried is worth at least 6d. If some way of salting or preserving the carcass could be found I would rather skin and store the carcasses for a few weeks until I have a boatload of skins and boxes of carcasses to take across. The idea of rushing small cargoes of fresh-paunched rabbits to the mainland daily or thrice weekly—the present custom—is too time consuming, when I need to be repairing the house and setting up our chinchilla scheme. But I expect it will have to be done for the present.

It's 6pm and I am going to the village to interview that nice quiet fellow John Edwards—the fisherlad who sat next to you in the boat in August, the one of the pair that always smiled broadly when spoken to, but was rather monosyllabic, but very experienced. I'd be happy to sign him on as my adviser and mate in the boat I must buy, if he'd be willing. The Codds say that most of the fishermen do little in winter here, except odd jobs, rabbit-trapping and making their lobster-pots ready for the summer.

Your idea of a bulb farm would be splendid if feasible, but the whole idea at present has been to raise chinchillas, and by hook or by crook we are (or I am) committed to the scheme. How are the chinchillas I left you?

I am nearly asleep in front of the fire, which is fuelled with 'culm', which is local anthracite dust mixed with clay. Culm making took place at Trehill yesterday in the big haggard, two large cart-horses trampling a lorryload of this clay and coal dust until it was very thoroughly mixed. Polly Codd is expert at making this mixture into about a hundred or so culm balls at a time. She boasts that the Trehill kitchen fire hasn't been allowed to go out in living memory. Just now there is a huge bucket above the boiler containing what they call 'hay-tea', for feeding to newly weaned calves. It consists of choice farm hay warmed up in hot water, with a dash of skim milk tipped in.

The gossiping Polly and her pipe-smoking laconic brother Jim are talking about a farm sale they attended recently. Such sales are like an endemic disease here, an autumnal fashion which sends the locals into a possessive frenzy. They dress up handsomely in their moth-balled best, Jim says a sale is better than going to the cinema—everything will be sold. Some poor woman bought 'a cracked piss-pot', it was lumped in with something else she bid for! I think it was Thoreau who wrote that if a tapeworm was offered for sale at a country auction, someone would not be able to resist bidding for it.

Later. The mason here—who is John Edward's uncle—told me that he 'lufes Skokkum', and takes it as a matter of course that I will employ him to mend the 'manor house' there. He told me he was a cousin of Bulldog Edwards of Orlandon (former tenant of Skokholm and to whom I paid forty five pounds for the rabbit-crop). When I told Jim Codd about mason Edwards his only comment was: 'He be very skilled, but terribly lazy and a noted liar.'

Jack, Edwards as he is known, was out when I called, but the mason was sure he would be the best boatman for me . . . 'Young Jack be a holy terror for salt water, spent most of his life in boats sailing this coast'.

I feel strongly inclined to tear up this straggling untidy letter. I also feel strongly inclined, when I think of the Beautiful Girl coming to our beautiful Island, to sing at the top of my voice, or stand on my head, or even (whisper it) compose a poem—which I suppose all true lovers do?

With undying love
Ever your R.

Tyr Bont

I've been absolutely longing to write to you all day, and haven't had a chance until this late moment. I promised Papa to help lift more stones to build his garden-seat by the tennis lawn . . .

Thank you ever so much for your lovely first letter. It is getting quite worn out already, I've read it so many times. Every morning that comes without a letter from the Loved One I shall have to pull out and read number One and pretend it has just come. It made me ever so much happier about you—I had only by slow degrees begun to realise you were no longer on your farm a few fields away. Now when I hear the familiar sounds—cocks crowing, ducks quacking, and your dog Nip barking, I tell myself no, it's not R. feeding them. And yet until your letter came I couldn't feel you were anywhere-sending a letter to Marloes seemed to be about as much good as throwing a message into the river, hoping it would somehow sail to you. Silly wasn't it— must be my lack of imagination, and of trust in the British postal system.

I hope you engage fisherman Jack—he has such an honest face, the sort that becomes beautiful after a short aquaintance. I liked Jack's sailing boat. I was silly enough to ask him why he called it the *Foxtrot,* and he said with a solemn face: 'She dances so nicely Miss!'

I shall picture you now, sailing away to the beloved island as we did, only two months ago—only that day you and I helped the fisherman to row, it seemed to me for hours on that winding course, because there was no wind. I loved every moment of that crossing, which Jack explained had to be so zigzag to avoid the contrary currents all along the beautiful mainland coast as far as the little red island of Gateholm, then shooting across almost to North Haven. I could see from the way Jack twitched an eyebrow at his mate that he was directing the navigation of his *Foxtrot*.

When I am alone now, especially in bed, I look at the Admiralty chart which you gave me showing every part of Skokholm coast, and study the run of the tidal flow and its strength at high and low water. I live again the delightful surprise of turning the corner into South Haven, yawning suddenly open—I am sure your Mother and Enid, Papa and Uncle were very glad to see smoother water lapping the landing steps! To catch fish was an added bonus!

That was a decidedly good augery for our future food supply! The more talkative fisherman promised us lobsters and crabs. With thousands of rabbits racing across the home meadow when we walked up to the buildings, I felt a wonderful glow within, wanting to start life with you that very instant, without even entering the tumbledown dwelling house. At least we shall never starve!

Although we missed the wondrous spring flowers you and Papa saw on your June visit, there was goldenrod and ragwort, and scores of little woodland birds on migration, and flights of swallows and martins. I fell instantly in love with the squat and venerable structure of the house, snug under its mountain. We can fix it up, never mind what the rest of the family think.

While I was cooking the fish it was wonderful to pretend it was just you and me doing the real thing.

I treasure the memories of sitting over the driftwood fire in the shadows of our future living room; (it looked so much more liveable by firelight!) . . . Those blood-curdling cries of the shearwaters as we walked up the little tramline to the lighthouse! The cacophony (can't spell it) was quite demonic, as they flashed past at terrific speed, in the red lamp of the lighthouse like rose-tinted falling stars. Uncle and Enid were most impressed. Uncle kept falling into rabbit-burrows, and was so exhausted that he leaned his back on a rocky outcrop and complained some shearwaters had started to use him as a 'take-off platform'!

I relive that visit, to reassure you that I have really and truly fallen in love with Skokholm and still can't believe my luck that you really want me to come out and share it with you! . . .

My dear husband-to-be, you need not fear, I shall always

rhapsodise about our island paradise. I do have gloomy moments, not about you or Skokholm, but about my own fitness to be an islandwife. Nature has some grimmer aspects: the scores of bird and rabbit corpses, the remains of the feasts of the great black-backed gulls; the peregrine falcon we watched, which swooped and killed a curlew. Nature on the island is red in tooth and claw, but not more so than our cat which catches birds and mice and grasshoppers, and loves to play with them, wounding them for long moments before crunching them up, or leaving them dead.

I wonder if you have been able to get over to the island yet? And how looks she in her autumn dress? I think you must have, in this fine weather. Lucky you! Please forgive squiggly writing but I am trying to wind up this letter in bed, which means either sitting up, when my back gets cold, or else leaning on one elbow and trying to keep the other warm under the clothes . . .

Ever your loving partner

D.

Trehill Farm, Marloes

16 October, 1927

This is going to be a brief and businesslike letter. I'm just off on another boat-hunt, but I remember my promise to write to you all about my first visit to the island.

First I have engaged fisherman Jack Edwards, plus the use of his boat *Foxtrot* for two pounds a week, he to find his own victuals. There was no bargaining for a lower wage (usually one pound a week, the Codds tell me). John hates bargaining as much as I do, and simply said he would be content with 'two pounds a week, as wages is falling like, sir.' I am pretty sure he was told by his rascally uncle to demand two pounds, which his uncle had told me was the minimum wage John had had as an experienced seaman aboard local trading schooners. In any case he is worth 2 pounds, though it upsets my balance sheet straightaway.

You remember I sent a copy of my chinchilla proposals for criticism to my brother in Burma, and today his reply came. I shan't send his criticism on to you, it's too dampening, and scornful of my business knowledge, which he has every right to be. But his remedy has arrived too late—he advises waiting at least a year before selling up my St Mellons farm, and just renting the island for a year or so as a holiday place! He talks of world recession looming up, when chinchilla fur and other such luxuries will be unsaleable . . . Enough said!

At 9.00 John and I launched the *Foxtrot* as the tide was ebbing in Martins Haven. We had quite a stiff row with his long sweeps before we could round in Jack Sound, then up sail with a rattling nor-easter behind us we flew south right to the landing place in South Haven. My first thought was to see how best we could haul a boat up. On close examination of the winch I inherited from the last tenant, we found it to be home-made from the largest cogwheel of a grass-mower, turned by the small wheel thereof, fixed to the axle of the rusty hand-crank. John said that to his knowledge it had not been used since Bulldog Edwards left the island thirty years ago! You can imagine how much it had rusted. Good old John scraped the teeth of the cogs and said most of them seemed quite sound. With a little repair of the sockets which hold the axles in place, he was sure it would do for hauling up a smaller boat than the *Foxtrot*. The broken rocks below the winch would have to be bridged with stout planks, on which we would place the greased hardwood sticks all local fishermen carry for hauling their boats up beaches and slipways.

It seemed rather formidable to me, and I wondered if we could not make a better landing out of the more sheltered North Haven, with its golden sand, and cliffs hung with more vegetation than any other cove on the island. But it will require too much labour to make a slipway there, John said.

Blacksmith's Landing—which is a steep-to rock path on the west side of North Haven—is often used for taking off stores in bad weather when South Haven is too rough for loading.

John and I made a thorough inspection of the old farmhouse. I think at first we would have to live in the old barn and to do so we would have to mend the hole in the very heavy island slate roof. I took measurements for doors and windows: at present the only light is from the gap in the roof and the original ventilation slits in the walls.

The island was red and green under the October sunlight, but there was no time to go bird-watching. Lapwings were crying on the plateau and ducks quacked from the ponds. I was very happy there, but we could not stay—nowhere to keep the *Foxtrot* safe. The lighthouse keepers saw us off about 4 pm, handing us their letters for post. We had a very stiff row against the wind to gain the Stack, then sailed by long tacks *for three hours* to get through Jack Sound as far as Tuskar Rock. Here the current was *roaring* angrily against the north wind, and we had a very nasty few minutes using those 18-ft long sweeps at the corner point known as the Haze. Actually it was very good practice for me—an emergency in which I discovered how many unused soft muscles were reluctant to help my aching arms! Tossing about, we had to row non-stop for a whole hour, making small progress. The alternative was to be drifted against the rocky shore, which I did not in the least desire. I was surprised at the reserves of energy which—seemingly at my last gasp—kept this frightened man of yours pulling! John of course seemed not to turn a hair. He is so expert with the sweeps; by crossing his hands he is able to pull two, his right hand on the handle of the left oar, and his left hand on the right oar. I tried to do the same, but caught a crab and fell backwards! John motioned to me to use one sweep only, a real relief to use both hands on one oar; he cleverly compensated by pulling with amazing strength on the 'one oar' side and less on the 'two oar' side.

Afterwards when we got safely to Martynshaven beach I was utterly weary. John however told me I would soon master two sweeps: ''Tis all a matter of taking your time, and care to keep up a steady stroke, always dipping the blades in a rising wave to get the best leverage. Aye, thee'll get the hang of it soon sir!'

Good old John—he is too sensitive to hurt my feelings by being rude. But mine was a thoroughly inglorious performance. Now my wrists are aching and swollen, so forgive any more to this letter. By now you'll be sick of this inch-to-inch story in dreary detail.

Always yours,

R.

The letter from Ronald's brother Ken:

Rangoon, Burma
16 September, 1927

My dear Ron,

I think I only met your Doris once, when home on leave. As I remember now she was petite, and crowned with a magnificent head of brown curls. You have my warmest congratulations on achieving such an ideal mate—I know you both love outdoor life, and know about all the birds, beasts and flowers. I am lamentably ignorant of such things, though I like them in the mass; there are however, some species I could cheerfully murder, such as the brain-fever bird which taps out its horrid call world without end in my garden. And I can't get up much enthusiasm for snakes—we have too many cobras, as well as some particularly vicious small snakes which lie concealed in the dust.

You ask for a 'business man's opinion' on your programme for making a fortune out of farming chinchilla rabbits on that island of yours. First of all you are asking me a very difficult question. I know very little about this island, beyond your rather vague but enthusiastic description of its scenic beauty, and its rich flora and fauna. I have a brotherly suspicion that you are a bit carried away with your desire to become a Robinson Crusoe. I don't want to be a doubting Desmond, but frankly I've never seen anything so simple-looking as your programme. In short it looks too good to be true.

However, let's take your programme item by item:

December to March 1928: 'Kill off completely all the wild rabbits on the island.' You say you think you can do this with traps, snares and ferrets, harvesting the majority, and if any are left, you will use gas to suffocate them in their burrows—after blocking up their holes . . . Yet the island is 250 acres, and you say that the whole place is a honey-comb of rabbit-burrows . . .

From this I should say that it would take an army of men to get to work in such a place, and extermination of the last few rabbits might well be impossible. But in any case your bill for labour in the first place would be at least two hundred pounds. Yet you put it down as fifty pounds, without allowing the cost of feeding and ferrying them! I've had considerable experience in hiring labourers, and shall be very surprised if you get any to work and remain contented on an uninhabited island for less than double the wage you estimate—one pound per week cash.

Then it seems to me that your estimate of an annual yield of 6000 chinchilla rabbits from 250 acres of rather barren rocky land is rather a high figure. However, you doubtless know, after your discussion with the late tenant of Skokholm, who I see is generously letting you off with a fee of 40 pounds for the coming winter crop of wild rabbits in return for resigning his lease to you. As a business man I am tempted to ask why he did not demand more than 40 pounds for the rabbit crop which he estimated (you say) at up to 5000 rabbits. But let that pass . . .

April 1928. 'To introduce 400 young well-grown chinchilla rabbits, say 350 does, 50 bucks. These should breed, producing 1400 offspring in that summer.' Well, I can't comment much here, for I know little about breeding rabbits. You always hear they are alarmingly prolific. So I hope they will do their duty! But what happens if you have failed to get rid of the last wild rabbits before April? Surely it would be fatal to allow them to mix with your valuable chinchillas?

Oct-Dec 1928. 'To kill off (harvest) 400 young chinchilla bucks. This will leave some 1000 does and 300 bucks. The 1000 does should produce a minimum of 6000 offspring each year from 1929 onwards, leaving each spring 1000 does, young and old, to form our permanent stock after 5000 had been marketed for their fur.'

I am not sure what Chinchilla rabbits weigh, but assuming a minimum of 4 lbs each the annual kill of around 5000 would gross some 20,000 lbs, which by my calculation is around nine tons avoirdupois. As you can't normally take tons of food from the land without replacing it with an equivalent tonnage (I am thinking of the rice crops of Burma which are heavily fertilised with tons of humus) you would be obliged to put back into your island rabbit-pasture the equivalent tonnage of fertiliser. Which would mean that you would have to ferry to your island nine tons or thereabouts of such a restorative. Your figures do not mention this cost at all—which at all events would be expensive in manpower and money each year. Still, if you believe your annual return will be a minimum of 2,500 pounds you may scrape a living by dint of a lot of hard physical work.

However let's examine your actual balance sheet:

Initial outlay—Capital required:

Pay to outgoing tenant, who offers to resign his tenancy, although he no longer lives there, and only rents the island for the sake of the wild rabbit crop, harvested by men he employs to trap the rabbits . . .	40.0.0
Sundries claimed by tenant Edwards, including secondhand boat winch . . .	5.0.0
Motorboat purchased . . .	50.0.0
Repairs to dwellinghouse . . .	50.0.0
Purchase of catching gear-nets, snares traps	50.0.0
Lease-rent to landlord, one year in advance . . .	25.0.0
400 young chinchilla rabbits at current market value of 5s . . .	100.0.0
	320.0.0

REVENUE	EXPENDITURE	
Half year ending March 1928		
To 6000 wild rabbits exterminated and sold at 10d each 250.0.0	Living expenses	56.0.0
	Boat expenses	25.0.0
	Labourers' wages	52.0.0
	Marketing rabbits and miscellaneous	25.0.0
		158.0.0
Year ending March 1929		
To 400 chinchilla bucks, pelts and carcasses at 10s each 200.0.0	Living expenses (3 persons)	156.0.0
	1 labourer wages (current)	26.0.0
	Boat expenses	20.0.0
	Marketing	26.0.0
		228.0.0

Year ending March 1930 (and annually thereafter)

To 5000 chinchilla rabbits,		Expenses as for last year but	
pelts and carcasses at		add extra for labour—total	52.0.0
10s each	2500.0.0	Increase boat expenses to	52.0.0
Deduct contra, say	500.0.0	Marketing expenses tripled	78.0.0
		Your living cost	200.0.0
	2000.0.0		382.0.0

Since you invite criticism, I must be blunt and say your method of drawing up a prospectus is so unbusinesslike that I feel obliged to advise you to engage a local accountant who may be familiar with the rabbit trade. For example, if you can buy 400 chinchilla rabbits at 5s each and later sell them at double that price then I think that whoever sells them to you for 5s must have a less optimistic idea of their ultimate value than you have.

I seem to be running on in carping vein, so I must end with a brief summary of the prospects as I see them—none too clearly from this distance. I have purposely looked at the whole idea in pessimistic mood because you are doing the opposite; between us we might cancel out some errors of view.

You say that even if the whole scheme fails you can still get a living from wild rabbits, sheep and fishing; but at best, it will be a thin living, and desperately tough in winter—you know how bad the winter weather can be on that coast. Personally, if I were in your position with an increasingly profitable farm, a snug slice of land to exploit and improve, and the prospect of marrying the only girl in the world, I would stick to the security of the mainland. I believe that you have no capital to speak of except the livestock and equipment of your ten acre holding, the sale of which will hardly cover the outlay on your chinchilla project—you say you can get 500 pounds for your business, lock stock and barrel. Perhaps it's not too late for you to hold on to your little farm, to buy which, and build that bungalow, Mother made the sacrifice of taking out a mortgage, which by the way, she has not yet repaid, relying on you to meet the interest with your rent.

My humble advice is that you abandon your island scheme, and consolidate on your farm for the present. I should be happy to contribute to the very modest rent of your island, to keep it in reserve for the future. It's a nice thought—to have a dream island, even if only as a holiday retreat. I shall be interested to learn what you *do* decide after all this,

Yours ever,

Ken

P.S. I have just read in the *Rangoon Times* that world prices are tumbling, with signs of a deep depression setting in. That will mean among other problems, that especially such luxuries as chinchilla fur will be hitting rock-bottom prices. On the other hand the demand for fish and farm produce can never cease as long as people are able to eat!

Tyr Bont
18 October

Dear Ronald,

I'm finishing off this letter instead of getting breakfast—there won't be time to write afterwards.

Sir, if you dare not to write down your adventures inch-by-inch, or leave a single lurid incident undescribed, I shall never write another word to you! Perhaps it would suit you if I carried out the threat, as I have only boring tittle-tattle to relate.

All the same TAKE CARE OF YOURSELF, you are engaged and under contract, and I won't have you taking foolish risks, sir.

This week has been a chapter of accidents, beginning Saturday night when, dreaming about you and the island I absent-mindedly dropped a whole pound of butter into the kitchen fire! And the last straw was Auntie Minnie telephoning last night to say that the cream she had bought from me to give an invalid friend tasted of paraffin—that fool Tom must have stood his milking bucket under the leaky lamp in the cowshed. I've discovered this morning our house milk is also reeking of oil. So that's that!

I cycled to Cardiff Library and spent a long time wading through a fat book on the management of rabbits for profit, but there was nothing about salting. I shouldn't think there would be any demand for pickled rabbit when there are always hundreds of fresh rabbits on the market? Have you read Simpson's book on rabbits? He describes what he calls the Wortley Trap-fence for catching wild rabbits. It is more humane than traps and snares, and can be set up to drive rabbits into at any time of day or night.

This book recommends improving rabbit-pasture by applying gas lime in November and salt in April. But I don't imagine salt is necessary on our sea-salted Skokholm? Is there a gasworks anywhere near?

If you haven't read this book, I can send you a copy. I found it most interesting. It says that at least 3 pound an acre can be made from wild rabbits enclosed in a properly managed warren. The land will remain sweet indefinitely with regular dressings of gas lime and salt.

Must go and get breakfast now,

Good morning,
with my love,
ever your D.

P.S. Warning—TAKE CARE OF YOURSELF, Ronald Lockley.

20 October, 1927

Dearest Doris,

I am writing this privately in the shelter of one of the Trehill straw stacks, where I feel nice and warm and dirty—before I wash for supper. Time by your beautiful watch—5.30pm. What a surprise on returning here after a long day travelling, to open your unexpected parcel. My dear sweetheart you are perfectly silly, yet absolutely splendid and generous to send me all those magic things—against our avowed rule to economise and save up for our island life. The cake is perfect, I've had a nibble already, and gave a slice to Polly Codd. As for the luscious fruit, I shall keep some to take to Skokholm. Thank you a thousand times. I wonder do they accept kisses by telegram?

In H'west today I ordered the lime, cement, timber, etc. for repairing the barn; also rabbit-traps, wire for snares and string etc. which John says are essential to begin the rabbit catching. At Milford we bought a new wire for the island winch, new boat rope, and fisherman John bought himself new oilskins and knee-high sea-boots; I followed his wise example.

October 19. At Solva today John approved that smallish motor-boat on sale for fifty pounds. He said it might be a wee bit small, but was just the job for hauling up at Skokholm and easily managed if necessary by one man. So I agreed to buy it if the owner, a Mr Swales, would deliver to Martynshaven as soon as possible. He gave us a short run outside the harbour at Solva and the little engine seemed to go perfectly. John says he will make a sail for it, so we shan't be absolutely dependent on the motor.

John is marvellous, turns his hand to anything practical. He is going to splice the end of the new winch wire to take a hook for hauling a boat up the beach, and is getting the blacksmith to fashion a steel 'tie-bow' which will be bolted to the boat's forward keel for taking the winch-hook.

You say, take care of yourself—I say leave it to John who knows all that is to be known of importance for island existence—boats, the sea, the tides and winds. He loves the sea, as I do. He has salt water around his heart, as the local saying is. On the way home John diverted to a little haven called St Bride's, where there is a rather gone-wild bed of osiers. He wanted to cut some to make a lobster-pot or two. He promised to teach me this skill—of making what he called a Cornish withy pot, larger and stronger and longer-lasting than the local 'twiney' pots, made out of hazel twigs and tarred twine by the locals. Must go indoors—too dark to see!

Now supper's over, and the light's much better! The folk here cheerfully spend a whole evening gossiping around the kitchen culm fire with only a feeble paraffin lamp burning. They are a merry young lot, intensely curious about my movements and plans. I didn't say much about the chinchilla scheme, since I am sure that they'd consider it daft. When I asked Jim Codd how he would farm the island, he says he wouldn't, but if he had to, he reckons sheep would be the easiest, keeping down the rabbits as low as possible by trapping and ferreting all winter, and fishing for lobsters in the summer. He reckons I could keep one breeding ewe to the acre, say 250, which should produce a like number of lambs for sale in the autumn. Allowing their fleeces to cover running expenses the lambs would be clear profit, a minimum of say 30s each?

Weather permitting we will sail tomorrow for Skokholm, with a full load of my furniture (save the mark!), and as much lime and cement and timber for repairing the barn as the *Foxtrot* will carry. Rabbiting will then begin. I have engaged Old Dick, a man of about 60 years whose sole occupation in recent winters is alleged to have been to trap rabbits at Skokholm for Bulldog Edwards. He lives with his daughter in Dale, where I interviewed him and agreed on his modest wage of 1 pound a week plus his 'victuals and baccy'. 'I likes Skokkum main well,' he said, and explained he liked to be by himself with no one to argue with him!

For warmth and cooking on the island, I've bought a two-burner Valor Perfection stove. It has a separate oven to fit on top—for roasting and baking bread, the ironmonger told me, 'if you know how!' Which I don't. I can always take a lesson from the lighthouse keepers.

Much love,
ever your Ronald

Tyr Bont

Dear Partner,

I'm writing this in bed again—the only place I can find peace and time to write to you these days. I discovered I had about two square inches of bread between us and starvation (you know I have refused to let the family eat bought bread or any not baked by me—I'm practising on them, so as to be perfect by July 12th, nice of me, eh? But what they think may not be so nice?) Therefore I had to make some scones quickly. A bakestone is a splendid thing, so quick in an emergency. It gets hot in a few seconds, we must certainly have one. I'm learning lots of useful domestic time-savers—one is that it makes absolutely no difference to a bed if you just cover it over when you're pressed for time. You can even leave it several days running—all this shaking and making is just a fetish, like daily dusting. However I've discovered that it is best not to rely on a lamp burning two nights without the wick being trimmed, for it will probably go out about 9 or 10 pm, and you'll have to fill it with smelly oil, when you are in the middle of baking bread—or writing a letter!

To return to commonsense. I am glad you have a Valor Perfection, for I can't see you managing a primus oven, not that you aren't capable, but they are so temperamental.

By the way, Papa says he is sure we have a large old grate in the lumber room somewhere. I believe we turned one out of the old scullery, and it might do for the island barn?

Please don't be in a hurry to tackle the house. I'd selfishly prefer to enjoy rebuilding it with you, perfectly happy to live in the barn at first. I really love that quaint old house 'built in a whimsical manner', as described by Richard Fenton.

But really I don't care where we live at this moment. A snug little weather-proof cave in the red cliffs, full of the song of the sea and bird cries would be heaven—with you. Don't lets bother about rabbits or sheep or bulbs. Let's live as the wild birds live, with plenty of time to stand and stare . . .

Oh dear, here I am, going off the deep end! The days here drag by, for all they're full of things to be done that don't get done. And you so far away . . .

Mama thinks I am that kind of particular fool that can only see the island through rose-coloured spectacles, thinking life there will be a bed of roses and lotus-eating. And supposing I do, I tell her, what is a bed of roses? As I've had to prune our roses here, I find them full of nasty thorns—not my idea of a gardener's paradise. I should tell her that the best time I had with you (don't laugh) was when we were working together on making rabbit hutches for your/our chinchilla scheme . . . but there are many more like birding in the Maes-y-crochan wood . . . and listening for nightingales.

What a lot of tosh I am writing—must be the effect of eleven o'clock and a glass of sherry but no tea in the afternoon. I'm sure if I read this over in a sane moment I'll be ashamed to post it.

I have imagined you setting off this morning—it was quite

perfect here, not a breath of wind, rather cold but sunny, with a light dawn mist close to the ground. I pictured you at sea loaded with a cargo for starting life on the beloved Island. Probably all wrong, we are very sheltered at Tyr Bont, but on the open coast possibly a gale was blowing? Do tell me all about the boat you eventually buy, and what you will name her. You are getting frightfully technical with your tie-bows and whatnot.

I've run out of things to write to you. I've read your letters dozens of times—they're getting tattered with such treatment, worn-out like the undersigned who is falling asleep. So goodnight.

Yours forever and ever,

D.

Trehill
20 October

Dearest Partner,

Yes, I have read Simpson's rabbit book several times. Probably some of the dates of borrowing from Cardiff library are mine! If you can get me a copy second-hand perhaps, I'd like it for our island library. I am going to try out a Wortley Trap fence on the island soon.

The Solva boat having been delivered to Martynshaven yesterday by Swales, on trial, I was up at 5.30am to load Jim Codd's large gambo* with my furniture. We went down to the beach at Martynshaven, loaded both boats, and by 8.30 set off for Skokholm. The motor boat towed Jack's *Foxtrot* in which I sat at the tiller to keep her in line with the motor-boat in which John was steering, Swales beside him. Later Jack told me that Swales was very sick yesterday when they crossed St Bride's Bay (I had taken Jack to Solva in my car so that he could navigate Swales's boat to Martynshaven.) It seems Swales is no seaman.

My agreement with Swales was for a three-day trial. I had to give

*Name for a long narrow horse-cart—made especially for the narrow gateways on Welsh farms.

him a post-dated cheque for fifty pounds, which I could cancel if the boat was unsuitable. But it was a calm day, and the motor behaved perfectly, chugging along manfully pulling the heavily laden *Foxtrot*. We made Skokholm in one hour, a good tide helping, before stowing away my possessions in the three least leaky rooms in the house. We made a bonfire in the old garden of accumulated trash—all the exuviae of fishermen who have camped here in summer during the several decades since Bulldog left the island. There was nothing of value or interest except a rusted pinfire pistol, and some mouse-eaten religious books. We burnt everything except the big driftwood bed John and the rabbit-catcher will sleep on when we settle in.

It was grand to be in my future home on such a day. A robin and a wren—the first I have seen on the island—were in and out of the roofless part of the house. I could hear mallard and teal quacking and lapwings crying from the direction of North Pond. There were larks—crossing the sea with us.

We proceeded to see if the motor-boat could be hauled up over the rocks in South Haven by that crazy handwinch, a feat accomplished with the aid of the new winch wire hooked to the tie-bow. The lighthousemen were most helpful, providing long planks from their store of driftwood, to straddle across the big gaps in the slipway. In case the cog-wheels of the winch slipped John had attached block and rope tackle to an iron ring between the boat and the winch which would prevent her from sliding more than a few inches downhill. However, the old winch cogs groaned, but held together until the boat was tight up against the barrel of the winch.

All was well, and we relaunched her into a flat calm sea, and with a favourable tide reached Martinshaven in only 45 minutes.

I am writing up my diary at Trehill. Time 10pm. Jim and Polly are away at another sale, and asked me to keep my eye on the young people here. The old farmhouse is full of cats and dogs, three merry serving-boys, and Molly, the farmer's niece aged five, and the young dairymaid Bronwen.

Tonight I found one of the serving-boys dressed in Polly Codd's pinafore, skirt, jersey and cloth cap in order to milk Satan, Polly's pet cow. This produced shrieks of merriment, but no milk, Satan refusing to 'let down' her milk to this hollow fraud and his good imitation of Polly's milking song and coaxing words!

Friday, 21 October

Last night to bed at 2am after talking to Jim and Polly, who were anxious to discuss the sale and their purchases, asking my opinion on the value of various articles. When you earn money, as these good folk do, by sheer grit and an 18 hour day, the spending of it becomes an occasion for immense deliberation, anxiety and excitement, and could lead to bitterness if the spending turns out badly for their future prosperity. Bronwen says her mistress Polly 'is being courted by a farmer' up in the Welsh (north Pembs.) so she is saving for her bottom drawer—'has been for years—that Welsh sweetheart of hers be a right cautious gentleman. Don't seem to have given Polly an engagement ring yet.' And more words to that effect! Trehill is worked as a partnership between brother and sister and most of the cows belong to Polly, while Jim controls the cropping land. He is a most amiable man, refusing to be paid for the use of his barn or horse and cart. I learn much local gossip round the fire, John always far from garrulous but with encouragement he comes out with interesting little bits of local history, for instance: Blacksmith's landing—so named because the Marloes blacksmith was dropped off there to shoe the horses and donkeys on Skokholm. According to John, Bulldog in his salad youth was attracted to take up the lease and farm the island at an opportune moment for him, when Trinity House began building the lighthouse. Bulldog supplied the horses to draw building materials from the landing to the lighthouse. The steps and crane in South Haven were improved to their present good state by Trinity House.

Bulldog made money out of farming Skokholm with seed corn, and 'roots as large as footballs' so Bulldog boasted to your father and me (when we saw him in June to get his permission to visit Skokholm). John tells me that Bulldog in his prime was a bit of a pirate and reckless . . . a loner, a big strong fellow who carried off a young woman he had fallen in love with to be his housekeeper. But when the babies began to arrive they went ashore to live. When the war was over, Bulldog had made enough money to buy his farm at

Orlandon. They never went back although his wife died pining for Skokholm they say! He moved all his stock to Orlandon—the larger animals being 'swimmed' ashore onto Marloes sands, towed behind the boat.

Much love,
R.

22nd

Dear Doris,

Yesterday a stiff sou'easter was blowing, which meant we could not attempt to tow a cargo to the island. All the cement and lime had to be stored in the only boatshed at Martynshaven, owned by Sturt of Skomer Island—not very weatherproof and without his permission. However we did enjoy a cruise in the motor-boat, as far as Skomer North Haven where if I had seen Mr Sturt, I would have asked permission to use his shed. But there was nobody at the landing place, and no time to walk the mile to his house.

By now Swales was agitating to go home to Solva, so I agreed, and off he went as soon as we got back to Martynshaven, with the cheque for 50 pounds in his pocket.

Today it gradually rained itself to a dry nor'wester so that although it was too wet to take cement and lime over, we towed the rest of my effects, food stores etc., over to Skokholm.

Old Dick looked positively majestic sitting in an armchair, wedged in the thwarts in the centre of the *Foxtrot*, John waving to him from the stern of the motor-boat! It was calm enough in South Haven. We unloaded everything and carried it up to the house. I envied Dick as he made his few preparations for settling in. He made us a cup of tea and I watched buzzards and ravens soaring overhead. But we had to take the boats back—too risky to leave them moored in wintertime.

What followed was my first DISASTER.

The wind had been getting up quietly, and John was talking of a nice breeze to blow us home. We certainly got it. A squall with catspaws sweeping Jack Sound, as the wind veered due north, just as we were trying to skirt around the notorious Haze Point and

Tuskar Rock, both named by the Flemish weavers who thought the boiling seas in Jack Sound looked like carded wool.*

The engine spluttered a bit as a wave swept our low stern, but recovered and we safely rounded into Martynshaven. But here the increasing north wind had caused a huge swell to roll up the landing beach, making the safe landing of two boats by only two men an utter impossibility—it seemed to me. With hindsight we might have planned it more wisely, by temporarily anchoring the *Foxtrot* off the beach. She is double-bowed and can ride waves better than the square-sterned boat. John decided we ought to wait for a lull, in the old fisherman's belief that every seventh wave is the wildest one. A futile hope, for when we tried to beach both boats together, a huge breaker filled my boat and *Foxtrot* rode down behind and would have hit us but Jack leaped into the water, grabbed the tow rope in the nick of time pulled her alongside mine. For more than an hour all we could do was to haul on the painter ropes, Jack to his and I to mine, heaving as each fresh wave hit the beach. For had we allowed either to be slewed broadside, much greater damage would have been done to them.

Soon it was dark and no one had come down to the haven. Each wave had slapped over the square stern of the motor-boat. *Foxtrot*'s sharp-bowed stern saved her from this fate, for she took very little water. But mine was waterlogged well above the engine casing. Finally the tide ebbed sufficiently for us to unplug the boats and haul them up above high-tide using a winch belonging to another fisherman by which time we were dead tired. On inspecting the engine I found the cooling water outlet pipe broken off, and the magneto soaked by salt water. It was a very crestfallen RML that crawled the mile up to Trehill, carrying the very wet magneto, now washed in fresh water, and drying in front of the fire. Jim Codd, who understands such machinery, has unscrewed all detachable parts and is drying them out.

'Mebbe,' said this good Samaritan, 'tomorrow, I'll come down to Martynshaven and check over the engine . . . '

It's midnight, and maybe I shall tear up this tragic letter rather

*Tuskar was the Tucker-man and the Haze was Wooltuck Point.

than trouble you with my difficulties? I am going to bed, to re-read your letters. I wish I was on Skokholm—Dick seemed so happy there saying 'Grand water for makin' tea, sir,' and 'Nobody to answer yer back, likes me own company best.'

Swales had no number or name on his boat, told me he called her *Elizabeth Maude.* Shall we re-christen her *Storm Petrel*? For she looked like one when she rested in the red rocks of South Haven.

Tinkered with the engine of our *Storm Petrel*, with Jim Codd. Half the young male population of Marloes, all dressed in their Sunday best, were strolling on the beach; all ready to give advice about decarbonising and putting the engine together again. But the magneto is still feeble and we can't mend the water pipe ourselves.

I have almost to learn a new language here in South Pembs, where Welsh is almost unknown, but fragments of their Flemish, Viking, and Celtic ancestry linger in their Norman-English speech. For example I learned today that pebbles are *popples*, rocks are *cleggers*, a short cut is *a squint*, a sea-swell a *runch*, a gap is a *slop*, a ditch is a *grip*, a boy is a *crut*, stupid or foolish is *dool* (so I could be a *dool crut*). All very expressive and even their replies are commonly emphasised with a sage nod and the prefix 'why-aye' for yes, and 'why-naow' for no.

Their voices sound softer than the rapid-fire gabble of the Welsh in conversation. The Marloes folk refer disparagingly at times to their northern neighbours, 'up in the Welsh', as with the complacency of the conquering towards the conquered. But they are just as religious—Marloes folk are largely chapel-going. Some consider it's a sin not to go on Sundays, when no one may do any work, even cook dinner or make the beds!

John says with a grin: 'But of course, sir, there's no Sunday in ten fathoms of water.'

Monday 24th, early morning:

Hurrah. It's calm and sunny, so must hurry to post and get engine soldered, load lime, cement etc., and sail to the Lower Island (local name for Skokholm) and stay there for many days I hope.

Ever your R.

Tyr Bont

Dearest Ron,

Its nearly a whole week since I have written to you. But I suppose you're happily on the Island, and won't be returning in a hurry this time. Which means I am impatient to hear what you've been doing. So now I pray you are back on the mainland, posting me your news.

A gale is howling around the house, setting every window and door rattling, even blowing the lamp out if you injudiciously open a door, as I did just now. Oh, I hope you are safe somewhere—at Trehill, and writing to me. I can just imagine how the gales are whipping the sea into a fury—terrible but glorious!

. . . the river is bursting its banks, and our fields are wetter than ever.

I am sorry you had such a bad landing at Martynshaven, and the motor suffered. You are lucky with John and Jim. I like the name *Storm Petrel* for the boat, so apt. And now there is a new moon tonight—a sliver of silvery white, so days of calm must surely follow.

All your rabbits are thriving. Carmen has a slight snuffle, and she always had a tendency to sneeze. Her hutch might be in a draught, but moving her to a warmer place hasn't cured her! Our man Tom has a 'permanent' snuffle, so I no longer worry about Carmen!! But I do worry over the responsibility of managing your/our chinchillas. I woke up in a fever the other night imagining one of your prettiest does was dying, after reading an article on the high mortality of pregnant animals. According to the schedule of chinchilla management, I shall soon have to start mating them. The breeding manual says 'look out for the does coming into season', but I see no signs, that is to say, they all appear stupidly content to eat and sleep!

I think your old doe Annabel was pining for you, or suffering the shock of being transferred to the care of a mere woman. She got another shock when I accidentally knocked over her nest-box and she crashed with a dreadful thump to the concrete floor. She went right off her feed for three days, so I gave her special tender lettuce, rolled oats and milk. Now she seems to have recovered, thank goodness.

Your stud buck suddenly went off the deep end yesterday—tearing around his hutch and kicking up his heels . . . I have rechristened him Swegn (is that how you spell it?) because he is going to live on our Viking island. I hope he'll enjoy being the founding father of all chinchillas, until he is old and it is time to turn him into a beautiful neck-stole, or part of a ninety-guinea ladies fur-coat!

Forgive my imagination running riot. Au revoir, partner, ever and ever much love from your lonely Do.

Trehill
30 October, 1927

Dearest Lady,

I have a confession to make—which will make you ashamed of me. It is a week since I have written, and I could have written every day, and posted letters to you, because *I have not been able to cross back to the island* during this time. I could have deceived you that I was at Skokholm and working hard for the whole week! If only I had been! Whereas I can relate only mundane news and disasters! Our Marloes Blacksmith fixed the water-cooler pipe back on the engine, and John and I got down to launch the *Storm Petrel* by midday—a trial run in case the trouble wasn't cured. Alas, it wasn't. The pipe soon leaked, and the magneto wasn't sparking properly. Had to haul up again, this time drove to H'west, where I had a strong elbow nut made for screwing into the jacket, and the magneto overhauled at an engineering shop.

The chapter of little disasters went on, frustrating in the extreme. Next day tried motor on the beach and then in the water. It ran well, but the SW. gale persisted too much to cross to Skokholm.

In pulling the boat up we somehow damaged the propeller blades. John tried to tap out the frayed edges, and decided that a hinged iron guard was needed to protect the propeller and stern-tube from future bumps. So our blacksmith made an iron guard contraption.

We have been twice to Milford to buy canvas, rope etc. for Jack to make a sail for S.P. and to Sandy Haven woods for an ashpole for the mast. Back to Milford for sail canvas, on to Neyland to see Rouse, owner of a large tug boat—who relieves the local lighthouses for Trinity House each month. I asked him to deliver some tons of coal to South Haven for me. But he was only agreeable to do so in the summer; he said 'too much delay in the winter might mean that the right moment to relieve the rock lighthouses might be lost.'

I've been for a long walk around the cliffs looking long at lonely and beautiful Skokholm. Wondered how fared Trapper Dick—and has he the sense not to trap rabbits this weather? Studied the heaving and eddying tide-races in Jack Sound, marvellous to watch. Saw seals, ravens and choughs. Lucky they, oblivious to the weather!

I have been helping Polly to milk her cows—not much good at this yet, but I must learn so as to be able to milk the goats we shall keep at Skokholm. Gale still blowing as I write.

In Trehill yard slates are flying off roofs, and the thatch off Jim's rick of clover hay. Jack has finished the ash mast . . . When we went down together to Martynshaven to fit a step and clamp to hold it, we essayed a brief cruise under the cliffs as far as roaring Jack Sound, to check the motor. That day I took Jim Codd in my car to Dale Castle orchard to collect a sackful of gale-blown windfall apples; while there I climbed the belfry of the ancient church below the castle in search of owl or bat but found only the rotten cradle of its one bell, and the dreary moan of the gale through the holes in the wooden louvres.

Today being Sunday, I have stayed inside and gossiped to Reuben Codd, Jim's young brother who lives at West Hook next door with his parents. His mother is a bible thumping lay preacher and young Reuben seems likely to follow her example, from the trend of his remarks, praising his mother for her evangelical eloquence. While the less religious Jim talked about his father with a chuckle as a 'Knowledgeable old sinner, he can't abide Mother's missionary hot-gospelling, and refusal to cook on Sundays. But they rub along very well, considering.'

Monday 31 October a.m.

Praise be—a calm sunrise, so look forward with glee to crossing this morning. Shall post this today. Must hurry away.

In haste, all love,
your R.

Tyr Bont

Dearest Ron,

I dreamed last night I was cycling along the Merthyr Road when you came up behind me. I heard your funny Talbot horn quite plainly, but you weren't in it—instead a man with a Monte Carlo hat and toothbrush moustache! Can you tell me what that signifies?

Just retired to bed, hence the pencil. Papa brought your beautiful chrysoprase pendant home from the local exhibition. Mama and Papa had noticed it in the exhibits and were surprised to be told it belonged to Doris Shellard, and would they return it at the end of the show to the owner! Papa said it was the most beautiful thing in the jewelry section—it is lovely—but I don't often wear it. I can't see it if I do! To think I'd let you spend such a lot on me without a murmur of protest when we became engaged. It seems absolutely wicked for I knew you'd have to be spending such a lot on getting our home on the island ready before we could marry. Tonight somehow it's helped to make you feel very near, and I'm wondering very much what you are doing. A letter from you is overdue. The papers are full of the great storms in Pembrokeshire, so please do write to reassure me.

I hope you don't mind me not sending you a birthday present in time for the 8th. I am saving up for it now, but I'm afraid I can't get it before about April. I think it fulfils all the rules we made about giving each other presents (which your pendant certainly did not!) But it is something we shall need for the house, not ornamental, but which we can both enjoy—I hope.

No, it is *not* a telescopic camera—even in my most extravagant moods, I don't dream of saving up to fifty pounds or more. I bet you can't guess what it is.

This is a silly letter, not a bit what I intended to write. My excuse must be that I'm a bit worried not hearing from you, and very tired, and it's after midnight.

So goodnight, with lots and lots of love.

D.

PART 3

November to Christmas 1927

Three men on an island

Dunlin feeding

Skokholm at last
31 October 1927

Dearest Doris,

At last I am living on the Island—in residence as they say. Time nearly 9 pm. I am sitting in the little east-facing bedroom writing on the little folding table (the house is fully furnished—ahem!) Jack is making wire-noose snares. In the armchair close to the fire old trapper Dick is dozing and probably wishing to be abed. The old house is very warm with two lanterns burning, and the Valor Perfection, on which I roasted two rabbits.

I've just been out to listen to the lapwings crying over the old meadows and ducks quacking and splashing noisily on the North Pond.

I am very happy to be here at last. We could only load two bags of lime, and our food and clothes. The motor only stopped once; I have not got my sea legs yet, I was nearly seasick bending over the infernal engine.

Having landed, the next job was to make the *S.P.* safe, by hauling her up to her berth in the red rocks. Unfortunately the great storm had swept away the improvised rocks-and-plank slipway we had built on our first visit. We had to re-improvise with laborious adjustment of large boulders and find more long planks to bridge the biggest gaps. Finally by noon she was fast against the ancient winch.

Dick, having trapped some ten dozen rabbits, which he'd hung in the empty leaking barn, was quite annoyed that we were not returning immediately to market them. Perhaps Dick was right, but I intended to spend at least one night on the Delectable Island. It looks so wonderful tonight the air being calm and mild, with pools of rainwater reflecting the moon and stars, and now and then a wisp of white cloud. There was a delightful moment when, hearing a twitter of birds at the edge of a large rainwater pool, I strolled near to find a posse of half a dozen small wading birds, perfectly tame and feeding. By their soft chirruping note they were clearly migrating dunlins.

Such is the magic of your future home, dearest partner. Through the broken window the occulting beam of St. Ann's lighthouse, five miles distant, flashes a regular beam, which blinks on the low ceiling over my head. Goodnight.

1 November, 1927
Aeolus, God of Winds, crept out of his red cave in Mad Bay, and shrieked his demon anthem around Skokholm all day, lifting the white skirts of Amphitrite and her sea-nymphs, and her son Triton rose in the hollows of the billowing snow-drift garments to blow his wreathéd horn. So that the *Storm Petrel* dare not leave her cranny in the rocks. A wondrous sight, but I am brought to earth by salty rain upon the house, I am obliged to patch our roof with ancient corrugated iron and drift wood held down by large rocks. But the rain drips steadily into the two rooms we inhabit.

Also had to make a mouse-proof pantry from a tea-chest. Old Dick tells me the mice arrived by accident when Bulldog Edwards was carrying cattle and colts into Skokholm. His boat being loaded with straw overnight in Martynshaven, mice got aboard. He added 'Some on 'em be big and 'eavy enough to spring me rabbit traps.' He has suggested we import a cat to cope with this invasion of the house, which occurs each autumn as the mice come in from the cold. He says that long ago when a cat was kept at the lighthouse, it went mad—'cos o' the terrible noise of the foghorn'. Anyway the keepers have made the lighthouse building mouseproof with excluder bars at the bottom of all the outer doors.*

Dick tells tales by our driftwood fire, which he carefully tends, adding another stick to keep the flame bright and his old bones warm. He is first to turn in, on the bed he shares with Jack, taking off his boots first, but not his clothes!

I'll draw you a sketch-plan of Skokholm Manor as it was—according to Dick—as far as he remembers when he worked for Bulldog. There's the remains of a large loft above the main room which used to be accessible by detachable ladder.

*[Interesting, because the Skokholm mouse is *Mus musculus,* the true mouse of the city but thrives in country buildings in the absence of its larger cousin the wood mouse *Mus sylvaticus.* What is even more curious and fortunate is the fact that there are no rats on Skokholm or Skomer, although there are reports of many shipwrecks occurring in both islands. But if the rats did leave these sinking ships, none have survived there. It is said the only rat to come ashore on Skomer was a pregnant doe which was seen as it left a load of stores on the beach. The then tenant Capt. Davies killed it stone dead with a well aimed pebble.]

Tuesday, 1 November

The day broke with a strong S wind, increasing to gale force, so we could not leave, for which I was thankful. Instead paid attention to the old farm buildings while Dick was around to indicate their use under Bulldog's reign.

I send herewith a ground plan of these (not to scale by the way)—Dick can't remember which was a cowhouse. The dairy shed has an almost intact roof; Dick hangs his rabbits there now.

I show the northern row of buildings in elevation. At one time, it is believed, a grain loft ran the length of them, but Dick said it has long decayed and its wooden floors have been chopped up for winter fires. The barn roof is almost intact with no more than three holes in its heavy tile roof—cut from the sandstone quarry near the lighthouse. The ground floor consists of huge flat slabs of red sandstone where the corn crops—mostly barley and black oats and a little wheat—were flailed by hand.

Peat was sometimes stored in the annexe to the house-porch, now roofless, but which you will remember we thought might be a convenient bathroom-cum-lavatory. I like the idea of digging peat; I think I have found the site of the old turbary near the South Pond.

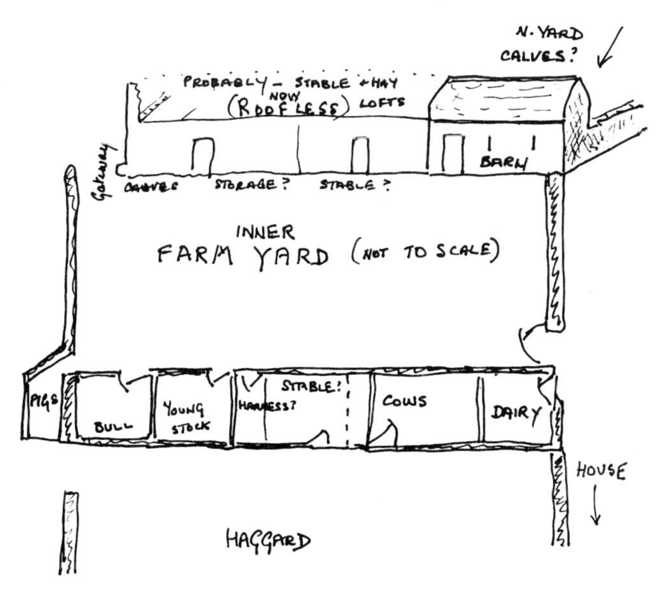

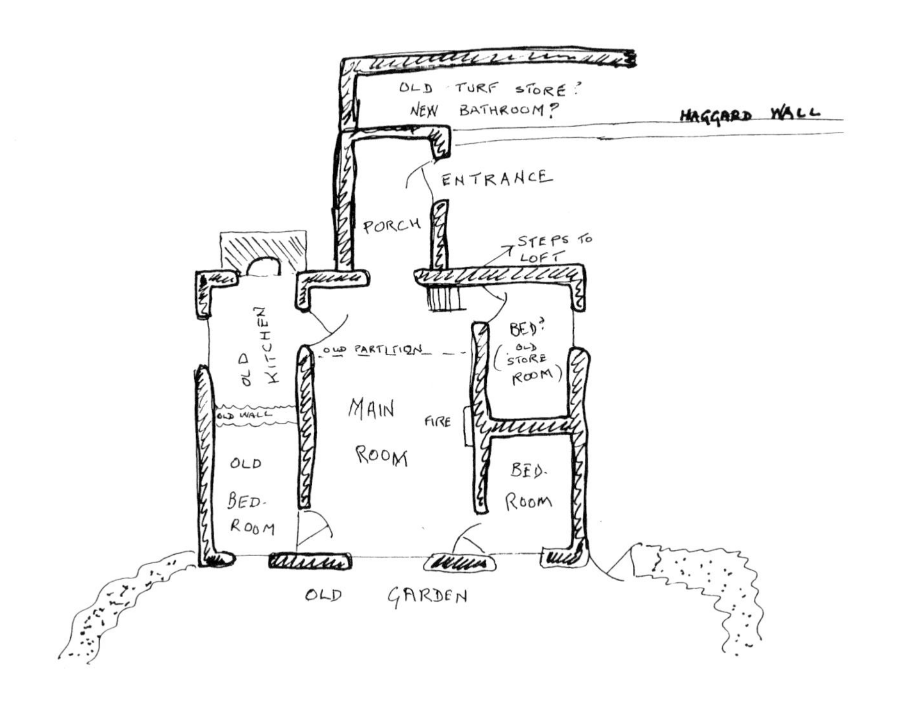

2 November

Dick caught 23 rabbits, including one fine black buck, fat, which I claimed, and we had the carcass stewed for supper. Its skin had a few white hairs mingled with its lustrous black fur. The earliest trapped rabbits were quite rotten, the best of these we skinned and threw the rest upon Bread Rock—so called because when the islanders were in need of flour for bread, they lit a beacon there. Buzzards, ravens and crows soon came to feast on the rotten rabbits.

Started to repair the enclosed garden in front of the house. Its protective bank walls are riddled with rabbit-burrows, so Jack began stopping these up and replacing the fallen soil and stones to restore the bank's height, while I dug deep some of the reddish stony loam, full of bracken roots, nettles and some hemlock. I put up a woodcock among these weeds, and followed its low flight to Spy Rock. The view from the top of this highest point of the Island was enchanting, a buzzard soaring in the updraught of the gale close over my head, mist still driving in from the south over the red and green plateau of the island, like the cold breath of Poseidon.

Today, Thursday, is still blowing from the SW with drifts of semi-horizontal rain. I stopped Dick from trapping. He had only 7 rabbits this morning—and a lapwing. I have pressed the crest in my diary to send to you! Dick looked so miserable I invited him to work in the shelter of the garden with Jack. I spend much time mooching round the buildings and making plans! There are gaps in the yard walls which I shall rebuild, I think it would be an ideal enclosure for the chinchillas. I have begun to dry-wall the worst gap, using the fallen stones, but it's a very windy place, and will need a strong lime mortar to hold it together. While I looked a lesser whitethroat (surely a record for time and place?) was feeding among the nettles. The Island proves to be almost a thoroughfare and resting place for many migratory birds, which today include many chaffinches, hundreds of lapwing, flights of mallard, teal and I think a few shoveller.

Am writing this 8pm on the table in the living room. Dick and Jack are chuckling over Saunders' *Manual of British Birds.* Dick, who can't read or write, trying to guess the species from the illustrations, and Jack not letting on until he can say Aye or Nay to Dick's guess!

I hope you are not bored with my day to day doings—the data of birds seen, numbers and habits etc, but you share my interests and I am always stimulated by the thought of sharing the future with YOU.

I don't express at all well what I am trying to say, but when we three males are together in the old house, and the ghosts of generations of islanders seem to whisper around us, we laugh together, as we reminisce about our day, the weather, all island matters and wonders, past and present—in happy camaraderie. I must be lucky in these two gentlemen, for such they are, loving nature, soft-spoken, with a faraway look in their eyes . . .

I like to go to Spy Rock at least once a day, and stand and stare over the whole island, or perhaps sit in a natural rock chair on the sunny side, dreaming that in a few more months I will hold you there—as I once did, remember?—and crown you Queen of Skokholm.

On Friday after lunch we threw 80 rabbits over the cliffs close to North Haven. Dick resumed trapping. Cleaned all accessible parts of the boat magneto and got the wayward engine to go perfectly. But my troubles were not over; after an abortive attempt to cross to the mainland, in hauling the *S.P.* back to her berth, the main plank bridging the big gap in the slipway snapped in twain—'twas rotten in the middle. And the boat hit a fang of rock tearing a hole in her side below her water-line. I finished an unlucky day by breaking my drinking mug in the house! Had to go to the lighthouse, and borrow lead, tacks and tar to mend the boat. Forecast by lighthouse wireless for the morrow is bad!

5 November

Weather deteriorating. Dumped more rabbits, but I was considerably cheered by sight of a dozen fieldfares (another first for the island) near North Haven, a snowbunting, and elver sized eels wriggling in the South Haven stream.

Dick has cleaned the well and covered it. This spring makes very good tea, being pure and issuing from the hidden rock (the local belief is that it comes all the way from the Prescelly mountains which we can see on our northeastern horizon). Old Dick believes this, and religiously collects a fresh bucket for our evening tea, first of all washing his trap soiled hands in a tub we have placed below the well.

Again a cold and cheerless wind kept us marooned. Dick collected 23 rabbits from his traps, but does not move any to fresh ground on a Sunday, which he and Jack spent in the weekly clean up and shave (cut-throat razor and hair trim), and pottering around, washing some of their flannel underwear and mending socks. I did much the same, though my efforts to darn were not exactly tidy. There were stonechats 'mong the usual starlings, thrushes, chaffinches, a raven and a buzzard. In Crab Bay I watched two handsome 'Dutch marked' rabbits; they wore white shawls and a white stripe between the ears and the tip of the nose, the rest of their fur normal black-brown. Probably throw-backs to domestic Dutch ones released long ago?

Jack cooked a delicious supper for us; rabbit and lapwing roast with slices of Jack's home-cured bacon, the bacon fat ideal for cooking in our paraffin oven. We have run out of bread, but still have plenty of ship-biscuits.

8 November

Crossed yesterday when heavy overnight rain calmed the sea. The motor started well, but suddenly failed off the Stack, so we rowed the rest of the passage. Without the engine we had to wait until the current slacked off in Jack Sound. So we sheltered in a gut on the E. side of Midland Isle. I could not resist landing there, and made a promenade of its green slopes. It would be an easy place to experiment with putting down a few chinchillas, as there were signs of very few wild rabbits—two were quite black, perhaps from inbreeding, Jack suggests. Philpin arrived in his delapidated van; the cargo of 106 rabbits made 97s 6d.

Forgive haste to post your letter (thanks for yours) and enclosed lapwing crest. At the same time I am posting the body of a snow bunting to the National Museum of Wales for sexing.

Ever and ever your R.

Tyr Bont
4 November

My dearest Ronald,

Write and tell me everything. You must be in residence now, and I want to hear every little bit of your adventures. I don't keep a diary—every time I've started one I've failed to keep it up.

You must let me know what other plants you want me to raise for feeding the chinchillas? And ourselves? I am taking some cuttings of raspberries and gooseberries, and have already planted out cabbages and carrots, for the rabbits. I have a new game. When I am milking I pretend I am milking goats at Skokholm. And when I am gardening I pretend I am with you in the island garden. Not always easy with some jobs, such as potting up chrysanthemums for indoors—I hope I shall never see a chrysanthemum on the island, they bore me so much.

How does your stove work? How do you keep yourself warm on these cold winter evenings? Who does the cooking? Have you started baking bread? There are ten thousand questions in my head, tormenting me. Yesterday I proposed to Papa that we ought to take a little holiday before winter really begins, and camp out on the island. But he shudders at the very thought! The weather is certainly trying, and the bits I read out from your letters about the storms, I fear, have helped to put him off. He promises we shall go there early next spring. Mama of course shudders, and still hopes you will give up the whole scheme!

Friday morning

There is quite a strong wind again this morning, and—a bad sign—there are flocks of gulls flying inland. Perhaps you are marooned on the island?

I have had a letter from your sister Enid. She must have felt the wrench of leaving the farm very much. She had no prospect half as exciting as ours when your farm was sold. It must have been very hard for her to go and live with your Mother in London after living for five years in the fresh air and freedom of your farm, with you to look after. Write to her often, I expect you do anyway. I miss her cheerful company too.

I bought myself a pair of silk stockings in Woolworth's, they were marked sixpence like most things there. But I did feel swindled when I was asked 6d for each leg! And they are going into holes already, so that economy did me no good!

Enid writes of hoping to look after you in the spring, before we are married. I hope she does for both your sakes, only I'm afraid she will have another wrench when I arrive and take possession. In her place I'm sure I would go and drown myself. As it is I shall be just a tiny bit jealous of your sister having you all to herself in the island spring. But you will be the lucky one, spoiled as you have always been by your competent and ever-loving sister whom everyone loves for her open-heartedness.

She asks about the bulb scheme. I have got a book on commercial bulb-raising, it says that it takes at least four years to grow a baby bulb to marketable size. I simply can't wait all that time. I'd rather grow sheep, and spin wool peacefully on our island!

Yours enduringly,

Do.

Back at Skokholm
8 November, 1927

Dearest Girl in the World,

I am twenty-four today, and realising my fondest ambition, which is to live happily forever on a bird-haunted island, set in a silver sea, with the prospect of being joined by the dearest girl in the world.

We loaded Jim Codd's cart with my barn windows, door, paint, boxes and bags etc., at Trehill, and went down to Martynshaven, where we filled up Jack's *Foxtrot* with same, as well as half a ton of cement and a bag of lime. With some difficulty we got this load off the beach, and presently had a fair NE breeze and a south-going tide to sail for Skokholm in 53 minutes by my watch—a grand morning's work! The rest of the day spent in unloading and carting up to the farmhouse, we stored the cement in the Trinity House hut above South Haven—with full co-operation from the keepers, and using their donkey and trams to bring everything as near as possible to hut and house. An hour was then spent in hauling up Jack's 23ft-long boat, probably the longest boat ever hauled up that crazy slipway.

How marvellous it is to be here. The island was very beautiful in the sunny cool easterly zephyr, which had brought in hundreds of new birds of passage: murmurations of starling, droves of blackbirds and thrushes, twitterings and pinkings of chaffinches and greenfinches, a kestrel, the usual stonechats, buzzards, crows, ravens and a pair of crying choughs settling at dusk to roost in North Haven cliffs.

Wednesday, 9 November

35 rabbits trapped, one combines the Dutch saddle marking with very long Angora-type hair. She was so pretty, with her ruby-wine coloured eyes that I kept her alive when Dick brought her home, and in spite of one leg broken—which I put in rough splints—I popped her in the remains of the upstairs loft for the night.

The migration of birds continues—this is the favourable wind for woodcock and lapwing, snipe and other game birds. But I see redwings, kestrel, and a peregrine falcon, which swooped twice at a raven. Just when I thought it would be killed the raven flipped over in mid-air and presented its talons to those of the falcon—almost as if playfully; they flew off separately with a sardonic croak from *Corvus corax*—a croak which sounds exactly like its scientific name!

We tried the Gassing Machine, and although it pumped clouds of heavy sulphur gas, not a rabbit was flushed, although all the likely exit holes were covered by Jack's purse-nets. We gave up and began erecting the Wortley Trap-fence. But I have my doubts about its long-term success in grounds riddled with burrows.

Thursday, 10 November

Sleety North wind. Restored a few more rotten sheets of corrugated iron on the house roof displaced by the gales, but the place remains leaky. The handsome Dutch-marked hairy rabbit did not survive the night, so I pelted her and we had a substantial carcass in a grand roast for supper at 6pm.

Dick had 37 rabbits and a woodcock in his 12 dozen traps, and Jack 17 in his new-set snares, making our highest total of 54. In the afternoon to North Haven, where Jack hauled up buckets of fine gritty golden sand as fast as I filled them. We got up about half a ton before the tide came in. We need this for concrete to fill the big gap in the hauling-way for the boat in South Haven slipway.

Friday

Pottered about measuring for repairs to house and barn.

Saturday, 12 November

Up at 6am, breakfast by lamplight and hurried down to launch *Foxtrot* , and loaded 96 brace of rabbits. We had to tack up to Jack Sound as far as the Anvil Rock at its entrance, but failed to beat the current under oars, so were obliged to beach on the pebbles at Renny Slip under the high south cliffs of the Deer Park—a new adventure for me. Having safely grounded his boat there, Jack performed wonders in carrying the rabbits humped on his shoulders up the cliff path there.

I went ahead to phone agent Philpin—after much delay he came and explained that 32½ brace had been condemned by the food inspector who had examined the last consignment, and produced the official notice of their rejection. I could only replace them therefore, but did not let him take the rest. Jack advised me not to bother with the unreliable Philpin any longer, but in future, to deal with the agent who collected the Skomer rabbits regularly twice a week by lorry at Martynshaven. Jack was rightly worried about his boat, still lying on the exposed Renny Slip with an incoming tide reaching over the jagged low-water rocks. As it was we had a stiff row to get through Jack Sound safe into Martynshaven, berthing in darkness by 7pm.

Enclosed a brace of rabbits, and, alas a curlew, woodcock and a fieldfare caught in Dick's traps.

Goodnight.
Your R.

P.S. While in Marloes this morning I picked up a letter from Charles Henry to say that he has been given notice to leave his employment at my old farm, as Mr. L. can't afford his wages it seems. He is getting in touch with you, as he is deeply interested in chinchilla rabbits, and has a pair himself, surplus from one of my first litters. I half-promised he could come and help on the island in the spring, which he longs to do. He is a good and cheerful worker, if a little dreamy at times, but for that—as great dreamers ourselves—we should be sympathetic.

Tyr Bont
6 November

To His Most Serene Highness, The Lord of Skokholm,

Greetings and Congratulations on his first Island Birthday, from a humble subject. His Lady hopes you will accept these few small tokens of respect and esteem. Sorry the cake got cracked in the middle turning it out of the tin. She hopes it will be edible, and enjoyed by all His Lordship's minions—the faithful henchmen John and Dick.

The vagaries of H.M. Postal Service, or the weather, or Your Lordship's preoccupation with Island affairs has troubled the undersigned—no letter or news from the Island in ages and ages. You must be held up there? I wonder how Skokholm fares now—no one can say you are seeing her under ideal conditions, as our critics loved to remind us all the time! You have passed that test, and your lovely letters reveal how happy you are. Yet when I brood over the tremendous task you have embarked upon all by yourself, I'm simply lost in admiration and envy. I just want to come and help.

I'm making, what d'you think—a tea cosy! I can't abide cold tea! At first I thought it would be a failure, but now I've knitted one side, it doesn't look too bad, and even Papa thinks it is passable, after poking rude fun at it. I've now got to try and finish it (groans). Why do I love starting a job, but hate finishing it? I'm afraid our house will be full of started things that will never be finished. You seem to admire those local lassies, have you fallen in love with one of them?

Many, many very happy returns of your birthday, with or without your Tyr Bont lady friend and admirer, and with all my love—D.

P.S. It is a dead calm night after a blustering day. I'm simply longing for dead calm weather. I have the queerest feeling that I'm not living at all—just existing from one day to the next, glad when each day comes to an end. It's the sort of feeling one can imagine a fly has when a spider wraps it up in silk, and hangs it up alive in readiness for its next meal.

I thought of how the sea and sunset and moonrise must look on our Island. That's the beauty of an island—the celestial bodies enhanced by the changing loveliness of the ocean.

Oh yes, one thing is, please keep the cake tin. It will be useful later.

It's so calm, surely there'll be a letter from you tomorrow?

Lots and lots of love,

Do.

Skokholm

14 November

Your letters are always a delight, thank-you a thousand times. I have negotiated with Nicholas, the other rabbit dealer, who willingly took (and contracted to take) all our rabbits. He paid me £5.14.7d. for the 62 brace surplus from the Philpin deal, and picked up a larger quantity brought over by the Skomer rabbiters. While in Martynshaven I got the motor in the *S.P.* going as if it had never been capricious, but could not run it for long out of the water because of overheating. Of course, I indulged in a stroll on the Deer Park, where I sat in the sun and read your letter yet again, admittedly distracted by the steady flow of the usual migrant birds towards both Skomer and Skokholm. There were little parties of eligugs (guillemots) off shore, and one gannet.

We are now back on the island, having got up at dawn at Trehill. Jim Codd loaned me two carts to take the timber delivered from H'west a few days ago, for making doors, floors and windows, and this filled the *Foxtrot*, with some to spare, which we had to put under cover in the Skomer boatshed (without permission, but Sturt's men said it would be quite alright!) Jim's young brother Reuben, a great hunter, came along, with his lurcher and three ferrets. With tide and wind we sailed across in 50 minutes.

In the afternoon we went ferreting; after two hours we caught only six and bolted about nine (which escaped)! The island rabbits seem very stupid—or very cunning. A walk up to the boggy plateau was more fruitful, the dog caught ten rabbits on the run. It seems ferrets may be of little value for rabbit control here. Reuben's first visit to the island demanded we visit the lighthouse and its wonders, Reuben fascinated by the huge clock mechanism which has to be wound up every hour to keep the lantern revolving—'to keep us from falling asleep' growled the keepers. They like to see new faces and hospitably gave us supper. I had planned that Reuben should have my bed in the little room—but he insisted we could share it. Result, a brief struggle between two large males in a single bed until I fell out and slept better afterward on the floor.

Tuesday, 15 November, Late evening

Reuben was out all day and caught 54 rabbits with his lurcher and purse nets, helped by the lighthouse-keepers anxious to take a few back when their relief boat calls tomorrow. As Dick trapped 36 and Jack snared 4 our total was 94 ready to be exported.

I seem to waste considerable time cooking for four hungry men.

At last to answer some of your queries, yes, please take any cuttings and plant out all cabbages, chicory, etc., which can be trans-shipped to Skokholm garden when eventually you do persuade your father that it is his duty to bring you over for a holiday (?) in the spring. The garden is almost dug over, although rabbit-burrows and bracken roots go down an awful long way in this friable sandstone soil. Cultivated fruit and vegetables are most important. We can try out everything you can spare, please. No flowers, of course, the island's wild display is all we need!*

I am so perfectly happy at Skokholm, in all weathers; but only at heart because of your promise to come and share its beauty with me. You can't help loving her guardian—the huge Atlantic Ocean, which stretches several thousand miles without land westward to America; there is a perennial wonder and attraction in its immensity. I see it in the wrinkled eyes of my companion Jack, and in old Dick too, when they stare at the sea in all its moods.

The Valor Perfection cooks splendidly—I intend to try my hand at breadmaking soon.

What do we have to eat? Here is our average menu:

0700 hours: tea, porridge, bread and honey or jam—Jack likes home-made dripping.

12 noon: Standby tinned corned beef, bread or biscuits (Ship variety—break your teeth unless dipped in tea). Cold potatoes if available.

*[R.M.L. relented on this issue!]

6 pm supper: rabbit, plover soup, broth, potatoes, cheese or what's available to satisfy the Skokholm appetite. Always tea, to end up, again before turning in. Dick has a big black kettle, and throws in a handful of loose tea from his food box. But in general we share each other's food.

Surprisingly Dick could eat all the birds he traps, thrush-size upwards. He is well aware that these gin traps are very cruel, mutilating birds; they are naturally attracted on this open windy island by the earth which he sprinkles to disguise the set traps. I believe some birds, such as wrens and pipits, actually roost in rabbit-burrows.

I am quite ashamed to say I have eaten roast blackbird and thrush offered me by Dick (he calls them 'poor darlints', as if genuinely sorry, but is doubtless a dissembling hypocrite, clever to sense and exploit your tender love of the living bird).

I have told Dick that we shall never use traps again here, because they are so beastly. 'Aye, sir' agrees the old man with a shake of his head!

I sometimes wonder if you ever read this stuff I send to you. Good night—it's bedtime. I see a lone mouse on the prowl. I wonder if they have already developed, during their half-century of isolation on Skokholm, enough sub-specific characters to be distinct? Like Darwin's discovery that speciation can be very rapid in isolation on small islands, like the Galapagos . . . GOODNIGHT. Maybe I'll post this with the lighthouse relief tomorrow.

Love from your R.

16 November, 1927

Dear Doris,

A pleasanter milder day, and sunny. The lighthouse tender called and unloaded winter coal, and a supernumerary to take the place of the sick keeper. I worked spasmodically on removing the debris of stones, rubbish and fallen tiles from the annexe to the porch which should make a roomy wash-place and lavatory. There are so many things to be done, it's difficult to know where to begin, but I am very happy, despite a decaying molar which gives fitful trouble.

Thursday, 17 November

I had suggested to Jack going ashore yesterday with the accumulated rabbits, not feeling that the SW wind would be gentle for long, but as Jack said 'twould be alright for another day, I perforce agreed; but this morning a howling SE gale was blowing in South Haven! So continued to remove debris of proposed washroom and did some backpacking of sand from the pile on North Haven cliff top, in readiness for making concrete for the barn repairs. Reuben's catch today was 37, including another black buck, fat enough for the pot, which I skinned. Dick had 24, and Jack snared 15. Dick brought home a meadowpipit and a water rail for me to identify. He called the rail a 'moory-hen' and said it would be too 'coarse' (meaning rancid) to eat. A curious *flat* bird, adapted to slipping through dense vegetation.

A wild sea surging in the sounds, yet more birds still arrived on the island—snipe, woodcock, starlings, a kestrel, etc.

Friday, 18 November

Again impossible to launch owing to the heavy ground swell, and the fact that Jack's *Foxtrot* is too long for launching when the tide is high, her stern is liable to get completely submerged before her bow leaves the slip and floats her hull off. A pity, as over 320 rabbits now await ferrying. I suggested going up on the night tide, so we launched her by lamplight while the tide was low but after we started to load our furry cargo, Jack cried out what he had been too shy to say earlier; ''Tis no shape goin' through tide races in the pitch dark!' Quite rightly he feared for his beloved *Foxtrot* , but the sea was calm enough to moor the boat off in South Haven before retiring.

Saturday, 19 November

Up early and loaded over 400 rabbits by 9 am, some now pretty stale. We sailed with the wind against the tide up to the lee of Midland Isle, Reuben loaning his strong arm on the sweeps to gain through Jack Sound; a notable experience for him who has never lifted a sweep before in his young life. But we had missed the new dealer so were obliged to leave the rabbits hung over the mast in Jack's boat.

Sunday, 20 November

A day of rest, but went down to Martynshaven and sold £12.9s.2d worth of the freshest rabbits to Nicholas, and brought back the stale ones to Trehill, for the boys to skin and make what they could of them.

Thank you, sinful child, for wasting time and money on this unworthy person, thank you a thousand times for the scrumptious parcel. It will take days to eat through all that food; but when I showed it to Polly her eyes glistened, and I asked her to take some of the riper fruit, and we all had a slice of the fruit cake and congratulated its maker—You, Princess of the Island!

I never know what to head my letters to you—Dear or Dearest Doris—'tis all the same, you would know what I meant if I wrote Dear Madam, or Most Celestial Princess . . .

Ever your humble servant

R.

The Lower Island
22 November

Dear Doris,

Discussing the chinchilla plan with Jack, who has never seen one, but has a great fund of knowledge on wild island rabbits, I finally extracted from him his opinion that it is virtually impossible to exterminate the last wild one, especially as so many live among the boulders and warrens hidden in the cliffs. So I have suggested the alternative as I see it. The experience with Reuben's lurcher and ferrets, and with Dick's horrid trapping has suggested to me that we give up the extermination attempt, and begin with chinchillas confined to a limited acreage enclosed on flat ground, perhaps the Neck and the Home Meadow, which will be easy to fence, then clear of the wild population by filling in the burrows and gassing them. Then put down the annual increase of young stock bred from the nucleus of chinchilla stock which we will keep in hutches. I hope to build a rabbitry in the shelter of the farm yard. Let me have your views on this.

We sailed back here yesterday, with a lovely NE breeze, and with her new sail the *Storm Petrel* whizzed through Jack Sound, and as she was sailing so well, I cut the engine and tested her as a sailboat only. She needs ballast, being flattish on the bottom, and we had only a light cargo of a wheelbarrow, and personal gear. A nasty leak appeared where it had been mended earlier, which necessitated bailing frequently. Dick meanwhile had trapped 65 rabbits in two days. We found him roasting some poor little blackbirds.

Tuesday, 22 November

Having told Nicholas I would fly a flag from the highest point every time we were coming over, I spent most of the day on Spy Rock, fixing a base for a flag staff—a 24ft pole we used to hang rabbits in the barn, held upright by three stay-wires I am bolting to the rock. Jack thought he could find a flag in his cupboard at home.

So please, dear wife-to-be, let me know what you think. I'd be honoured if you would design and make me a flag, which should be fairly large—say 6' x 4'—to be seen on the skyline from the Deer Park or St Ann's Head. I suggest a black and white storm petrel?

Five choughs gyrated above Spy Rock as I worked, enjoying their splayed wing aerial display, and later saw *nine* over the Home Meadow. The usual migration of thrushes etc. continued, including *four wild geese* circling the pond and gaggling noisily, but did not alight owing to Dick's presence nearby.

Jack had a useful day, mending a leak in the *S.P.*

My rotten tooth seems cured, but the old Talbot car seems near the end of its tether, neglected and battery run down. Think I may sell it?

Goodnight. Will post this tomorrow, when we plan to come over with 126 rabbits.

With all my love.

R.

Tyr Bont
10 November

Dearest Ron,

Just at the moment I am too tired and cold to write much as I'm sitting up in bed, with a hot water bottle keeping my lower half warm!

Tomorrow I will get a copy of *Fur and Feather* magazine and hunt up any skin merchants advertising there. No one locally knows of a good method of preserving rabbit flesh, except in salt or ice. I imagine they would keep in brine for a short time, like pork, but keep them too long and the brine gets to smell horrid. Papa says he has a Jewish recipe for smoking meat, but can't find it!

Friday Midnight

Just got to bed—with *Fur and Feather*. Shall write tomorrrow to three addresses of skin merchants. Meant to catch this evening's post, but too busy baking bread, also Vi arrived and we gossiped, hence this late hour. Goodnight. The lapwings are crying rather desolately over the frosty meadow by the river. I can almost believe I am listening to your island lapwings.

I am sure you are right about tackling the repairs to the barn first. It's for you to decide. Please don't be in a hurry to repair the old house. We can do it together next summer I hope. Meanwhile it seems sensible to set up the roomy barn for storing and living. How I wish I could be with you. Please describe *in detail* how you will fit it out.

I'm so happy today, I don't know quite why, except your letters have such a ring of joy and confidence in the island's future and you are happy in spite of the stormy winter. I played lacrosse today in a match at Whitchurch . . .

Sunday night

This is a perfectly hopeless letter, I'd better tear it up. Nothing of interest in it.

Love Do.

Letter to Ronald from Mrs Shellard:

Tyr Bont
27 November

My Dear Ronald,

No, I did not know it was the duty of sons-in-law-to-be to write to their prospective mothers-in-law, according to all accounts they are too much disliked to have much to do with each other beyond what politeness demands? Anyway I was very glad to have your letter, my conscience was already pricking me for not acknowledging your very nice present of Skokholm produce. Thank you very much for this, it was thoroughly enjoyed. Harry said we did not allow it to hang long enough—the birds I mean—but it was long enough for your Charlie, he did the plucking, and when he brought the curlew and woodcock to the door I noticed he was holding them well away from his nose! The trouble is Harry wanted to paint their speckled colours, and would not release them for days—he took so long to get them down on canvas . . .

Charlie seems a thoroughly nice boy. I do wish Harry would get rid of some more stock soon, as Do will be up to her eyes in rabbits after Christmas, and we do not want to keep the tiresome Tom in employment any longer.

I shall be sorry if you cannot spend Christmas here, but of course your family in London has priority. Vi and her children are here, and I have persuaded her to stay on with us until after Christmas. All join with me in sending you our kindest regards.

Affectionately yours,
Edith Shellard.

Dear Ronald,

Sorry my last letter was so scrappy. I really had lots to ask you. First, are you able to sell rabbit-skins, and if so, does it pay? Second, I don't approve of black for a flag—it savours too much of the skull and crossbones and would not show up so well as white on a landscape, or seascape? What about pale blue like a summer cloud, with a flight of black, white-rumped storm petrels heading towards the staff? I suppose they do fly in little parties, because of course we must be technically correct?

Maybe my notion is too high-faluting—I don't suppose one can buy tenting the colour of clouds—fancy going to a shop and saying 'Have you any summer cloud in stock?'

Would you like a real Welsh Dragon flag to go on with? Rather moth-eaten, but Mama offers to patch it up on her sewing machine. You shall look at it when you come. I feel quite stirred up inside when I realise I shall see you soon.

I think we may be giving up the farm soon. I'm undecided whether to get rid of the fowls as well, they are paying quite reasonably. Please advise me, I've been thinking about the problem of having fresh eggs on the Island. Plenty of gull's eggs when the gulls are laying—exactly when is this—May—June? In which case, should I breed from these pullets and bring the next generation to the Island?

Eggs are fetching 4/3d a dozen retail in the shops—I should lose all my customers if I charged that. People seem to think that the farmer is bound to sell his produce dirt cheap at the door. Don't you jump for joy when you realise that you have finished with those townsfolk who come to the door for fresh eggs and poultry, expecting you to let them have everything cheaply? I chortle when I think of next summer. But if I breed from these pullets I'll have to think of a new cock for them—I can't mate them to their brothers!

That's all I have time to say, to put in with Mama's letter.

Goodnight, my love.

D.

P.S. I'm afraid I shan't have very much time to write in the near future—I mean up to Christmas. I'm awfully busy, so please don't be too disappointed with these scrappy notes. I suppose if I did not write at all I should deserve nothing from you? I notice that as my letters get shorter so do yours.

Early Next Morning

Oh dear, what a mean thing to say—this is such a miserable letter that I shall post on Mama's only and burn mine—Ronald dearest, it's so dull here. No adventures, no excitements, nothing to write about of any interest.

No, I'll post it as you will have to find out about my indecisions, and the sooner the better. On a brighter note your letters give me the feeling that you're as happy as a lord on the Island. I read bits of your descriptive diary to Papa and Mama, I hope you don't mind. I wanted to share these splendid sentences with someone who could appreciate them. Papa certainly did, but I felt afterwards I had given something very precious away. How selfish—I gloat and think how unlucky other women are not to have a live serial island story to look forward to—and soon live with.

Now I feel better, your repentant D.

3 December, 1927

Dear Doris,

Wish you had been with me beachcombing today. I spied a stout long plank among low water boulders in Peter's Bay, and bethinking how useful 'twould be in future building operations, did clamber down the cliff to retrieve it. When Lo! a wondrous cave opened before me. Therein did enter and discovered it haunted by a monstrous jellyfish with long octopus-like trailers, which floated in the clear water of a pool in the floor of this magic cave. Penetrating further with quaking knees did see the skeleton of a ship jammed against the walls of the cavern, and sundry great pieces of her timbers criss-crossed like scaffolding from wall to wall. Over these did clamber into a great murky recess far above the tide-mark (limpet line), where did speculate on the possibility of making a home for a certain (now enchanted) Faery Queen. Reluctantly decided against it as the air in this dark cavern was too stagnant!

The jellyfish was also stagnant, very dead, so letting dead sea-devils lie, I took one piece of wreck timber with me. This cave is the best discovered so far, ideal for when we want to be alone, or avoid income tax.

5 December

I was recently offered a Sealyham terrier, one of the real breed from the Pembrokeshire village of Sealyham, a good rabbiter 'twas said. However I declined it in favour of a kitten. As you know I like cats only in their proper place—wild on Scottish moors. This time I was swayed by the thought of the havoc it should make in the armies of mice invading our house. So now we have a kitten in residence—the first to be landed in many, many years.

Went for a walk to Marloes then to Dale.The estuary and sands at Dale were full of gulls arriving to drink and preen after feeding in the ploughfields in the company of curlews, oyster-catchers, redshanks, snipe, larks and starling. I wanted to warn the St Ann's coastguards not to be alarmed at the sight of a flag flying over the top of Skokholm. It was still flying—they had not seen it! Of course, they excused themselves, they had not expected one in such a place—rumour had reached them that the (madman) Lockley had long ago abandoned the inaccessible island! I could see the flag with my naked eye—a cheering sight! They said that birds never strike the lantern of St Ann's Lighthouse, because it exhibits a fixed (occulting) white light, non-flashing.

The long walk home along the cliffs to Trehill was glorious, Skokholm in view all the time—buzzards, choughs, stonechats, buntings, furze and white scurvy-grass flowering, and I saw two weasels playing behind a hedge-bank.

You ask what do I do in the long evenings? I write up my diary and nature record—and keep you up to date! It's generally 8.30pm before I can get out my pen. We come in just after dusk, wash off the daily grime and salt in a tub we have placed under the eaves to catch whatever rainwater it will—always salty from the gales. We are very hungry for whatever's going, usually rabbit—and any unfortunate trapped bird. With the driftwood fire going, and the Perfection stove cooking, it's often very warm in the little house (wind tends to die down at night). One gets very sleepy after food, and inclined to yarn for the rest of the evening. I recognise I am very lazy then, but I am also very impatient—impatient that so little has been achieved each day.

Today I have been cutting up two long iron V-bars found under boulders in South Haven after the last storm. We are going to bolt them as a form of ladder to cover the biggest gaps in the rock slipway below the boat winch.

I haven't yet had time to make and bake bread. At first I hadn't time to wash my own clothes, and sent one parcel to Mother in London. Her deserved reply was to wash them and return them with a box of soap to do them myself in future!

Your R.

Ashore
5 December, 1927

Dearest Do,

What's the price of aeroplanes? We crossed from the Island yesterday, but can't return today, owing to a southerly gale blowing into Skokholm harbour. Hopeless harbour in any strong wind from SW to SE, the swell rolls in from the open Atlantic like a majestic hymn with the loud pedal full on. Its not too difficult to launch the boat if we do so at low tide, when the little beach of red pebbles is sheltered by a fortuitous but immovable slab of rock. But then the landing steps are more exposed.

What we did yesterday was to launch the *S.P.* at low water, with the sail ready to hoist as soon as we got out into the swell, and sail smartly round to North Haven, (sheltered under the cliffs from the south wind) to collect the rabbits assembled there by Dick at Blacksmiths Landing. As I believe you love romantic adventures you will like this part of our island living. But perhaps you will have too much of a good thing? And your brave heart will quail at having to face roaring angry tides, leaping white horses, and furious persistent winds and rain? I hereby give you fair warning—to think it over before committing yourself to a wild unapproachable island, beautiful in calm, most savage in storm; and to cap it all a selfish incompetent husband.

For undoubtedly I am selfish. Although I love the sea the more it seems to challenge me, a woman must think very differently? With these almost incessant gales of late I have had more leisure to consider life on a lonely island from your point of view, that of a cultured woman brought up in a sheltered environment, with all the amenities of a gracious home—and a farm of your own to command. Are you sure you really want to exchange peaceful secure country life for the uncertain future on a wild rock in the ocean? There are times when I am afraid for you, tying yourself to this headstrong, not to say impecunious and selfish Lockley. Be warned—it's not too late to withdraw! Goodnight.

It's now Thursday Dec 8th. I began this letter in the Griffin Inn, three days ago. I have been to see the lady who inhabits an old fort above Dale Roads. She breeds chinchilla rabbits, among other animals—you'll like her, she is an eccentric by the name of Miss Bland who adopts waifs and strays and animal casualties, including two orphaned young girls!

I am seriously thinking of erecting a hut at Martynshaven to store belongings and sleep weatherbound ashore. This dependence on locals must stop. I am making enquiries of the agent in H'west, to see if I can lease a small plot for a hut, close to the road.

Mother writes that she has invited you to come up with me to London for Christmas. Please, please do come. I was afraid to risk asking you off my own bat, as could not see how seven of us Lockleys were going to sleep in that small flat. But Mother evidently solved the problem, and Dad has sent me a list of trains, so I expect to travel up on the 23rd, and travel back on the 27th. So you must come. I'll pick you up on the 23rd and we'll paint London red.

Ever your R.

Skokholm, 9 December

My deepest apologies. In the hurry to get off yesterday I forgot to post this letter and did not realise this until I came into the island house at dusk. Having spent the afternoon in sowing the slag in two places—one cwt on the centre of the Neck, where I intend enclosing a patch of heather grass to put down some chinchillas, and the other cwt in the home meadow, to enrich the grazing there too.

Saturday, 10 December

Filled up the fissure on the west side of the barn with new mortar of lime and sand. The original mortar in these walls has reverted to pure earth and blows away to nothing on being touched by my trowel. Yet the ancient walls still hold upright in most places, resisting the gales. Of course mice get in fairly easily, and snails, which love the dry shelter, where they shrink back into their shells and hibernate for the winter. I enjoy winkling the sleeping *Helix hortensis* out with a flick of my trowel, for the thrushes to dine where they fall into the yard. There are plenty of thrushes on passage here among other migrants. As I worked a kestrel dashed after a stonechat, which sought cover inside the barn—second time a wild bird has sought human protection in my experience.

When I asked Dick what had happened to the fine black rabbit pelt I had some days ago stretched out to dry on a board inside the barn, he was reluctant to reply, but at last muttered something about the young supernumerary light-house keeper, landed at the last Relief to replace a sick permanent keeper, was rather too fond of mooching around the buildings.

So you see, Doris, a little crime has reached the island—from the mainland. Discussing this by our evening fire, Jack told me later that Dick was certain that the lighthouse lad had pinched the pelt during our absence ashore.

Sunday at Skokholm

I tried my hand this evening at breadmaking. It proved a failure —too heavy-handed with the dough I expect. It was suggested I feed it to the gulls on the north pond, but even they rejected it and parts of the loaf floated there for ages! John is teaching me how the tides and currents run around the island. Usual day of rest, cleaning and washing clothes, shaving, etc. Jack uses a cut-throat.

Monday, 12 December

Patched one hole in the barn roof, placing fallen tiles back on new laths, smearing the joints and overlaps liberally with concrete. We left after noon on the favourable flood tide, passing through pods of porpoises.

Goodnight, I shall go to bed with your letter—glorious prospect! But I am specially glad tonight because I have been offered a site near Martynshaven on which to build a little hut for storage and living in when we are marooned ashore by bad weather on the mainland. I shall inspect the site with the landlord of West Hook on whose land it is situated. Will report in my next letter.

How goes the Tyr Bont Rabbitry?

Very much love R.

16 December, 1927

Dear Ronald,

The thought of the great gales and stormy seas appals me, and as for the selfish incompetent husband, he is not to be thought of—to whom are you referring?

If you believe one word of that the sooner we part the better—why do you suggest such things? I wonder if I had not wanted so much to pioneer on the Island with you, whether you would have asked me to marry you? I think not.

About Christmas, just supposing you were coming here, instead of going to your family in London, I am sure your family would be upset? I haven't dared to suggest to Mama that I spend Christmas week with your family in London, because she would hate the idea that I wished to spend my last Christmas before marriage anywhere but at Tyr Bont. It doesn't really matter to me—I am not sentimental about Christmas, but I know you will understand how I feel about the old folk. Surely you'll be able to spare one night here on your way to London? I shan't be happy until I see you before Christmas.

I'm awfully tired tonight, it has been a dull drizzly day, no wind —I feel stifled. But I expect you have sailed back to your beloved island without a care in the world?

Lucky you! Goodnight, and send me happy dreams from your eyrie on Skokholm.

xxx D.

Dearest R.,

Another letter for you! I told Papa about the Deerpark hut plan, and he thinks it would be a good spec, to rent it and put up a little house on it to live in. I told him I did not want to live on the mainland. 'Oh!' he said, 'I wasn't thinking of you. Do you think you are the only person in the world!' Jolly well squashed!

I think dear Papa is inwardly fuming, with over work at his surgery at this time of year, and wishing he was holidaying with you as he used to do, and just a wee bit cross with me planning to abandon the dear old man. Anyway he has been rude to Mama too. He did say earlier that we would have to get rid of the farm because of my leaving, but today he was quite cross when Mama broached the subject. We had a four-handed set-to, three females against one dogged man. But only succeeded in making the air blue and everyone exceedingly uncomfortable.

Now Mama has told me to go ahead and sell anything that is fit to sell. Whatever we do seems wrong—I sold two heifers at the local market, and got a very poor price for them, but they were actually getting thinner on the winter grass. Oh Dear, I didn't mean to burden you with my troubles.

I agree with you about a cat. Perhaps after surfeiting on mice this winter it will go mad—like Dicky says, a lonely tomcat looking for a non-existent queen in the spring! I hate our cat for killing wild birds, but it also kills rats and mice, and purrs so nicely on your lap on a winter evening. But on our island, with thousands of resident and migrant birds, not so good! I am thankful that you have decided that gin-trapping is too horribly cruel to be used again. I've just read in the paper about the beastly slaughter of quails in nets and snares in Egypt.

Do you suppose we could naturalise quail at Skokholm? According to my bird book quail migrate as far as Britain and sometimes breed.

Young Mary has just trampled all over this letter, and I am ordered to put her to bed. So goodnight for now, with unswerving love.

D.

Skokholm
13 December, 1927

Dear Doris,

I should much like to know what you are so busy about that you find so little time to write, Madam. On arrival back to South Haven, went for a ramble and found one of the lighthousemen helping himself to some goodly planks which had washed ashore. He was quite rude when I said I required his fine planks for house repairs, he argued that all jetsam on the island was the property of those who placed it above high water. He may be right, but I said I would confiscate that fine plank, and invited him to help himself to all 'firewood' jetsam he could bring ashore. I cruelly reminded him that we had regularly posted and collected his letters when we went ashore, if directed c/o me at Marloes. In the end we became quite amicable, result—this week a sack of lighthouse coal appeared mysteriously outside the house!

You say nothing at all about how the rabbits are getting on? It's time to have the adult does mated, please note.

17 December

I have got on with repairing the whole roof of the barn, with a bit of help from John—finished it today. All done with original heavy sandstone slates. Each one has to have its own oak peg—wedge-shaped to fit the hole in the top, which meant that we had to cut and shape replacements for the rotted ones. The pegs hold the slate in place on the underlying lath, the smallest slates at the top of the roof. A good layer of concrete is applied to each row of slates, and the whole roof afterwards grouted with a fine smearing of cement-and-island-sand mixture.

Days of the week have no special significance to me; working happily alone, it is an effort to remember what day it is. I do not look forward to going ashore. Once I have looked for a letter from you, I am anxious to return to Skokholm quickly. I have been to the lighthouse for a lesson in Bread-baking and tonight I turned out four large loaves, which swelled up beautifully. We ate two of them too greedily.

You ask an impertinent question: would I have asked you to

marry me if you had not wanted to come and play Crusoe on Skokholm? The reply is, would you have promised to marry me if I had not an island to offer you? I think not!

Several lapwing caught in the rabbit traps. I shall send you some, with a couple of fat rabbits. The old house is so draughty that we have had to rig up a big floor mat and some canvas as a screen around the fire. Jack, Dick and I must have been a comical sight, for we polished the cutlery (together with the *S.P.*'s magneto) and kept ourselves warm with driftwood and lighthouse coal.

Sunday, 18 December

Bitterly cold for the day of so-called rest, which I spent largely in rambling after driftwood, and cogitating and counting birds—the huge flow of lapwing flying before the east wind. There was a touch of ice on the North Pond, but in the shelter of the garden a dunnock and our tame robin and one twittering greenfinch seemed happy enough. Surprised a water-rail, which ran down a rabbit-hole—a curious wraith-like bird which although it migrates long distances, prefers to run and hide rather than fly when you stumble on it.

Monday, 19 December

Still it blows more furiously than ever, and a frost holds enough to carry my weight on pond ice—yet the wind is so strong in over exposed parts of the pond that lanes of water are rippled open, where ducks and gulls swim. I counted five teal and a mallard there. Flocks of lapwing fly west into the open ocean, some slightly north-west might conceivably reach Ireland, but those I saw heading more southerly are likely to miss Paddy's Land altogether.*

Birds seemed uneasy today. Numerous snipe were lurking where the ground was soft enough to probe with their long bills. Stonechats were hunched up miserably as they perched in the heather. Herring

*[This actually happened. It was later recorded that several lapwing—one ringed in Cumberland—were recovered in Newfoundland, 2200 miles west, having been storm-blown there before the same easterly gales which, according to the meteorological office, prevailed across the North Atlantic. The lapwings, not native to Canada, died in the thick snow and ice there.]

gulls were impudent enough to dig into rabbit-offal where Dick had paunched his catch. There were fieldfares, redwings, greenfinches, more water-rails, a kestrel, buzzards, while blackbirds and song-thrushes abounded. It is evident that birds are carried west by this cold easterly and become concentrated in this far west point of South Wales.

The frost was too severe to risk making concrete—in Boar's Bay the long icicles hung from the little stream tumbling over the cliff there. Yet in a sheltered niche near the boat winch I found a primrose in bud.

Wednesday, 21 December

Wind changing and calming down. Thoughts of being marooned over Christmas were put away! Oyster-catchers came inland, chattering to each other this morning on the rock behind the house. I suppose we shall have to cross today, though I feel strangely reluctant to do so—with the island so full of interesting migrants. Only the thought of your letters awaiting drives me across just now. So much to do before we leave the Island for Christmas, and so little done—to report to you.

I'm apologising in advance, soon I shall have the joy of holding you in my arms—seems such a long time since I did, and I'll be shy —

But ever your steadfast R.

XXXOOO

17 December, 1927

Dearest Ronald,

It is disappointing that Ann—the first doe to be mated, and the only one that looked like producing a family—has failed to do so yet. According to my book she should have littered three days ago. I had great hopes when she started filling her nest-box with hay by the mouthful, and there was some of her belly fur mixed with it. It is evidently a false alarm (what the manual says is a pseudopregnancy, all in her imagination?) and she's not really thinking of offspring!

I'm awfully sorry, I did warn you that I would probably make a hash of coney love affairs. These chinchillas refuse to react according to the procedure laid down in the manual of rabbit-breeding. They always seem to behave with placid indifference when girl meets boy—just a polite sniff when introduced, then a munch of greenstuff. No love, more often a fight, when one of them bolts for cover—into the nest box, and sulks there. Signs of love in a lone rabbit are said to be by stamping, so when Beatrice began stamping a few days ago, I was about to bring her a buck, when I discovered her looking angrily at our cat staring at her through the wire-netting, alarmed, not lovesick! Sorry to be so stupid. Perhaps rabbits prefer to mate at night, privately? They are nocturnal in the wild.

I've just been re-re-reading your recent letters. I am longing to see that big cave in Peter's Bay. I simply must come back with you after Christmas—I don't care what people say, our mothers are so Victorian! Only ten days to Christmas! I want to jump out of bed, and waltz around my room, but I might wake the sleeping household up, and Vi's baby would start yelling.

This morning when the sun peeped out for half a second, I heard a rush of wings above the garden. It was a big flock of starlings going west straight for Skokholm! I sent them my love for you. Then Mama came in with tea, and I told her and Vi that I planned to return after Christmas with you. Vi remained neutral, but Mama got quite nasty about it—so did I! Oh bother!

I must go now and feed the chinchillas and pray Ann may yet have babies.

About baking bread, I'm now expert, you'll be glad to hear. But I only bake once a week—on Saturdays. To freshen a loaf, dip it briefly in water and pop it in the oven. This turns it into new bread right away—quite marvellous! You evidently need a lesson in bread-making. I'll show you when you come.

Ever so much love from D.

Tyr Bont
18 December 11.45pm

Dearest Ron,

This is the last letter you will get before I see you—in five days time! It is getting more and more difficult to find fresh green food for the hutched chinchillas. This afternoon I was out with Vi and Mary, gathering rabbit-food along the lanes. We got absolutely frozen—like the hedge-parsley.

There's a thick mist today. We can hear a foghorn moaning far away in the Severn Estuary. I think all hope of me returning with you after Xmas is doomed. Vi offers to come, but I couldn't possibly drag her away from her family.

Soon, we'll be able to talk over everything together. I refuse to believe that the weather will be so unkind as to prevent you from crossing.

Thank you for two fat rabbits with lapwing sandwiched between. We ate them tonight while they were fresh, and before Papa got ideas about painting the very beautiful plumage of the peewit—as he calls it.

Enid has just asked me to stay in London with her after Xmas, and go with her on the lacrosse tour. If I go anywhere after Xmas it will be with you to Skokholm—if you'll have me.

I would have bought a raffle ticket for you at the village Christmas 'do', but I was afraid that you might win something, then if your name was called everyone would look at me and I should blush—stupid creature! There were lots of things that would be useful to you just now—Christmas cake, puddings, a whole ham . . .

As for your idea of my confiding my troubles to you, I have none, except I'm not with you and that I cannot breed rabbits, both I have already confessed. If our chinchilla scheme fails I will be quite happy to be a shepherdess wife to a lobster fishing islander.

Goodnight,
ever your D.

P.S. There are bullfinches in our River Woods, and other seed-eating birds—or are they siskins . . .

From R.M.L.'s diary:

Spent the night of 23rd December at Tyr Bont, before proceeding to London for Christmas with parents and sisters. Brother Ken still in Burma . . . Arrived back at Tyr Bont at 10pm on Dec 27th.

Wednesday, 28 December

Spent the day with Doris, instead of going to Pembrokeshire immediately. We took bus to Rhiwbina, walked over the hills to the *Travellers Rest* at Thornhill in the snow, had tea, bread and cheese at 2pm, then walked back over Black Cock Mountain, passing all those wild haunts I knew on youthful expeditions years ago. On the way back to Tyr Bont, bought four ferrets, picked up my terrier Nip from L's.

There followed a frank discussion with Do's family as to our future prospects and hope of a living on Skokholm. Mrs S. against the isolation, Mr S. supporting my progress so far. Doris and I said very little, having long agreed that whatever happened we would become man and wife on July 12th 1928.

PART 4

January 1928

New Year, new plans

Blackbird, blue and great tit

Tyr Bont
30 December, 1927

Dearest Ronald,

Here I am writing in the bedroom where you slept last night . . . It still seems to echo your footsteps. I can't write very coherently. My joy in our lovely walk over the mountains is a mixture of happy thoughts and sheer physical tiredness—my legs still ache from trying to keep up with your stride. I'm now reproaching myself for keeping you up so late—poor boy, used to living a natural life and retiring probably before 10pm. Here I never seem to get to bed before midnight. Mama has made them all play whist again—I can hear their chatter and laughter downstairs. Thank goodness they took pity on me, and did not ask me to play. I have no card sense but I know your family are all keen bridge players.*

Trehill
30 December, 1927. Early am.

Dearest Partner,

You see, I have returned quite safely with Nip and the ferrets, and am leaving at noon for the Island.

Of course I forgot to take the Welsh Dragon Flag with me, so will you post it when time and inclination permit? It will do until your Three Storm Petrels Rampant arrives—it was fun making up that clever cut-out. You must decide what shades of colour are best.

Your obdt. humble servant R.

Skokholm
31 December, 1927

Dearest Doris,

New Year's Eve was a lovely sunny day with a mild spring like air, the frost having quite thawed, and a pleasing moon at night. Though it was bitterly cold crossing yesterday. South Haven, when

* [Mother always hated cards. Ronald, on the other hand loved all card games —though his bridge was far from conventional.]

we landed, was hung with fairy tale icicles where the two little streams 'fled over the clift' as John described them.

Nip and the ferrets crossed to the island in fine style, despite a lumpy sea. Nip a good sailor, tho' he evinced a desire to swim the last quarter-mile to the island, and but for being tied to a thwart, might have leaped into the tide as we approached the Stack.

The old flag we left flying on Spy Rock was of course torn to shreds in the Christmas storms—my fault for neglecting to take it down in the hurry to get away. Also the pebble landing-beach washed right out by the ground-seas; but it will gradually return in fine weather, John says.

Early am 1 January, 1928

Happy New Year to You, loveliest Girl in the World! A thousand Kisses and Hugs.

Remember this is the beginning of the most auspicious year in my life!

Please give my best New Year wishes to all at Tyr Bont.

Last night at 12pm Jack and I walked up to the Lighthouse to wish the keepers all health and happiness—prosperity they have already—an assured income, and a pension at 65. Only one was awake—because he was on duty. Over a cup to tea we heard the New Year wireless messages. On the way home we could see all the lights: St Anne's, St Govan's, Lundy, Smalls. Sth Bishop and the red of Skokholm. Such a lovely moonlit night, the Island full of bird cries—soft quackings of mallard, querulous bell-notes of teal, plaints of peewits, whistling of curlew and wigeon, scraping of snipe and piping duets of oystercatchers. The last are already coming inland to claim their old nesting-sites, but only by night. The sea was calm, the shore laced by a just visible white line of surf . . .

Jack was agreeable to trying out the ferrets in the garden hedge, where some holes have been opened in our absence. But we only netted three. We adjourned to the patch on the Neck which I propose to clear and enclose for the chinchillas. But not a rabbit appeared, and only with difficulty were the ferrets recaptured before dusk; they, like the rabbits, found it snugger to lie doggo underground. Meanwhile I was delighted to watch little flocks of migrating birds arriving on the easterly wind from the Mainland, . . . I identified a solitary turnstone near the Stack, a pretty Arctic-born miniature of the lordly oystercatcher . . .

Tyr Bont
5 January, 1928

Dear Ron,

This is a horrible pencil—don't try to strain your eyes over the writing, for it won't be much loss if you can't read it. I wonder if you have had the fall of snow we had? It started Saturday morning, and was very thick, tho' it lasted only a couple of hours. Everything was a fairyland afterwards, so breathlessly pure it made me feel a blot on the landscape. Even the wire-netting was transformed into crystal lace. The birches were a dream—silver filigree against the delicate blue of the sky.

Your sister Aline called, skates in hand, so we swept the snow from a goodish patch of the pond in River Field; but not enough, I fear, to make figures-of-eight!

Suddenly in the evening it began to thaw. It rained all night until not a scrap of snow or ice was left. An old chair I had used to steady myself when skating was left sitting in the middle of a huge lake in River Field! I waded in to rescue it this afternoon, carefully watching the tops of my gumboots, but forgot that there were holes in the back, cold trickles seeped in. Ugh!

Time to go to sleep. Goodnight and a very happy New Year.

Love forever.

Do.

Thursday

Just had your letter. I did not think of you wandering about Skokholm New Year's night, so I wasn't with you in spirit. I felt when I'd read your lovely letter that I had missed a wonderful spiritual experience—not that you had been at all forgotten. But I was so excited by your account that I fired a salvo out of my bedroom window—wasted three bullets of my little automatic pistol. I wondered afterwards if I had killed any of my own chickens because the cocks crowed in response! It's a good thing I have a pistol, isn't it? To protect me from a fierce islander.

It is now on guard on top of your letters. Is that a good omen? I've been trying to find some eloquent words, from the depth of my heart—to wish you all the happiness that you believe you are going to achieve with your humble wife-to-be, but I am embarrassed, and never was any good at eloquence . . .

Enough said! I am yours forever and ever, your islandwoman Do.

P.S. I am very doubtful about the cake—it feels too heavy. Give it to the gulls.

Skokholm
4 January, 1928

Dear Doris,

There's a splendid moon this week, and I am quite moonstruck as a result. Whenever there's a moon you can expect mad letters from me. I feel inspired to write you reams of romantic rubbish, restrained by the fact that I have so little time in which to scribble it.

The last trip on Jan 2nd through Jack Sound was 'wussern' as they say round here than Belloc's 'Nona'. 'Twas a day of unrelenting misfortune. First when we lowered the *SP* down our patent iron-runged ladder, we found that the little beach was so washed out we could not launch her while the groundswell pounded on the exposed fangs of the rocks. So with halting steps and much fist-shaking at the snarling seas, we had to haul her up safely again. Jack was quite philosophic as usual, but I did not care to be outwitted by a mere groundswell when all the sea outside seemed calm and inviting. Besides, we had packed the boat full with rabbits, sundry parcels and the outgoing lighthouse mail. At noon when the tide came in full and the rocks were covered we tried again and got away on the crest of a swell that sucked us out from the creek to the open sea. Next the engine failed; it had been wetted by a big wave in launching.

Now as we approached Jack Sound where the dangerous Horse or Cable Rock and its shallow circle of tossing water lies in mid-sound, snap went our yard in twain! So we had to row the rest of the way to Martynshaven through a boiling sea of reefs, eddies and the cauldrons which surround the Black Stone, the Benches, the Anvil, Crab Stones, Tuskar and the Haze. There was a big surf gathering to hurl us upon Martynshaven pebbles, so that one of us had to take the painter, jump ashore, and hold the boat head on to the beach, while the other ran to make fast the winch wire and turn the handle like mad, while the man at the boat strove with all his strength to prevent breakers throwing her broadside. After all that Dick was not there, nor in Marloes, nor in any of the pubs!

So we did hie back hurriedly to our beloved boat, nor recked me of Dick or any of his accursed kind. What cared we but to return to the beautiful island? With a new yard and a new-faced moon, what more could this man want (save a letter from the Gracious Princess)? For we loathe to stay by night in that evil den of gossip which is called Marloes.

We lifted our new cutch-dyed lugsail which moonlight had turned a deeper black-red, and the tip of the new yard pointed straight to heaven and impaled the North Star. We knew not which to admire—the moon, the sea, or our vessel, in this ecstasy of a sea-symphony of celestial sound and vision . . .

And when we glided into the Island haven the curlews of the land were crying a welcome.

The moon, you see, has quite got into my blood. I wandered alone around the cliffs, longing to share each wonder with you. I could see in my mind's eye all colours of the day by moonlight—the red rocks, blue sea, white surf, whispering bracken, silent grass and the ghostly pale patches of lichen. When I returned to South Haven the sea in the cradle of red rocks was very still and the air so warm that I had a great desire to dive into the sparkling water.

It was as I expected liquid silver would be—very cold! I dived twice until I tingled warm, interrupted finally by another bather by the light of the moon. A mermaid? No, just an inquisitive immature seal!

Local news from Skokholm hearth

Today Ronald Lockley, Seignieur of the Island, was engaged with his Aide-de-Camp John d'Edwards in hauling sand from the famous low-tide deposits in North Haven. The Sr was also observed to begin inserting new windows in the venerable walls of the Barn, and speculation was rife that the whole structure may soon fall upon and slay him.

John d'E, in the absence of Trapper Richard, put down a few wire snares—partly to provide provender for supper, and so far reckons to and does bring home a dozen conies each morning. Have caught a chill from sweating in North Haven getting sand, or was it the silvery swim?!

A sick keeper was taken ashore by Trinity House and a jolly jack-tar took his place pro-tem.

The ferrets have not been a success—in fact only seven rabbits bolted in two ferreting days, using purse nets over their burrow entrances, Nip stands by to leap upon any that escape (he captured four of these). At present we can catch more by roaming over the central plateau and flushing rabbits which lie up in the withered bog-grass, which Nip is good at chasing, the ground being too wet for burrowing. One ferret has been lost for two days now, which is a worry, since John muzzles them with string—to prevent them killing underground. But he says a muzzled ferret gets so hungry it invariably surfaces and is glad to be picked up and fed in its warm hutch. The stupid rabbits simply won't bolt; they squat at the blind end of a burrow, presenting only their rumps to the ferret, which comes to the surface frustrated, with its claws full of fur. If it manages to free itself of the muzzle it will kill and gorge itself, and sleep underground on a full belly.

I wonder if you have read as far as this?

Your kind confidence in our future success may be sadly misplaced. For I too have had moments of despair, reaction to my normal joy in living here. I remember the arguments and foreboding of your wise mother when we talked about the island at Tyr Bont—only last week, though it seems months ago. What do people really think of You, a gracious lady wasting her talents as mate to a madman—for such I am told I am—on a remote island. Do they say, 'Oh, those romantic fools! That young Lockley with his forlorn hope of clearing the 250-acre island of the thousands of rabbits. In a few years or sooner he will have spent his capital, and be driven back to the mainland—to a London job at 2 pounds a week, no wild birds, no wild flowers, no sun, no moon, no stars, no noon, no pleasant time of day to stand and stare . . .'

This is not exactly a cheerful letter for the New Year. My present touch of the blues is perhaps engendered by a Christmas letter from my wise brother thriving in the tropical heat of Burma! He tells me of herds of elephants his firm uses to extract timber, especially teak, from native forests, they also export shiploads of rice. He sends his good wishes, which he asks me to convey to you. The general tone of his brotherly advice is much the same: he reiterates that we are very unlikely to clear the Island of the wild rabbits, that I have no business to isolate any woman on a desolate storm-swept rock!

I ask myself again, 'After three months' experience of island living, and studying the behaviour of these insular rabbits, do I really believe I can exterminate them?' Answer: Not without employing a large gang of men, an expense too great for my small means. But I must press on with my idea to clear the wild ones from a more or less level area of the Neck, and/or an acre or two of the Home Meadow, once we have rabbit-proof fenced these sites with wire-netting some four feet tall and dug into the ground to resist burrowing. In the last century, when both Skokholm and Skomer were farmed properly, with crops, the hedge walls were kept in rabbit-proof condition by the farm labourers regularly patrolling the boundaries, filling in any attempt by rabbits living in the outer heathland to invade the field crops. To prevent the rabbits leaping over the hedge-walls, these were topped off with projecting layers of cut heather and gorse.

The present failure of traps, snares, longnets, gas-machines and ferrets certainly has meant rethinking our former rather naive plan to exterminate the wild population. It has been proved and I now admit that of all these methods the cruel steel-toothed traps have caught the largest number of rabbits—approximately 2000 marketed. This is two-thirds the normal Skokholm crop, according to old Dick. The Wortley trap-fence is far too laboursome to set up, especially on a windy day, so we have had to give it up.

Please comment on what I now believe is our only alternative plan of management of the chinchilla stock you are helping to build up. I will bring them here—I hope next month. By that time I will have built a rabbitry of hutches to house them in. I will house the breeding does in the hutches first and place the immatures in the outdoor enclosures, where they will live on the summer grazing. By the autumn, when there's less grass, we shall be marketing all the bucks, keeping a few of the best stock. At the same time we shall experiment with turning a few loose. Possibly some may escape from the enclosure, but that won't matter much because we shall be catching a majority of the rabbits living wild in an operation concentrated in October and November—when pelts will be at their best, and both wild and chin rabbits would be marketed, for both flesh and fur.

A big rabbitry of hutches and two grazing enclosures would mean a large garden to grow vegetable food and this would entail eventually employing more hands. In turn this means we should have to build accommodation to match—fortunately there is a good range of buildings still with their stone-walls intact, which we shall repair and reroof.

I have talked this plan over with John, and asked his advice. He is always modestly reluctant to give it, but has said it sounds interesting; and has hinted that he would be pleased to stay on this summer as boatman and general handyman, as he is so helpfully now. Of course, I instantly agreed!

I shall be impatient for your considered reply.

Just now I can't work fast enough. I am torn between the desire to move to the barn, the need to build rabbit-hutches; to dig and plant the garden or to tear down the rotten roof of the Manor cottage. All tasks suited to my present enthusiasm but bedevilled by the need to cross with rabbits and collect building materials, and act as general cook and houseman.

Next time we cross, if Dick does not turn up I shall no longer bother with him.

Please give all the relevant news to the others at home, as I'm quite exhausted in writing this. And so to bed.

Goodnight my love

—Ronald.

Ashore 8th

Thank you for posting the flag, and the cake, and the honey—what luxury! And how nobly the Red Dragon of Wales flies in the sea breeze above Sky Rock! It really is a beauty, splendidly large to be seen clearly from the mainland. In fact it gives me the feeling that it symbolizes to the outer world what our lease specifically grants us —'the peaceful possession and quiet enjoyment' of our island home.

Letter from Ronald to his brother, Ken:

Skokholm
6 January, 1928

Dear Ken,

I am sure all you write from the tropical sunshine of Burma is wise, and I value every word of it, though it sounds slightly unreal to me.

My boats are burned. I would assure you that I never thought life could be so rewarding, so clean, vivid and exhilarating until I fell in love with two things, an island, and a woman of like enthusiasm for island living. I realise now that the majority of men, even outdoor men such as farmers, foresters and fishermen, lead very prosaic and frustrating existences shackled to modern civilisation. Here I am right up against nature, seeing, living, joying in daily, hourly contact with birds and the sea.

All of which I know will help to confirm your view as to my sanity in taking on the Island. I see your point of view clearly enough—that of a successful business man who perhaps worries about his impecunious brother spending his last penny on an untried and doubtful speculation. Your brother who finds it tiresome even to keep a record of his receipts and expenses; I do enter, in the back pages of my daily nature diary, occasionally, with little joy, a record of the money got from selling rabbits, and with appropriate gloom the outgoings. I think the difference between us is that you started your career at the opposite end of a man's life, you are now gaining wealth by hard work in order to enjoy a life of ease in retirement? Whereas I am enjoying a life of happiness now at work in an environment I love, but may well be a pauper by the end! . . .

Of course you are probably right about the rabbit-extermination plan—we are having many difficulties. All the means we have tried so far are mere palliatives, and the most efficient is the accursed bird-slaying gin trap.

Meanwhile we plod on quite happily in a small way. The new plan is to fence off an accessible flat area from which we shall clear any wild ones and put down chinchillas, keeping a breeding stock in a large rabbitry . . . I shall let you know what transpires in due course.

Meanwhile we are having requests from family and friends to be allowed to visit the island next summer. At least our cheerful sisters write enthusiastically about their young brother surviving three months of the stormiest winter on record (according to the wiseacres of this coast). I think they have got a little excited about some notoriety in the *Western Mail,* a cutting Marjorie sent me, in which I am described as 'the loneliest man in the British Isles!' Unfortunately this has resulted in readers writing troublesome enquiries—to which I do not normally reply, unless they enclose stamped, addressed envelopes!

On some days of howling wind and rough seas I do get a little depressed, but it doesn't last. For example I am not feeling too grand today—caught a fair chill two days ago by sweating while hauling sand for repair work. I have an excellent boatman, and between us we are working hard to rough-repair the large old stone barn sufficiently to make it light with windows and its roof watertight for a temporary dwelling while we rebuild the little island farmhouse. My chesty cough is rapidly disappearing—there are no alien germs resident on this island, where modern contagious sicknesses are unknown—so the lighthousekeepers assure me. To demonstrate my unbusinesslike nature, I have been tremendously pleased to find the island is a treasure trove for the ornithologist, not only in the thousands of summer nesting seabirds, but in the continuous migration of smaller woodland birds passing over the island . . .

I like your amusing description of the offal-scrounging kite snatching up bacon and eggs from your breakfast plate! Do write more such natural history anecdotes to your Admiring brother R.

Tyr Bont
4 January, 1928

Dear Ronald,

Goodness knows when you will collect this letter for there is half a gale raging outside and it sounds as if it has come to stay.

You may rejoice to hear that I telephoned the auctioneer on Monday, and he is coming tomorrow to value the remaining farmstock. Another step towards freedom and the Island?

I suppose I ought to be glad; but strangely I am rather sad. I only hope that someone will buy the animals who will treat them humanely. My trouble is I get too fond of my farm beasts.

I'm not selling the fowls yet. I am making up a nucleus for the island flock. Please will you send for that cockerel from William Cook of Kent (your mother's relative) so that I can breed some fresh blood into our Tyr Bont fowlery. I shall quite enjoy being a hen-wife on Skokholm, and as your cook I shall want fresh eggs. The gulls' eggs won't last long, unless we put enough down in pickle for the winter.

I'll be very careful and dust the hens with Keatings powder, and disinfect the nest boxes regularly from now on, so the fowls won't bring obnoxious parasites to the island! . . .

6.30 Thursday morning

Still blowing, so you may not be able to cross today.

I wish I had not sent that cake. I have a feeling it will turn into stone. However perhaps it's just as well for you to be forced to sample some of my dismal failures. I own to quite a lot, as I learn to be kitchen cook. Cooking is infinitely preferable to housework; probably on fine island days I shan't do any at all. For you must realise I'm not in the least houseproud like Mama. As far as I can see baking and washing are the only chores that will have to be done more or less regularly. I'll do them on wet days. During an anticyclone dirt will accumulate.

I asked Martin what he thought he would do if he had to farm Skokholm. He thought arable farming was the best option, especially growing seed corn crops—wheat, barley, oats, which would thrive best in the open windy terrain where their isolation would ensure freedom from disease contamination from other strains. He would combine seed grain production with small livestock—pigs and poultry, easily transported by boat, and their manure would provide the necessary humus for the grain crop; plus, he thought, as much wild bird guano and seaweed as the island afforded . . .

No letter this morning and blowing great guns once more. How I long to watch the waves battering the red cliffs of Skokholm. Mad Bay must be an awesome sight. I hope everything is all safe on the Island, and the barn roof still intact.

Ever your faithful partner

Do.

Trehill
10 January

Dearest Lady,

The sea is quite savage today—great white mountains of swell driven by the sou'west gale. I am obliged to remain ashore, and so at last I am going *to build a hut in Martynshaven.* In the West Hook farmer's field on the slope running down to *Storm Petrel*'s berth. Our sleep in the little lodge I shall build will be lulled by the waves breaking on the beach—which will have a delicious soporific effect. It is very sheltered, Jack and I have often sat above the beach there, talking and eating our grub after a stiff crossing; in a few minutes we are both taking catnaps. Some of the old bewhiskered lobster fishermen, coming to tend their boats, will sit and gossip agreeably for hours with you, and presently they too drop off to sleep. There is one lovely old fellow, with a white beard touching his waist, by name Warren (Edwards of course) who rides a high-seated donkey cart, often with another white-whiskered fishing crony, or his black bearded son, a most picturesque sight.

I intend to design the hut quite simply, based on a plan of the store hut maintained above South Haven by Trinity House. Two rooms, one 10' x 15' for living in (with two bunks), the other 10' x 10' as a store. I first spoke with the owner of Skomer about putting a hut inside the solid gate of the Deer Park, but typically he was not in the least encouraging.

I finally selected a site which I'm sure you will approve of. John advised me not to be too close to the beach because in summer it stinks of rotten fish bait and mounds of decaying seaweed. We found an ideal place just under the brow of the hill, providing shelter from the south and west wind, but giving a splendid view northwards over the haven beach and the wide arc of St Bride's Bay, as far as Ramsey Island. This gorsey slope is part of West Hook Farm, owned by an interesting character, ex-farmer turned taxi-driver, and dealer in rabbits and any livestock he can bargain for—the Codds speak rather disparagingly of Tommy Reynolds, but he was politeness itself when he came down to tell me I could build my hut *anywhere* on that unwanted slope. 'No charge, no charge,' says Tommy shaking his red nose, 'help yourself to a few yards for your store hut. You're a gentleman Mr. Lockley, glad to be of service.' So was hatched the perfect gentleman's agreement, by word of mouth! No documents necessary; (undoubtedly my brother would have frowned at such un-business-like deals). I have agreed to hire his ancient limousine in case I need a taxi for transport of friends to the train or anywhere in the county, and later he secured from me the right to purchase the Skokholm rabbit crop. Tommy used to farm West Hook but has lately rented it out to an old retired couple but Tommy runs a few dry stock there himself.

Tommy was so airy-fairy about the site of the hut and no rent that I felt it necessary to visit West Hook farmhouse and advise the tenants about the deal. I encountered a very old lady in the home meadow, sitting on a three-legged stool milking a raw-boned cow of advanced age. We agreed on a sub-rent of 7/- a year. 'Shurely sir, us'll be plaised to have nice neighbours down there in the haven. Jus' drop in at any time. We do make butter, and grows a few vegetables should thee want some, like.' I wish I could reproduce her rich slow, restful speech here.

I feel quite excited, and shall stay ashore now until the hut is built and occupiable. I have ordered all the timber and other building materials, and they will be delivered to site. So now you'll be able to write to me every day! Jack and I, plus a carpenter, should be able to build the place within a week—I hope? As Dick is now home in Dale and eager to trap the island rabbits I shall take him over and leave him on the island alone—as he likes to be.

What we need rather urgently now is a winch for hauling the *Storm Petrel* up Martynshaven beach. Nearly every fisherman has his own which no other man may use without permission of the owner. Jack uses his uncle Warren Edwards's winch, it is old, almost broken-down, from a wrecked schooner, Warren said. He kindly lets me use his too, until I get one of my own. Apparently good secondhand winches are obtainable at a breakers' yard. I wonder would your Papa look around at Cardiff Docks for one? He would know the appropriate size.

Love as ever R.

Trehill
11 January, 1928

Dearest Lady,

Haven't much time to write, but do so in anticipation of you doing likewise—that's my selfish motive.

Thanks for the enumeration of your vices, which however scarcely merit the name. I shall not dare to enumerate mine, for fear of losing you. In fact if you were guilty of all the imaginable horrid and desperate deeds 'twould make no difference, I would still love you. Just a few of my minor weaknesses are selfishness, laziness, occasional brutality, sentimentality, to say nothing of great impatience and lack of commonsense. The subject is now closed.

We began work on the Martynshaven hut yesterday, and got most of the foundation dug out, down to the bedrock in parts. As the prevailing sou-west wind was howling and screaming we were able to select the least windy place under the brow of the hill, convenient to, almost touching, a bend in the lane. Jack sensibly pointed out that it was easy here to unload a cargo from the beach or a lorry from inland, direct into the hut. I have asked Edwards the Post, also known as Edwards the Shop, to deliver my mail here (everyone is Edwards here, even Lord Kensington, who once owned the Marloes peninsula). They are an inbred lot, formerly hostile to newcomers. But I find them quite delightfully hospitable, and with a dry humour worth listening to. Already I have ideas for a sketch or novel of this fisherman's community . . .

Tyr Bont
Wednesday night, 11 January, 1928

Dearest Ron,

Its 11.15. and I'm very sleepy but simply must write or you will think me mean after your gorgeous long letter. Then it was a nice surprise to have another this morning, though it was only what niece Mary described as a 'tweeny' one. She demanded that I must read out the 'tresting bits' in both letters.

Early morning

This morning I was wakened by alarming shouts, clanking iron and rushing water—I rushed into Papa's room to see what it was about: he told me men had been working most of the night while the road was free of traffic, (and had kept him wide awake, and he'd only just fallen asleep, 'THANK YOU'!) They were joining up the big water main to the small one which passes through our wood. You can imagine that our poor steep little lane is almost washed away. What boring news but an explanation of why I happened to be early . . .

Now it is nearly midnight and cold, but it's been a gorgeous day. The river was steel-blue, and golden green where the banks were reflected. Spring seemed to be very near, in the songs of the birds, and the celandine leaves unrolling, even a few flowers peeping in the lane. Here winter heliotrope has been in flower since before Christmas—I think you saw this? It seems to have survived the recent frost and snow. Goodnight.

Friday morning

How does your Martynshaven mansion progress? Papa was rather disappointed that it is not big enough to garage his car! Does he expect a Crystal Palace? But he does approve the whole idea, and wants you to send a sketch of its exact position—it must be, he says, on the other side of the little stream where he picked watercress last year when you and he were waiting to cross to Skokholm for the first time.

Time for me to get up. Goodbye and fine weather be thine.

Love from your sweetheart D.

P.S. I don't think even liquid gold would have lured me into your mid-winter sea! H-how l-l-long did you stay in? My teeth chatter at the very thought.

The winch was one of the things I have to ask you about, Papa knows of a suitable, almost new, winch at a secondhand chandler's in the Docks. We had a grand argument as to whether Haverfordwest or Milford Haven is the best place to rail it to. Do we just address it to Mr Lockley, Milford Haven? I daresay if we put your address as Atlantic Ocean it would get to you just as quickly? . . .

Papa is just shaving so I've five minutes to write a little more. I've just discovered that one of the young Chins is blind. Its eyes were still shut, so I gently rubbed some olive oil on them and got them open. They had some matter in them and the eyes looked cloudy. I don't think she is one of the best ones—her fur is more or less smokey, not clearly ticked like the others. If she really is blind, what should I do? . . .

Ever so much love from Do.

13 January, 1928

Dearest Ronald,

Have you any ideas for a banner? There is a Women's Institute Exhibition in October, (when I hope to be faraway on a certain island) so I thought I should gracefully slide out of being there. However, the president of St Mellons W.I. admired the design I put on the Spy Rock flag which is now finished except for some braiding to take the halyard; I could hardly protest that I knew nothing about designing and embroidery, tho' I did boast the design was yours.

Any suggestions will be welcomed—you ought to have heaps of inspiration on our beautiful island. I thought to incorporate the local saint's head in the design, although as St Melon was reputed to be a vegetarian, like St Francis of Assisi, he ought to be chewing a lettuce?

By the way don't make me the excuse for employing a man and a boy. Not that I don't think YOU may need them—especially now. But I know I shall be as happy as a queen all by myself on Skokholm; in fact I shall be pleased to get rid of everyone at times, and have a few days in retreat like a well-behaved nun. Perhaps you won't trust me with lighthousekeepers a mile away at the other end of the island . . . ?

. . . Mama and I had tea with Muriel and her mother yesterday. Mrs D. hinted that Eunice's marriage was as disastrous for her daughter as mine would be to you.* I was stung by this analogy, but to my surprise Mama came to my rescue, and said you were a nice young man and there were plenty of opportunities on Skokholm for making a living.

It was such a nice speech for Mama that on the way home I thanked her, and suggested that I ought to join you as soon as possible and help with the repairs and the chinchilla scheme. In fact I said I wished to marry as soon as possible—now that you had repaired the barn and were building a little lodge on the mainland. She made no reply, but went early to bed, saying she had caught a cold up in the draughty Davies house!

A couple of days ago Mr L.'s wife came over the field from your old poultry farm, to tell me that she'd had a terrible fright. In the middle of the very stormy night she awoke to someone knocking on the back door, and with it she could hear a dreadful rattle of chains! She thought her last hour had come—I can just imagine her clinging to L. and vowing she wouldn't stop another hour in such a terrible lonely place. But it turned out to be simply an unpruned rose tree banging against the wooden walls of your bungalow, and as for the chains their watchdog had ripped himself free of his kennel, a large chunk of which was still attached to his chain; the frightened animal had come to the bungalow door seeking shelter and human

*[Muriel Davies and her mother ran a farm near St Mellons and were great friends of the Shellards. During the 1914-1918 war they employed a German prisoner of war, Muriel Davies' sister, Eunice, fell in love with him and in 1919 went away to live on his rather primitive farm in Germany. She never came back except for holidays.]

company! Mrs L. is such a pretty young woman, but a town bird lost and lonely in the country.

Can't stop to write any more just now.

Love from D.

Evening. Hook
13 January, 1928

Dear Lady,

Have been working on the foundations of the hut in Martynshaven. The carpenter is coming tomorrow. It's been a lovely cool sunny day, and we have missed a chance to take Dick to the island. I noticed that the lighthouse relief was accomplished today. We needed a load of sand for the concreting, so I hired a horse and cart from the Codds, and sent Jack and the carter off to St Bride's Haven, while Dick and I continued on the hut foundation.

You'll delight in St Bride's Haven, with the ruins of its ancient chapel. At one time in the last century there was a large net fishery of herrings centred at St Bride's. The present large church was built a little way inland—as the ancient chapel and old graveyard were perilously near to being washed away; in its disused state, the chapel was adapted as a salting house for fish. The superstition is that the good Lord God punished the fisherman for desecrating His chapel by removing the herring shoals from St Bride's Bay!

A local booklet quotes:

'When St Bride's Chapel a salt house was made
St Bride's lost the herring trade.'

I have twice wandered around this now almost deserted and correspondingly beautiful Haven, seeing seals in the bay, and birds of many kinds. A little way inland is the ruin of a vast mansion hidden in an extensive gone-wild plantation, former home of the lord of the manor. In the haven nothing remains of the old port except a cottage about to fall into the tide, and a few stones of the old chapel, and the odd gravestone tumbling upon the sandy shore near an old lime kiln. A marvellous 'sweet Auburn' sort of place to me, and it will be a favourite picnic place for us on days when we may be weatherbound ashore.

As I sat on Martynshaven beach, just Dick and self sharing slices of your cake, I felt almost like Thoreau did when he was building his hut beside the beach at Walden Pond. Only instead of the newspaper in which his (Thoreau's) lunch was wrapped I had your letters to read. A wonderful combination—your news, your cake, the grand view, the sunshine, and dear old Dick's slow but witty comments at intervals. He greatly approved your cake—called it 'main good', and fished about for more information about 'thy lady love, sir.'

Among other tit-bits of information I prised out of Dick was that there were still plenty of herrings visiting the bay in season, but the local fishermen are too lazy to go after them. As a boy he remembered that the Martynshaven boats would be 'loaded ter the gunnels wi' 'errins, so the carts 'ad ter be backed inter sea ter unload 'em. 'alf of 'em was never sold. Farmers came down and took away the rest for manurin' their fields.'

Dick remembers when the only cottage in Martynshaven, now reduced to a shed where Sturt of Skomer keeps his car and hangs up his rabbits for the dealer, was occupied by a farm labourer who raised a family of a dozen children, and kept a 'main girt big garden' opposite it, on West Hook land—just below where we are building. He said there was an old well there too, now overgrown and needing 'cleaning up'. So, having made some tea from water in this well (flavoured with duckweed), I invited Dick to clean it up this very afternoon. Which he did, straightening the old retaining walls above the flagstones and removing a number of frogs and small life. It now only needs a cover to shut out the light to discourage the growth of algae. (We have such a screen to protect the Skokholm well.)

Considerable interest is being taken by villagers in Lockley's hut. Half a dozen idle persons peeped in, polite but curious, some hinting that they would be happy to be employed in the work! Which they delayed by their chatter, always interesting but inconvenient to progress.

Jack delivered a massive cart load of St Bride's Haven sand for the concreting before dusk, the good fellow.

There are buzzards and choughs flying about Martynshaven, and just as I was leaving for Trehill I heard a little owl calling from some rabbit burrows opposite—on the slope of the Deer Park.

Great excitement at Trehill, with preparation for visitors, cake-mixing, polishing etc. I gather that at last Polly's sweetheart from up in 'the Welsh' is coming for the week-end. I am invited politely but firmly to sleep at her parents' farm a few fields to the north known as East Hook, which I have now done.

Here, listening to the three resident Codds—Reuben and his parents, I learned that Jan 12th, was Old New Year's Day when Marloes and Dale boys used to beat the village boundaries making a great noise with a stick and tin can, until they found and captured a 'Cutty Wren'. Each parish had a special box with a glass roof, in which the unfortunate wren was placed alive. This box, decorated with coloured ribbons, was carried from door to door, so that each household was by tradition obliged to pay a coin as tribute; if it did not, dire consequences might be expected, described in a short ballad sung by the Cutty Wren carriers.

The custom has died out recently, it seems. But Marloes celebrates in a big way the day after Christmas, when there is the festival of St Stephen's, with fairs, dancing, and travelling players known as Guisers. This can last until New Year's Day.

Edwards the Post, who keeps the only shop in Marloes, has offered to lend me an old book—*The History of Little England beyond Wales,* by Edward Laws, in which the quaint customs of southern Pembrokeshire in the last century are described and well illustrated. It was published in 1888. I have only dipped into it—a huge tome, and so valuable that he says he would prefer I did not take it across to Skokholm, 'because the salt air be main bad for books'.

And so I must close.

Ever thine R.

P.S. I have seen a peregrine falcon several times about the Deer Park, where no doubt it picks up migrating birds very easily. Jack told me to look out for 'poison vipers' (as he calls adders) in the ferny slope between the site of the hut and the beach. It looks ideal for them—undisturbed fern, bracken and gorse. I told him that on no account was he to kill snakes, that I would show him how to pick up his poison viper without being bitten. Too cold just now for snakes to be abroad anyway.

[Undated]

Dear Ron,

Charles and I have been having a most strenuous day. I'd been down to the village posting letters and sundry parcels, and collecting hedge parsley on the way back, to be greeted by Charles with the news that the roof had blown off the top of the fowl house, and was reposing several yards inside the meadow! A freak gust of wind had taken it clear away, yet it was hardly damaged at all—just one plank smashed and the felting torn. However we had to dismember it and put it up plank by plank. We could do nothing else in the strong wind but work quickly before rain set in.

What a wonderful view one gets from the top of a roof. It is astonishing what a few feet of extra height makes to the amount of horizon one can see; or is it that one's eyes get jaded, so a raise in eye level makes the view take on a new dimension—a fresh prospect; like looking between one's legs, your upside-down eyes see colours more vividly?

You have trained Charlie very well. He gave me good advice on how you used to arrange your long and short planks when building a shed so that the joins do not all rest on one rafter, which would weaken the structure. I feel very bucked that we got that roof firmly nailed back, and that I seemed as good a carpenter as Charlie, and better at hammering in the nails straight; he holds the hammer by the neck instead of by the shaft! After being more or less regarded as a ninny at carpentering by Papa it is having a good effect on me that I can do a man's work with a hammer as well as a man, albeit he is only an overgrown boy!

But the whole little adventure was good, and working in the wind on the fowl-house roof blew away my cobwebs, so you probably won't have any more morbid letters.

Don't you think we are all Sentimental Tommies at times—acting in a certain way because of something we've read about or seen, or is expected of us? Bernard Shaw says that half of us would never fall in love if we had not read such a lot about it in books. Shaw liked to shock us as a practising cynic, of course, but you don't have to believe half he says. Surely love is really one of the few instincts we are born with that lasts into old age, or don't you like such a divine feeling to be called instinct?

Oh dear, why am I moralizing (are there two lls in that word?) I just want to be happy, have lots of physical work to do, and not puzzle my simple brain too much with the injustices and miseries of the world. You may find out more about me if I write enough such letters!

I nearly ruined a good skirt last night trying to get a newly weaned calf I had forgotten to feed into her pen. She ran away at high speed and in trying to intercept her I fell full length in a mud-puddle. At that I was so exasperated that I picked up a switch and beat her back into the yard. So you see I am not to be trusted with dumb animals. Of course it was my fault, I shouldn't have tried to tackle her in my tea-time clothes. But you are sure to find the episode funny, as Papa did when Mama told him. Seriously, I hate people who fly into a temper and ill-treat dumb animals.

This is poor news. It seems ages and ages since I had your last letter, and even when I get the next it won't be in reply to this one.

I can't write any more in this strain. Goodnight.

Yours—if you still think you want me? Do.

P.S. I heard a missel thrush singing in the wood with a gale blowing. Hasn't it a wild and vigorous cry, repeated with emphasis, and frequent pauses as if for a reply? The name Stormcock suits it admirably.

[Undated]

Dearest Ron,

Do you like your letters addressed Mr Ronald Lockley, or Ronald Lockley Esquire? I know Esquire is supposed to be correct for a gentleman, but I always think that it sounds pretentious. I remember

Uncle Jim nearly had a fit one day because his daughter sent a letter to her harmony doctor addressed plain Mr. Farjeon. I don't suppose that gentleman would even have noticed it.

For 3s 3d I have bought a sou'wester at a local sale, looks quite new, useful for island living I hope. Not used yet, it's been rainless with a brilliant night sky filled with stars.

When the auctioneer came to look at the livestock he asked me if it was true that we were selling Tyr Bont, so what could I say except that I supposed so, but nothing was definite. He said he had a client who wanted a place in the country outside Cardiff. The next day another auctioneer rang Papa up with the same question. Papa was so cross! But seriously though I don't think he will ever make a move in the matter, so it's just as well that Mama has started the ball rolling. We may be homeless soon, so expect three forlorn Shellards calling on you to take them in.

The air here is quite blue as a consequence. Mama has challenged Papa to find her a flat somewhere near his surgery, but he says he is certainly not going to live in town, and intends looking out for some place on the coast, preferably an island, provided it is connected to the mainland at low tide, and near enough to Cardiff for him to drive to work on weekdays! How impossible!

How does the HUT progress? I have to confess that large piece of new felting we put on the fowlhouse roof was today ripped and is flapping in the wind. We are not to blame for a bad repair as Papa had said he'd get some battens, but meanwhile the nails would have to do. Of course he forgot to get them!

It feels good to put the blame on someone else!

It's half past midnight. Goodnight.

Saturday morning

If there's no letter from you I don't think I'll post this—not that it would be much loss to you for there's nothing worth reading in it. It's such a hard job to scrape up fresh news writing so often—especially when I spent a large slice of yesterday in town . . . Ever so much love Do.

East Hook Farm, Marloes
14 January, 1928

Dear Doris,

Quite wicked weather today, impossible to work on the Hut, 'sleetin' an' emptin' rain', as the carpenter observed. I don't like employing a carpenter, but have no tools here at Martynshaven except spade and pick-axe. Except that this local carpenter (8s a day) keeps his tools sharper than I do, I doubt that he can build much better than I (doesn't say much for him!) I am too impatient; but try to be patient, carefully studying his style and making him economise on the wood, and mortise and tenon every joint.

I have thought long and deep about adding a garage, but concluded it would be too expensive, also there is no easy entrance for one, the slope is too steep, suitable only for the stonechats which perch every day now on the tops of the gorse, cursing our presence with gentle chirping.

Thanks for your nice letter just received. Please address all letters to me at Skokholm Island, Marloes. The postboy delivers each weekday just now and I have promised I will put up a postbox as soon as the hut is erected.

As Charles is so eager and ready to come, I will send him a telegram as soon as I am ready to collect him from the train at Haverfordwest. He is to stay and help you as long as you need him; just tell him to be prepared.

Am writing this in East Hook kitchen, with a pile of unanswered letters. I am too sleepy to tackle more after this one to my sweet partner. So forgive brevity.

The weather hardly inspires me to write—there are distractions—young Molly (Codd's grand-daughter) talking fifteen to the dozen, Mrs Codd washing up in a huge enamel bowl on the next table, she humming a religious air, and old man Codd asking me endless questions. I enjoy their spontaneous hospitality (I can't get them to accept any fee for housing and feeding me and I have a feeling they'll be insulted if I persist.)

So goodnight, with love and kisses, your R.

P.S. The gloves should have been yours for Xmas, but weren't ready. They are from real Skokholm wild black rabbits.

Sunday

Another day of wild wind. I want to go down and work at the hut, but dare not, I should never be forgiven by the Codds or the whole village for working on a Sunday. Mrs Codd is a substantial-sized motherly woman and a great worker, but only on weekdays. She is a chapel lay-preacher, and told me she intends giving me a 'Testament marked wherever *the Blood* is mentioned,' and also a *Traveller's Religious Guide.* For which I shall of course, be *appropriately* grateful—and I hope, penitent in the reading?

I like East Hook better than Trehill, it's so much quieter, off the haven road and close to the cliffs with a lovely view of Ramsey and the Bishops and Clerks rocks to the north. Old Mr Codd is a quite delightful pagan and doesn't approve of his sanctimonious wife's lay-preaching—told me she was a 'hot-gospel lady'. He is a very handsome man in the Flemish style, never goes to chapel, and I am quite fascinated by his soft short curly beard, the result of never having shaved in his life. Perhaps it is not too late for me to grow one as soft and silky? I shall try in the next few weeks while you are out of sight, . . . Shaving is a bore.

I thought to pay Charles his 10s a week, but allowing that I will have to house and feed him, I propose to pay him 20 pounds a year, plus food and lodging and train fare home to Cardiff and back for his holidays (a fortnight annually seems to be the custom here, according to Jack, who always takes time off to help with the local haymaking!)

Monday

Fancy you proposing to put a man's face on a Women's Institute banner! Why not a Cuckoo Clamant? Like most women the cuckoo is excessively assertive, cunning to deceive, determined (to put her eggs in another female's basket) and flirtatious, though admittedly it's the male cuckoo that 'cuckoos', that repetitive song! Sorry, have no other ideas.

The Skomer boat came out with a big load of rabbits on Friday, three men rowing, but failed to get back against the westerly, so you see, other island folk have the occasional setback too.

Waiting to go to a life class:

4 High Street, Cardiff
[Undated]

Dear Ronald,

I am making an attempt to write a better letter, even if it will be full of my woes and on the only paper I can find in Papa's office. First we haven't got rid of all the farm stock. The cow Gyp was entered in the sale, but when it was honestly announced she had one of her quarters obstructed, no one offered to buy her. After the market the auctioneer advised me to fatten her for the butcher! But as she is in calf we shall have to wait till that's born; and I suppose he or she will have to go to the butcher too.

It's a rotten business having a general farm, and I'm glad you aren't having one on the island. I don't think I will let you after all this.

If you'd seen that cattle market. Pens of calves—poor shivering orphans just a few days old, bawling for their mothers . . . the cows herded tightly together in pens. I wish some of the people who laugh at vegetarians for not eating meat could be forced to witness a cattle auction of such low standards as our local one. But I am just as bad, I like milk and butter, to say nothing of home-cured pork, your Skokholm rabbits and game birds. I swallow my prejudices along with the island bunnies' fat flesh. Sounds disgusting?

Must go. Forgive this gruesome letter. I knew it was going to be unpleasant, and yet I did not like to think you were looking every morning anxiously for a promised letter and not getting one (what conceit!). But I know you get plenty from your family and your birdwatching correspondents, not dismal news like mine—this one written with a pencil which has just lost its lead. So I must stop.

Thursday morning dawn

I must post this letter today. I've found something more cheerful to write about. It's going to be a fine day. The sky is full of stars slowly fading as the sun colours the eastern sky. A little owl is squawking close to my window. This owl always reminds me of nightingales and owls in Maescrochan Wood. Do you remember it was such a gorgeous night, you hugged me, pretending it was cold? Now that's more cheerful!

But still I must scold you for sending those gloves. The absolute cheek of you accusing me of extravagance when I gave you a couple of cheap books which might be good reading on the Island, and you said I have broken my vow not to give each other presents. You have broken your promise much more thoroughly. For I can read the books, but you can't possibly wear my gloves!

My pencil is the limit. I'm writing on the wood most of the time—gnawing it makes it worse.

Good morning and may this one reach you soon, in sunshine and no wind.

Much love as ever.

D.

P.S. I've just found a cheerful subject in Beatrice's hutch—she is the crosspatch which scratches me when I open her door. She is almost purring this morning. I don't know how many babies she has, and I was a bit scared to look closely into the squirming mass of naked infants, and she clearly did not want me to. Just squatted with her back to the nestbox and a twinkling nose-smile as she gazed at me almost benignly.

Papa has at last bought the winch for you for two pounds. They will put it on the goods train to Milford Haven Station, 'to be called for'. The GWR will let you know when it arrives. Hope that's all right.

Do write more about the progress on the HUT. What are we going to call it?*

Ever yours.

Do.

East Hook Farm
17 January, 1928

Dearest Doris,

I think you are very brave to write in a black mood. I know I

* [In those early days I do not remember it being referred to as anything but 'the hut', but as additions were made it sometimes became 'Skokholm Lodge' and is now 'Lockley Lodge'.]

couldn't. It's quite possible to have black moods on the Island, especially in dreary weather, or thick wet mist and the perpetual moan of foghorns from lighthouses and passing ships.

Glad you are becoming a good carpenter—you will need to be when you get to Skokholm! You write that you want to live a life of physical exertion, forgetting mental worries and be a natural animal. You'll find it easy here—all the high-falutin' notions I ever had quickly vanished. I eat and sleep and work on an enormous scale, especially the first. I devour food unreservedly. It's really more fun to be an animal; not to bother with being a cautious minded 'arian or 'ologist of any description, just to live in your own sweet way your own sweet life. I own it's not complete without a mate, but meanwhile I live in hungry anticipation. It's good to be in love, to be inspired by love, to work to exhaustion, to eat to bursting, to be tired, and able to sleep profoundly, to be all sensual adjectives.

About the Hut, we finished the concrete floor on Tuesday morning. As I was working at the floor on Monday morning who should turn up but Jack's uncle the mason, who began by telling me I was doing it all wrong! So I challenged him to pick up a trowel and show me how; the crafty old sinner at once produced a mason's float from his bag and proceeded to put a fine surface on the wet concrete. I was weak enough to agree to let him work all afternoon on the job. I am sure his main impulse was one of curiosity, as he asked a lot of searching questions about what I proposed to do on the island, etc.

He (justifiably) praised his nephew Jack; without children of their own, he and his wife adopted Jack as a young orphan, and brought him up to be an independent young man—'a damn good crut' were his words—and had taught Jack not to swear when he came home from serving on local schooners and ketches! That trade has greatly diminished now and he likes his nephew working closer to home.

As we gossiped and worked together, between us we finished the floor. On looking at it today in its hard state both his and my portions look equally well—or evilly—finished!

Jack meanwhile had been rebuilding the gap we had to make in the stone-faced road hedge, and made a neat job of resetting the jambs of the future entry from the road to the Hut. Over a cup of tea the verbose mason had some hair-raising tales to tell us about the many wrecks on this coast which he had seen. In particular that of a French barque which was driven ashore under the Deer Park cliffs: 'Us Marloes Gulls be ter-ble wreckers, nor does we care for them Frenchies we wus at war wi', in me father's time.' He told us when this wreck ran aground near Renny slip the crew tried to swarm ashore over the ship's bowsprit, but they were knocked off into the big waves one by one by the Marloes men using big sticks . . .

Quite fascinating and I am trying to remember to record such stories in my diary.* I am learning a great deal of folk lore and fact. One is that when a drowned foreigner is washed ashore and can't be identified the body is buried in a special Strangers Plot set aside in the corner of Marloes churchyard . . . 'They's a main trouble,' concluded the mason, 'often rotten with long drifting in the sea. I mind one me father an' me picked up, 'ad lost is 'ead, but we claimed the shillin' reward for puttin' 'im above 'igh water by carryin' up 'is corpse in a laverweed sack.'

On Tuesday evening we returned to Skokholm, taking Dick (who had a hangover!) and a young nanny goat which I bought for 10s from the Marloes schoolmaster. It is a pretty cream-coloured Anglo-Toggenburg with neck tassels; she is now tentatively getting to know the lighthouse flock.

All was well, more or less, after our long absence of eight days, Nip and the kitten residing at the lighthouse. The southerly gales had, however, stripped some of the roof off the south side of the house, and the mice had engineered tunnels in a home-made loaf hanging from the ceiling. But Peter the cat was set to work and caught several of the culprits that evening.

Wednesday was unmentionable. A rather wasted day cleaning the house, cleaning the motor in the SP (it's working well at present God b.p.) and looking for the goat, which had abandoned the Lighthouse flock and walked alone to the Neck—as if she knew home was in that direction.

Now we are back ashore today to work on the Hut. Its going to cost about 20 pound in materials, excluding our labour. I think you know it will be of corrugated iron outside, lined with matchboards inside and packed between with straw and sawdust. Sorry we can't

* [Alas, I find very few of these stories recorded in the R.M.L. diaries.]

afford a more pretentious palace, but at least it should be warm and solid. And you shall alter and enlarge it as we can afford it.*

Tyr Bont

Dear Ronald,

I passed three students today in the lane while out gathering rabbit food. They had their heads together discussing the properties of some gas or other and I couldn't help comparing them to you. That is what you ought to be doing—going about with other men your age and not thinking of tying yourself to a wife. Don't you sometimes feel you are too young to get married and saddled with the worries of a woman and household? Don't you feel the need to be free a bit longer? Because if you do, we must wait a while. I've got an awful fear that I am rushing you into marriage too by appearing too impatient . . .

It's close on midnight, which may account for my latest sample of introspection. Only this lonely spinster felt she simply must give the wild islander the chance to escape longer—if he wishes to.

Did I tell you that on wet days Charlie and I have been clearing up the cart shed and burning all the unsaleable impedimenta thrown there for the last ten years. The clouds of dust we raised today made Charlie's face comically filthy, but when I came to look at my face in the bathroom mirror my hair was quite a stylish grey. I have no inspiration tonight, so with love from your still faithful partner, goodnight.

This is a letter of scraps. Mama and I went to see *Ben Hur* at the Cardiff Cinema. First time I've been for many moons. It was very fine—in parts, but lingered too long over the sloppy uninteresting sequences, and flashed off on the interesting bits before you had time to appreciate their significance. I can hear you saying, how *critical* you are! I can't say I'm interested in watching two strange faces, smothered in cosmetics, hugging and kissing in long-drawn out close-ups, frequently repeated. The chariot race was terribly exciting by contrast.

Goodnight for now.

* [It was altered and enlarged from time to time and finally a garage built at the corner of the road below.]

Saturday

Here I am sitting in the train for Malvern. They were short of a player for Saturday's away match? Rather pathetic wasn't it? So here I am squandering my hard-earned allowance in trainfare when I should be saving up for many more important things. Money seems to melt away as fast as I earn it. This train is rather jolty, so my writing will be rather more illegible than usual—if that's possible.

I never have time to get the family breakfast on match days. Papa had to make tea, and catching sight of my rather meagre lunch of cheese sandwiches, he made me swallow an egg and sherry cocktail saying that that was the sort of food to play lacrosse on, then said he'd like to have come with me, and to be sure and score the winning goal!

Ugh! Sherry and egg is horrid so early in the day! Now I've got a beautiful headache, whether it is the sherry, or yesterday's frivolity I don't know—probably both.*

I'm very anxious to hear more about the goat. 10s seems very little money to buy a whole nanny-goat for. Is she milking and in kid? Eunice told me of a nanny goat who milked for 4-5 years without having had another kid, and was still giving about 8 pints daily. It seems to me like a fairy tale. But the length of lactation period interests me. How splendid it would be to have hardly any problems of disposing of surplus kids each year, and no dry period. One might even dispense with keeping a smelly billy goat on the island most of the time? They can be dangerously aggressive as they get older . . . *

I've just been to chat with the rest of our team in the next-door carriage.

The weather was awful this morning but breaks are appearing in

* [My grandfather was what today would be called a 'fitness freak'. Each morning he stood in a bath containing 6 inches of piping hot water. Taking an outsize sponge, he would proceed to squeeze water all over himself straight from the COLD tap! After a brisk towelling he would smack himself all over. The sound of these smacks reverberating all over the house absolutely fascinated me when I was a small child. His first course for breakfast was invariably a barely coddled egg drunk straight from the shell!]

* [The lighthouse billy-goat had an evil reputation and large horns. Fortunately one could usually smell him coming and head for safety in plenty of time.]

the clouds now, so the lax pitch may be less slippery. We've just passed some market gardens. I hope our rabbit food garden on the island won't look so depressing? Which reminds me we ought to grow lots of spinach beet. I've discovered the chinchillas love it, and it's easy to grow—a most useful winter green. And chicory, which is grown in France for table rabbits and used as a substitute for coffee. It can also be blanched, if properly earthed up. In fact I have bought it in Cardiff, at 1s a lb. It is really delicious as a salad.

It will be grand to have a well-ordered rabbit-cum-herb-flower garden running down the meadow—your 'pleasance', with a lilypool beside the spring. I have my doubts about it being that grand or keeping it weeded, but meanwhile I join you in pleasant dreams about these plans.

All my love and loyalty to my romantic husband-to-be,

Ever yours,

Do.

East Hook
23 January, 1928

Dearest Doris,

'Tis nearly February and too little accomplished. Pray for fine weather and sunny days to dry up this damp Marloes country.

It is thrilling to have your sweet letters with all the little groans and challenges you like to tease me with.

For instance you ask me if I want to back out of my promise to marry you on July 12th next. True I have no right to marry until I am sure of a comfortable living, but if your query signifies you want to wait, or even give me up I must respond with the same offer to set you free of your promise to marry me. Now is the time to have your doubts, six months before the event!

But I must warn you again of the terrible fate that awaits you in living on Skokholm. Old Mrs Codd tells me that the landlord's agent told her that he was horrified when he learned that I proposed to incarcerate a real 'lady' on my lonely island. The mason told me that when I first began boating to and from Skokholm three months ago, the whole village prophesied that I would either be scared away by the wild sea, or else drowned by now! But lately they seem to have calmed down, taking things for granted.

Of course, as the mason hasn't hesitated to point out, I am fortunate to have Jack as a weatherwise boatman, and a restraining influence on my inexperience and ignorance of tides etc. For me there is just that element of risk in crossing in bad weather which adds to the pleasure of sea-going then, and the beautiful calm days are an added bonus to that joy. I have loved every voyage in the *Storm Petrel*; except perhaps that one in which I was sick in bending too long over her obstinate engine in a choppy sea.

My knowledge of marine engines is almost nil, and John's not much better. Some days the motor will not go at all—it's too sensitive to the odd wave which splashes inboard. There are times when I would cheerfully chuck the whole contraption overboard. When not in action its idle propellor drags behind, its blades acting like a sea-anchor. Fortunately the *SP* proves to be very sea worthy, ideal in size for easy handling among the rocks, and light enough to haul up the steep slipway—the only safe place we can keep her during bad weather.

No, the goat is unmated, but there is a billy running with the Lighthouse flock, so we should expect her to kid in the spring and provide us with milk by the time you come, by which time I hope we shall acquire more nannies. This will be your department; I'm not very good at milking, Polly tells me.

I laughed at the nonsense in your letter about the three students discussing the properties of gas in the lane. I never had any bosom friends at school, no one really liked the things I did after I grew out of the 'birds'-egg collecting stage'. I spent all my spare days in prowling about the woods and fields *quite alone*. You are the first fellow-spirit in love with nature that I have ever known intimately. So I have achieved my two great ambitions: an island, the other being the prospect of living there with that fellow spirit . . .

As for the gloves, the products of the island are not included under our no-presents agreement.

Dick killed a buzzard he trapped on Sunday; he hates hawks as they attack his trapped rabbits. I was very angry and forbade him to kill any hawks in future. It was even useless as a specimen for the

National Museum of Wales, with its skull smashed in. This buzzard had only been caught by one claw, and could have been released—old Dick did apologise, saying he did not know I wished to protect hawks. And tried to make amends by saying he believes that some old buzzards are aware of the danger of scavenging birds caught in traps. He's seen them hopping around cautiously first watching the poor trapped bird struggle; if both of the victim's legs are broken the buzzard may wrench it free and carry it off. A hideous business, but for the revenue from the trapping I would give it up right away.

What is the solution? If wild rabbits keep up their profitability, and there is a huge trade each winter in Pembrokeshire catering for the demand for flesh and fur in Birmingham and the West Midland towns, then it seems to me we ought to engage more men to catch our island rabbits as early as possible in winter. I am still trying the ferrets, but with no real hope of netting enough to make it worth the cost of manpower. I think I shall have to sell them soon.

East Hook
25th

Dearest Doris,

While out ferreting along the cliff top Reuben flushed a dog-fox, and after a wild chase aided by his dog and gun, he at last brought it down. I helped him skin the poor thing, which he intends to send away to be dressed and made up as a lady's stole (tho' I can't see his mother wearing it—his sister Polly doubtless would).

I have tried to persuade him to be more discriminating, but he slays every wild thing, from hawks to partridges, wild geese, ducks, even moorhens and any strange looking bird.

He recently shot a bittern, that rare and beautiful bird, on Marloes Mere. It has now been stuffed at the taxidermist's in H'west, where I saw it in the window. Yet it is difficult to be too abrupt with Reuben, he is such a helpful youth. I seem to have lost my boyish hunting instinct, and prefer simply to collect records of the living fauna and flora. I tried to explain this change in me to the Codds; Mrs praised me for it. Mr C. annoyed his spouse by saying 'was not

Abel the chosen of your Lord God of Genesis?' With a sardonic twinkle in his eye! She lavishes attention on young Reuben and ignores her husband, a man nevertheless noted for his husbandry on the land. Yet his wife takes no seeming interest in this skill; at meals she always serves young Reuben first. She told me he was an intensely religious boy, and she had been training him to become a lay-preacher. He certainly has the gift of the gab!

What other news can I send you on this newsless day? Heaps of sweet thoughts—which might bore you? I begin to like Martynshaven more every day I am there, wet or fine. It's so peaceful and always some interesting bird when I look up from work. I want summer to come quickly, while I work hard here and on the island all day long, so that I can get tired and fall asleep and not think of you too much until you are really here.

Glad Beatrice has turned up trumps. How many young chins are there now? The more the merrier. Hope the winch comes while we are building the hut, so we can put it up at the same time.

The hut takes longer to complete than I expected. Haven't got the roof on yet, and spent an exasperating day nailing the corrugated iron on the side sections. I have rarely used this material before, now I am painfully aware of its nasty habits when you cut or maltreat it. One needs thick gloves—which I haven't got. Think now, too late, that I should have used weatherboards outside. I got the local carpenter to measure up for two windows, but he seems to take days to make them, although he promised to bring them down within twenty-four hours of taking away the wood to his workshop. I suppose I am too impatient, and wish I could take time to do things slowly and well, like your father. It was a fortnight ago that we began to dig the foundations for the hut!

A windy morning turning to a sou'west gale this afternoon. As it is also a high spring tide today I shall have to go down just before high water (9pm) to check if the *Storm Petrel* is safe where she lies on the beach. I'll be glad when our own winch arrives. Jack and I have marked out a place for it well above the highest known tide in Martynshaven.

Just back from the beach, and am writing this by candlelight, having almost run out of notepaper. The boat was safe though the surf roared and rattled and sucked at the pebbles below. A fascinating place by moonlight, where all the spent waves, born in the seething cauldron of Jack Sound, come hurrying home to die.

Well dear lady the stars are now shining, the wind is sighing, Skokholm lighthouse glows red, the Bishop light flashes white in the nor'west and little sparks of luminescence twinkle in the bay below this old farmhouse on East Hook cliffs.

Ronald.

Tyr Bont
27th

Dearest Ronald,

. . . I had a nice surprise in your letter this morning. You can't think what it cost me to write and offer you your freedom. I think that if I hadn't known deep down, that you didn't really want it, I would never have offered. You see what a poor creature I am! I want you and by that wanting I gain my freedom to live with you! I hope you will understand what I mean? . . .

Just off to lacrosse practice, happy to do so because you want me to get as much social life as possible before being isolated on an island! Very dutiful of me, isn't it?

I'm most intrigued by Mrs Codd's attempt to talk religion to you, but I'm not sure why she should underline everyplace where *The Blood is Mentioned in the Testament.* Could you enlighten me? A lot of blood is shed in Genesis . . .

I can't stand the sight of Charles Henry, I'm so jealous he is going to the island which must be looking lovely today. Here the clouds are racing gloriously across a blue sky. There are two layers, the lowest a roseate grey and smokey as they fly very fast, but the upper are intensely white and slower—only 'white' seems inadequate to describe them, they are so bright against the patches of blue sky—not the intense blue you get in summer, but a fresh lighter blue . . .

Just listen to me rhapsodising when I ought to be out feeding the rabbits. There are now 21 young ones. The one I thought was blind after much bathing with boracic solution has opened one eye, but has a very bleary outlook on life at present. One of Jennifer's also has one eye closed which I'm bathing. What is the matter? I am beginning to think the rabbit shed is too draughty?

Very much love from Do.

Tyr Bont.
29th. Sunday in bed

Dearest Ronald,

I'm afraid you will never get a respectable letter from me, decently written in ink, for my bed seems to be the only place I can find time to write to you, and I'm liable to spill ink on the sheets then. Having bathed and annointed my face with cold cream, and wound up my watch, and put on your ring, and got into bed, I felt at last in the right mood to write.

I've got to be jolly careful you don't outbloom my countenance with that ruddy cherubic complexion of yours. Don't you dare hide it under a beard, no matter how silky and curly it may grow!

I'm sure I did not mean to chatter about all this when I started this epistle! So do say something more useful—woman.

Now we are turning out the lumber room, packed with forgotten items put in there over the years, as too good to throw away. I wish you were here to see if any of them could be useful on the island.

1. A complete open fireplace, like your Skokholm Manor one, only unbroken.

2. About 20 lbs of assorted galvanised chains.

3. A small portable folding bed that can be shut down flat (hangs on the wall).

4. Cow cake crusher. Papa thinks it could be adapted as a boat winch?

5. An old dentist's lathe.

Can't remember what else just now, I'm getting too sleepy, so goodnight with much love.

Monday morning

We won our lax match on Saturday. Lacrosse is an exciting game, you are always on the run trying to catch the elusive flying bird of the ball. I have not played a lot lately, so I now feel quite weak in the arms, using so many unused muscles.

Your little owl is very loquacious this morning in our shrubbery, and I can hear Mr. L's cocks crowing away on your old farm. I must get up.

Eunice is home, so Davieses came to tea yesterday, and talked about the Island; we discussed the floors on Skokholm. It was suggested we had *painted* wood floors to our house. I said it would be a pity to hide a beautifully grained wood floor under paint, and that unpainted wood was so easy to wash and dry. Papa came in and advocated clear solignum, which would help to destroy any woodworm and one can wash a solignum floor and restain it, better than putting beeswax on and polishing it. What do you think? I'm afraid I'm not a houseproud person. On wet days my dear man, you may find the house untenable and will be driven to live with the rabbits because of a wretched housewife who has put off all the housework during the fine weather. The floor of the living room will be wet then and smelly, and the bedrooms piled high with furniture waiting for the solignumed floor to dry, and you wanting to get to bed after a hard day's work outdoors.

Such is the gossip of three women over tea, all I can think of to write to you just now. Underneath their talk I ungenerously detect a touch of jealousy that I was the lucky one—going to be married to a romantic islander? . . .

I must post this, so au revoir for now.

Ever your D.

Beatrice has achieved only three offspring—lazy crosspatch. I enclose two cuttings which may be of interest.

Part 5

February 1928

'My Brasail' and other dreams . . .

Buzzard

Feb 4th

My dear Doris,

We both must have been studying cloud effects by your recent letter—thankyou. A terrible thing happened today. I was sitting on Martynshaven beach eating my lunch and reading your letter when a rude westerly wind suddenly snatched your precious missive from my hand! It ran along the pebbles ending up in a rock pool where I captured it, not too illegible with salt-water. Thankyou for the cuttings. Flax growing sounds an attractive possibility or side line, but there is always the problem of the wild rabbits. Do they eat flax?

What a shock to learn you use cold cream on your rosy countenance! Perhaps I should use a hairnet to control my unruly hair? For your information my beard grows apace but alas is not at all silky smooth—it bristles horribly.

Anything you unearth in your lumber room might be useful to us, but we must first consider the trouble and cost of getting it down to Martynshaven. I suggest for the present we manage on what's on the island, be Crusoes. One of the pleasures of island living is what gifts the wind and sea throws up on our shores—one day I found a crate of oranges, always there are useful planks, sizable boxes and unlimited firewood for the trouble of climbing down and lugging it up the cliffs.

Anyway at the present rate of progress—nil—on repairing the island house, the interior painting and staining won't be even begun before July 12th. But on an island we shall, I hope, be content to live on 2 pounds a week, which is what I calculate it costs me at present—in purchased food and fuel.

Interval. 9.15pm

Tea, home-made scones and backchat provided by my benevolent hostess Mrs C. and her dear silver-whiskered husband. We've gossiped until we are sleepy and now the old couple have gone to bed. We had to go out to look for a ferret Reuben lost this evening, and to lock up the poultry more securely in case the lost ferret raided their roost. Reuben took me down the cliffs to show me the large entrance to a badger's sett, although he had always supposed it to be a fox's den. But I could see by the bundles of dead bracken and withered grass and orderliness of the burrow entrance that it was the occupied sett of the local Brock family. They had just spring cleaned and taken new bedding below. I asked Reuben not to shoot badgers. He was reluctant to promise not to, but I hope I convinced him that they were not only harmless, but beneficial in devouring bugs and snails, and would dig out the nests of such vermin as rats, mice, wasps, also snakes. In fact I made out a great case for the protection of this harmless and handsome wild creature.

The exterior of the hut is more or less finished. The interior can await days when I shall be marooned ashore.

Lately I have been working on the barn with the help of the mason and Jack. We have hauled tons of sand and put in some windows.

Thanks for your letter. Make them longer please, with local gossip as I do mine. Every word is precious to your R.

Tyr Bont
2nd

Dearest Ronald,

Forgive the superlative but I am still overjoyed that you don't want your freedom any more than I do. I do wish I could come down to the island NOW. I lie and listen to the wind raging around the house, singing in the tall trees, and rain on the roof, and try to imagine that I am at Skokholm and that it is the sea I can hear. I feel poetical, and try to remember poems about the sea to make me go to sleep quickly.

Today I saw a huge flock of gulls—probably herring gulls—flying or rather staggering, wings awry, towards the Severn Sea. They were being blown sideways. I held out my arms and called to them to take me with them, but they took not the slightest notice!

What nonsense—probably ungrammatical too.

I'm half-asleep, dreaming about flying with the gulls. Goodnight.

Morning

I wonder if anything will come of flax growing? It may be a good crop for farmers generally, and sounds more profitable than sugar beet which the Government has spent millions on promoting. Flax might help the flagging linen industry? The trouble is one is always reading about new plants and crops to revolutionise agriculture, and then they seem to die an untimely death, one never knows why.

What a nuisance that the *SP*'s engine is so unpredictable. I suppose it is necessary to have an engine at times, altho' you seem to manage without one successfully enough. You enjoy sailing so much, by your letters, that I am very envious living my dull earthbound existence. I vote we have a really fast sailing yacht when we can afford one. When our ship comes home let it be a grand yacht fit to sail around the world—or at least like Belloc's *Nona* sailing off the Pembrokeshire coast.*

To change the subject. Have you thought again about Charles' wages? Mama thinks 20 pounds and his keep rather too generous, I did not think it too much, but Mama says experienced labourers on Vi's farm only get 40 pounds yearly, and they have families to support. However I expect you've already decided. I just thought that I'd better tell you—rather belatedly it's true, but I kept forgetting.

It's getting late.

Very much love Do.

Tyr Bont

Dear Islandman,

I've just been re-reading your recent letters, cherishing the sweet things you write now and then about me. I wonder do you forget them as soon as written by your facile pen dipped in the ink of

* [We never had more than very small outboards. Father bought a rather derelict Cornish lugger c.1936. We had high hopes of sailing in it to the continent but she got wrecked off the Devil's Teeth a few months after we bought her.]

exaggeration? Well, I won't remind you of them in case you did not mean them.

I am so very glad you will leave the floors and interior to your humble spouse-to-be.

Papa thinks we'll have to have a pantechnicon to move all my goods, plus the rabbits and the chickens, down to the island. I think if this place is sold he would like to dump most of his precious woodworking tools on you—his workbench and moulding planes etc. Where is he going to put these in the flat—which Mama has set her heart on? I can't imagine Papa in a flat, can you?

About fowls. How many do you want on the Island? I am assuming about a dozen laying hens for the winter, tho' you may put down a few hundred gulls eggs in pickle. I've been repairing my one available pen to accommodate your Kent cockerel and a dozen of my laying hens. Your letter about it being nearly February shook me into action, if I am to produce February hatched chicks, which I am told are best for winter egg producers. I imagine a dozen wives is enough for your young Kent cockerel to manage? How long have they to be mated before I can safely use the eggs for hatching?

By the way I've just realised that this cockerel of yours will be no good to us on the island, for he'll be the father of the pullets we'll have on Skokholm, so please, please, let me have the bill for him. We'll have to get an unrelated cock later.

It is simply pouring again, so I can go on writing to my island man with a clear conscience. Not altogether clear, however, for Mama is patching my old pyjamas. She has just said I ought to be doing it, so I shall know how! I am scornful of the idea that I shan't know how. I'm sure anyone can sew on a patch though I expect it will take me ages, as I shan't have a sewing machine. Never mind, I shall bring any mending to be done while you are gardening or fishing or watching birds. Mending in such circumstances takes on a rewarding glamour.

Forever yours Do.

5 February, 1928

Dear Doris,

. . . Perhaps as your mother hints, 20 pounds is a bit on the generous side, but then he will have an unusual job—living on a lonely island. I shall expect him to earn it, just as I expect Jack to earn his 2 pounds a week. That is the top wage for a good male labourer locally, but Jack is an exemplary and highly skilled worker and worth double—I would have been lost—probably drowned without him. I hope we have enough money to employ him after the rabbiting is over. He has fortunately agreed to stay with me at present, to help restore the house and continue as boatman, lending me his *Foxtrot* (the apple of his eye) without charge. I doubt if he owns anything much else of worldly goods where he lives in the village, too much under the thumb of his uncle and aunt, where he does much of the work on their small-holding. He is obviously happiest with one leg in the sea.

So you'll do your mending in the boat when I am fishing or watching birds. Good. I'd rather wear rags than see you slaving at domestic duties. I very much hope that instead you will find time to carry on your painting skill.

I forgot to tell you I was delighted to find our buzzard has a new mate, soaring in tandem in the air over the home meadow. Two song-thrushes singing and several larks. Guillemots and some razorbills coming close inshore preparatory to landing and inspecting their cliff nesting sites; interesting courtship games, pairs swimming towards each other, then suddenly diving. From the top of the cliffs you can watch them zigzagging under water with jerky movements of their half-opened wings.

Nip likes to accompany me when I make my daily visit to the North Pond, when he helps to flush any snipe or woodcock lying in the bog grass cover. Occasionally he catches and eats a rabbit on his own. The lost ferret turned up in a trap, fat and well, one leg rather lacerated, but is recovering. As a means of controlling rabbits ferrets are quite inefficient. Island rabbits so seldom bolt. I shall probably give the ferrets to Reuben.

There were more clusters of frogspawn on the North Pond, which I have enlarged as much as possible, by damming up its outlet to Mad Bay cliffs. Rather fun, as the pond is on a flattish depression, so damming it at this wet time of year makes it twice as extensive for visiting wild fowl. You remember on your August visit it was low and bright with red persicaria; we also saw the charming bog pimpernel in the wet ground. There's no sign of these plants as yet, but plenty of signs of wild ducks and the nocturnal visits of wild geese which leave their cigarette-like droppings and downy feathers where they preen beside the pond.

About that acre of rabbit food: I propose having it fairly close to the buildings, handy to the rabbitry hutches I am going to build within the shelter of the old farm yard. It is all at present under rabbit bitten grass and dead weeds (nettle and hemlock), but must be fertile from centuries of grazing and never being ploughed up.

It would have to be fenced and made rabbit proof. I envisage eventually it being surrounded with a strong tall hedgebank protecting the crops, where we could grow hardy trees such as sycamore, hawthorn, blackthorn and pines (*P. sylvestris*), which I have noted growing in exposed places on the mainland.

No more now. I must go to bed, having used up two candles in the kitchen tonight. Everyone at Hook has gone to bed. This paper is my dear hostess's. She brought it to me specially to write to 'your loved ones at home', and thoughtfully placed a bible on the table close to my left hand. God surely guides this good woman!

Goodnight to the very sweet Queen of Skokholm. It's 11 pm by your watch.

With heaps of love,
ever yours R.

4th Friday night at Tyr Bont

Dearest R,

I've just been renewing one of the miseries of my youth, or rather childhood. You'll never guess. Seaming pillowslips. I begged and begged Mama to buy the ready sewn ones, the sort like a cylinder, but she utterly refused, saying the unsewn type were of better quality and much cheaper. Mama always used to give us pillow slips to seam when we were naughty— is it much wonder that Vi and I both hate sewing? All the old troubles were still there—cotton getting in the same tangle, and the needle getting stickier every moment until it creaks when you push it through the tough linen. Mama took pity on me just a little by starting a new seam, we also had the wireless on which helped to make the time go faster—the weirdest 'modern' music imaginable. It just seemed to go on and on non-stop without arriving at a climax, and just as you came to a bit that seemed more tangible, it would go off the rails again. I enjoyed being bored with it! It was a concert at the Queen's Hall by a conductor called Schoenberg. It will be interesting to read what the critics say about it.

I wonder if you are home on your beloved island? I expect so— it's been dead calm here with incessant rain until about 4 pm.

Muriel, Eunice and I made an expedition after birds yesterday. It was a lovely day with a jolly keen wind down on the moors by the Severn. We did not see much that was unusual except little flocks of shelducks resting on the edge of the mudflats. I shouldn't have known what they were but I could see they were ducks when they flew and showed a red breast band; when they rested on the edge of the sea they looked more like gulls.

We recorded some skylarks and pipits, but not sure which pipits they were. Redwings were easy enough to identify from their red underwings, but fieldfares looked like missel-thrushes—there were flocks of both . . . We went such a long way along the muddy shore that we simply had to tear home against the wind, so as not to be late for dinner. One good thing, Eunice had no breath left for her usual obstruse arguments! Goodnight.

Oh, I forgot—I baked you a cake. I've looked hard at it and hope to goodness it isn't as heavy as the last one. It's to celebrate the opening (I hope) of Martynshaven Hut. Please let me know what it tastes like—the absolute truth please. If it has too many raisins or peel, or too much sugar or spice, tell me and I'll alter the recipe accordingly.

Goodnight once more.

Sunday night

I had a fright this afternoon. Your sister Marjorie and friend Pat with her dog called in for tea, Marjorie had to go back to London by the evening train and Annie put the cake I'd made for you on the table before I could stop her. You should have heard me reluctantly inviting our guests to taste your island fruit cake, but praying they would prefer the sponge cake which Mama, realising my dilemma, brought to the table—which luckily they did. Poor you, I'm sure you'd prefer Mama's sponge but you won't get the chance!

The evening entertainment ended with our labrador Punch attempting to eat up Pat's little West Highland terrier. Luckily Punch did not get a good grip on his neck before I grabbed my brute—thank goodness.

How are your fingers? Do be careful with that beastly corrugated zinc—it can be poisonous. I suppose you haven't any iodine? You ought you know.

Just struck eleven, so sweet dreams be yours.

Ever your D.

Dear Island Man,

I could almost find it in my heart to be sorry that Martynshaven Hut may be finished—I miss your more regular letters. Selfish of me of course, when I know you are delighted to get back to Tir Nan Og.*

Did you ever read a poem called 'Hy Brasail'—all about a rash youth who sailed away—

> He heard not the voices that called from the shore,
> He heard not the wind's menacing roar,
> Home, kindred and safety he left that day
> And he sped to Hy Brasail, away far away.

* [Correctly Tir na n-Og (Irish, literally 'The land of the Young ones') a folk tradition associated with the Isle of Rathlin. Probably my mother got it from a lyrical poem by T. Gwynn Jones. However it became a 'pet' name for Skokholm when my parents were in lyrical mood!]

The island smiled on the far horizon, and lured him on, and this is what happened to him—

> Rash fool! for a vision of fanciful bliss
> To barter thy calm life of labour and peace,
> The warning of reason was spoken in vain,
> He never revisited Ara again!
> Night falls on the deep midst tempest and spray,
> And he died on the waters, away far away!

Pooh! How can they possibly tell—he may be living blissfully on Hy Brasail. I don't suppose anyone else was courageous enough to sail after him . . .

I believe I've not written to you since Mama has been ill. Somehow she caught a dreadful cold, I have prevailed on her to stay in bed—so she must be feeling rotten. She seemed on the verge of a nervous breakdown just before she caught this cold. I'd been cross and snappy and so preoccupied with my own particular worries that I had not noticed that I was jangling Mama's nerves, and she already fretting about my departure, the sale of the farm, and her anxiety about her future.

Must stop now, and try to make something tasty she might eat for her supper. Will finish this letter in bed.

In bed

Just midnight so I won't write much. But feeling more cheerful because Mama actually drank a small cup of beef tea and nibbled a little piece of toast. So I think she is getting better.

A simply glorious night, with a brilliant moon and stars looking twice as large as they should. They are too bright I'm afraid—a sign of bad weather to come.

Goodnight with much love as ever,

D.

[Undated]

Dear Lady,

We are certainly not going to catch 4000 or even 3000 rabbits. We will be lucky if we market 2500 this year, which local trappers say is a poor one. Last spring trapping was begun here very late, in February, and went on too long—till the end of April, by which time, Dick says does would be in all stages of breeding; this destruction spoilt the crop for this winter. Sounds feasible.

When I asked Jack about shearwaters beginning to nest in the burrows he admitted a considerable number were caught in the gin traps, from March onwards.

By now, Jack and Dick know I am a rabid bird lover and protector. But it was clear to me that hitherto they thought very little about the cruelty involved. For centuries generations of local men had exploited the sea-birds on these islands as a natural seasonal crop. The fat fledgelings of both shearwaters and puffins were harvested for human food in the last century by the use of nets and other devices—Jack says, 'seabirds make good bait for lobster pots!'

Adult sea-birds make rather tough eating, but the young squabs of shearwaters and puffins, are deliciously tender, he said. To extract them from the depths of their natal burrow a rather diabolical device is used, in the shape of a pliable wand, up to 6 ft long, one end of which has a wire noose, which serves to loop around leg or neck of the hidden young bird. If this fails the other end has a sharp chisel-like point. I got Dick to show me how it was done, using a dead rabbit pushed well down a burrow, to demonstrate.

Dick pushed the wand down until it touched the victim and invited me to twist the wire until the split point was firmly engaged in the rabbit's fur—'Thee mus' keep twisting the wire all the time so's it'll screw into the fur real tight, so's the rabbut's 'elpless an' thee can draw 'ut right into the open.' Which I did. With this device any live shearwater, puffin, rabbit and even a ferret can be screwed forth, once contact is made with the poor creature's skin.

A medieval torture device! But I can imagine hungry castaways on the island might survive tolerably well using this device, probably it is as ancient as man's association with sea-birds burrowing on such islands? In fact it might be worth keeping for my/our museum of island curiosities I am beginning to collect e.g. a few flints I have found scratched out from rabbit burrows. I sent two flints to the National Museum before Christmas; the geologist there replied that as Skokholm is entirely a red sandstone island, most likely the flints had been dropped by prehistoric human visitors, and asked me to look out for signs of their dwelling huts. There are several on Skomer and some on Gateholm, visible today as a ring of heavy foundation stones. So far I have found none on Skokholm—if any ever existed, most likely the stones were robbed to build the present house and farm.

Goodnight for now, your sleepy R.

P.S. Before I forget would you kindly ask your father to visit a boatbuilder's yard at Cardiff Docks and send me some copper nails and rooves for repairing the *Storm Petrel* properly (that crack is still held together with canvas, pitch and tar). We need a gross of copper tacks ½ inch long and half a gross of both 2 inch and 1¼ inch copper nails, with rooves to match for riveting. Sorry to trouble you, but they are not easy to obtain locally.

8 February, 1928

Dearest Doris,

Got ashore last Weds., after days of steady sou'westers and drizzling rain, which we spent largely in embellishing the interior of the barn, plastering over draughts piercing the solid walls, where the dry inside earth has drifted away; and in building up a splendid hearth and chimney against the eastern wall.

I have been to see Bulldog Edwards (the late tenant of Skokholm) to examine a disused kitchen range which he offered me 'for a song'—a very rusty song for 1 pound. It has a big oven and boiler, and might be ideal for the barn. He was in a very affable mood as we sat by his 'modern' stove and drank tea! Told me that I could place my winch (when it comes) where his old, now derelict island boat *Primrose* is still resting, tight against the bank on the side below the hut. I learned that it had been a wonderful island-going boat, and that no man who owned a good one would ever break it up when he had finished with it. It must be allowed to 'go to its last sleep in peace',—a nice thought. Which explains the number of broken-down boat remains lying among the nettles at Martynshaven!

Thank you very much for all your letters, and the splendid cake. I have handed some around at East Hook, and intend to celebrate the opening of the hut in the Haven of St Martin tomorrow, weather being entirely unpropitious for returning to the island.

So sorry to hear about your Mother and hope she has recovered by now. Please convey all my best wishes—and perhaps apologies, as I suspect we egotistical lovers (as you suggest) are somehow to blame for her worries. Love can be very selfish?

. . . Damn this East Hook pen, dripping ink one moment and dry the next—it's stopping the flow of eloquence I had reserved for your benefit!

I liked your poem 'Hy Brasail'. I am sure that is what I shall do if anything happens to YOU. I'll sail away on an easterly breeze of course to whatever land I may be blown to, and if a great storm rises I will go down quietly with the sinking sun. Or if we are still together on our Island and the bailiffs are coming to take possession, we will quietly sail away together on a holiday I have long planned with my heart's desire—away from the island haven, past the Stack and north through Jack and Ramsay Sounds, far up the Irish Sea (you'd better get out your chart), and reach the Hebrides, where we shall visit many uninhabited islets beloved of the seals and wild geese. Then, leaving the sheltered waters of the Minch we shall pass the mighty Butt of Lewis and set sail for lonely Ronald's Isle—which you will find on your map marked North Ronay. Here is the Hy Brasail of my boyhood dreams. It was once inhabited by a Gaelic community who were so isolated that they knew not the use of money, and lived like hobgoblins in snug houses of turf *under* the ground, safe from the storms sweeping the harbourless island. Here wild sheep still roam, providing us with wool for our garments. And a huge herd of grey seals come ashore to whelp in the autumn, and we shall learn their ways and their musical songs. Here, hauling our boat safely up for the winter, we shall live happily ever after, fishing, gathering gull's eggs, keeping a garden, making cheese from ewe's milk and You will be the Island Queen dressed in brown lambskin matching your crown of curls.

Forever and ever yours—
Prince Ronald of Ronay.

Tyr Bont
Thursday night

My Dear Gentleman,

I am so happy tonight, my heart is like a singing bird—because it's nearly February. February, March, April, May, June. Can't it be June? Do say it must be June. I can't miss June with you, it's the nicest month in the whole year.

When will the chiffchaff come? I found spring this afternoon when I sallied forth to collect rabbit greens. You will say I make too much of a song about gathering rabbit food. Well, you're right—it is the joy of prowling the lanes at this season of burgeoning wild flowers and birdsong.

I was out early this morning while the lanes were still in shadow, and when the rising sun tipped the hedge-tops it made more shining gold the newly-opened pussy willows. There are masses of snowdrops full blown in the garden and celandines in the hedges. Many larks now sing all day long. I wonder are there celandines on Skokholm? I know there are larks. Please do write more about spring arriving with you—you've told me so little lately about the Island birds and flowers.

I must see that badger's sett at East Hook. Please don't let Reuben shoot any more. Tell him your sweetheart wants him to show her badger babies on a summer evening stroll there.

Ann has achieved a family of seven. I think Carmen is going to have her family any day now—she's bulging in the right places.

You'll be glad to learn that the baby I thought blind has one normal eye open now, the other is rather bleary; and Jennifer's child still has one eye closed. Liddy's are 5 weeks . . . I shall have to place them out to graze soon, and the 'weary round of procreation' will begin afresh for Liddy. Poor little thing, she isn't going to enjoy much of a break from being a matron. She's a charming character, very friendly. Gets up on her hind legs and tries to open her hutch door on seeing me, sniffs like a cat with winking nostrils at my fingers. No doubt cupboard love, yet when I fill her waterbowl, she will rub her chin affectionately against my wrist.

Do you know that we spend at least 1s 6d a week on stamps—doesn't that extravagance appal you? It offends my economical sense.

What a wild boisterous night, how the sea must be roaring and tearing at Skokholm! We have had a thunderstorm too—the first clap was more like a roar; I thought our big elm tree had been struck. After a bit I saw a huge flash through the kitchen curtains. I turned the lamp very low and after a few moments was rewarded with the sight of the landscape lit up with brilliant violet light. It was like looking through a camera when you take a snapshot . . . I wondered if it was anywhere visible to you? Lightning always excites me, yet I am also a wee bit scared, a queer sort of terrified elation.

I'm writing a lot of tosh and it's midnight. Goodnight and happy dreams be thine.

Love Do.

5 February

Dear Ronald,

I am writing in bed and using ink, so I only hope this new nib won't drip!

Mama is definitely better thank you, although she can't taste a thing. In one respect that's convenient for me, since I can conceal all sorts of nourishing items in her food . . . On the other hand it was disappointing that she could not taste an extra special pudding that I made, it had four eggs and a whole wineglass of sherry in it.

Fearful extravagance, but at least Papa enjoyed it saying it had character, which he put down to the sherry!

Here is half this letter already filled up with food, but one thinks of little else when one has an invalid to look after. Doctor says she must stay in bed as she definitely has bronchitis.

I am glad to report there are now 34 rabbits in the rabbitry here, and every adult doe has a family except Carmen. The doe with the permanent snuffle, Doreen, has 5 and has stripped her undercarriage naked to provide a warm nest . . . sign of a good mother?

I'm fed up with Beatrice, she still stuffs up her nest box with everything she can lay paws and jaws on, with the result that there's hardly room for her babies and they are always very damp.

That is my report as your lieutenant in charge of the chinchillas. The young ones are growing at a fast pace, and Charles and I are busy making new runs and outdoor houses to put them out to graze, away from their dams. We are adapting some wooden grocery crates, with an inspection lid on top, a pop-hole to let them out by day, and shut them in at night. We are using 2 inch wire netting four feet high pegged to the ground with tent pegs and held upright with metal garden stakes. The whole outfit can be moved to fresh grass when necessary.

I'm sorry not to have sent this letter before, but DV it will arrive with the boat nails. These were delayed because Papa failed to get the washers from the Docks, but found some in a Bute Street Chandlers shop. So they should arrive by Thursday mail with you.

What with the weather, the rain, the mud and wrestling with rickety gates and doors, roofs that leak, and general delapidation outdoors, resulting in everyone being cross and on edge, topped by the sale going so badly, if I hadn't had you and a mudless Skokholm to think about I would have drowned myself in the large rainpond now half-filling the river meadow.

You ask my advice about planning the rabbit-food garden. Please don't overdo this, as I like to think I shall come in time to help in its design and execution. Of course you will have to make a start, and plant enough greenstuff, seeds, etc, to feed the chins over the autumn and winter. Only I do long to be with you to share the joy of planning and planting.

Goodnight.
Love from Do.

P.S. Please don't think I'm an inveterate grumbler, but since I said I had worries I had to rake up some trivial ones—but I have NONE AT ALL about you or the Island.

Part 6

February 1928 *(cont.)*

Moving in to the hut

Young raven

Martynshaven
12 February, 1928

Dearest Rabbit Queen,

Everyone calls you Do, 'Doe' which is quite absurd, at least I find it disturbing. How can a queen of an Island be Queen Doe? Might as well call you Lady Rabbit Queen, which you are anyway! . . . I personally prefer Doris.*

This is my first letter to you since sleeping in the Hut, written as I sit on a heap of bedding and clothes amid bundles of match-boarding, straw bales, sacks of sawdust, tools, stove and utensils. I've moved in! What a mess! It's raining and blowing from S. so I can't put anything out of doors and too much of a crush indoors to tidy up, the porch crammed with 96 rabbits hung up and awaiting the dealer.

Most mysterious weather yesterday, extraordinary sky colour which looked like the end of the world. This made us apprehensive about putting off for the island, having been marooned ashore since Sunday. However the wind being SW and strong but veering westerly, we motored out towards Skomer, and to gain our westing, we went down through the Little Sound instead of Jack Sound. In this narrow sound the tide rushes like a river in full spate, no convenient eddies to take advantage of. We were swept south as you might shoot rapids, right out into Broad Sound. And so to Skokholm after a battle with the wind and south stream off the Stack, which fain would have carried us to St Ann's Head, and even up the Severn Channel towards Cardiff perhaps!

We stayed only long enough to take off the rabbits and pack some items for living in the Hut, for I still did not like the look of the weather, and the current by now had changed in our favour for sailing back to Martynshaven. Which was just as well as the *SP* was loaded to the gunwales. This morning confirmed our fears; the lightkeepers will be groaning too, they are overdue on their relief.

But I am far from groaning, I tell you all our misadventures

* [This was an ongoing disagreement between my parents as long as I can remember. Because my mother hated her given name so much and family and friends had always called her 'Do' Father lost the battle—but on occasion would pettishly bring it up again.]

because it's only fair you should know about them, yet all the while a wild, wild song sings within mc. And all because I've felt surer than ever that you are steadfast in your promise to come and live with me . . .

I have ordered the right wood for the rabbitry from Fishguard. The Haverfordwest firm is much too dear (half as much again in price). But shall pick up my old Talbot car and relicense it. It's been lying in a H'west garage all these months. I need it now for transporting goods for the repair and rebuilding, if I am to have Skokholm in any shape for YOU and the chinchilla enterprise.

You are exciting me with your news of the number of young rabbits you are rearing. You will soon be hardup for room, so the sooner I can take them here the better. As soon as I am ready I will send for Charles, and he can bring them down with him.

The hut is very warm, lined with straw, shavings and sawdust behind the interior matchboarding. I won't need pictures—the two windows frame sea and landscapes of surpassing beauty.

I've taken over an ordinary simple three-bar grate for the barn, the one Bulldog Edwards offered me complete with a big oven and boiler for 1 pound collapsed in a heap, like a rotten skeleton, when we attempted to load it!

My best wishes to your Mother please for full recovery. Thank your Papa for copper nails and rooves. In the meantime, faithfully your devoted servant, Ronald.

Evening

Motherly Mrs Codd made me stay to supper at East Hook last night as it was wet and wild. She further expressed her fears as to the proper airing of the hut, etc. Tho' I prefer my new mainland abode, I gave in gracefully, somewhat greedily thinking of a good square meal, which I would not be eating alone! When the good lady cleared the table she handed me, once more, a writing pad for 'your daily letter to the Loved One.' She said this with such profound sincerity that it's clear she is a perceptive woman. So you are getting a bonus tonight.

At the public library in H'west, being short of reading matter, I borrowed a book on Sir Richard Steele (he died almost exactly 200 years ago). I quote 'The insupportable labour of doing nothing'. 'Every man is the maker of his own Fortune.' 'Few can grow old with a good grace.' 'Woman seldom writes her mind but in her Postscript.' 'To love (a lady) is a liberal education.' 'Reading is to the mind what exercise is to the body.' How true. When he addressed his letter to his sweetheart wife Prudence, and signed himself 'Yr/most obedient obsequious servant. *Pray date yr letters.*' Which sentiment I respectfully endorse! So dear wife-to-be—N.B.

Most of my favourite books, like Thoreau and Hudson are in that crate I left with you when my farm was sold; don't forget to pack them in the load of impedimenta for Skokholm. Only five months now! We shall read them together in the winter evenings.

Jack and I celebrated the opening of the Hut by eating slices of your latest cake. Since you have asked for a criticism of your cakes I passed the request on to John—he said it was 'main good' but just a trifle too sweet for his tooth. My only criticism is that it is too full of good things—too axtravagant; but no doubt you'll learn to be less so on the island, with just flour and blackcurrants—which are said to thrive in salty air. Reuben has given me a bundle of cuttings for the Island. East Hook garden at the moment seems to consist of currants, gooseberries and the inevitable rhubarb, but early potatoes thrive here, for late frost is rare.

This south wind moans around the house. Around our Island the cliffs are white with leaping spray, and foam blown upwards must be flying from the breakers. I've often seen this foam travelling like snow overhead; when a sou'west gale is blowing South Haven is carpeted white all the way over the winch landing and covering the bracken above, and now and then a lost ball of foam will alight in the wind eddies about the garden and house, and settle like a rare snow bird upon the windows.

Tyr Bont
Friday night

Dear Lord of Skokholm,

Why don't you come and fetch Charles and some of the rabbits?

Quite apart from the joy of seeing you, I do badly need your advice and approval of the chinchillas families mustering here for their Island destiny. (Oh hypocrite, you will say, you only want a glimpse of your future husband—which is perfectly true.) I'd give anything to fly down and see the hut, even cross for a day to the Island. But how can I? I am tied by one leg to rabbits and chickens and to poor invalid Mama. I can't leave her—she won't allow me to!

What about Liddy—do I mate her again at once or give her a rest? She is looking rather thin. She was one of the maiden does and has 5 offspring alive and well-grown.

Really, although I may grumble and ask questions, I do enjoy caring for these interesting creatures; each proves to be as different in character as humans are. I can manage them all at present if Charles goes to help on the Island. Will it be all right if I amalgamate some of the litters now weaned, and let them run together in the same grazing pen?

Otherwise I need more hutches and enclosures for what Mama calls my Rabbit Kindergarten.

Papa is awfully sorry the winch took so long. He only discovered it was still in the warehouse in the Docks when he rang them up and made a fuss. They apologised and promised to send it at once.

A new page but what can I write about? One of my hens is sitting on a dozen eggs at last. I have 'Keatinged' her thoroughly and painted the skin over her naked breast with mercury ointment to destroy the lice which all my chickens have, despite regular dosing. Do rabbits have lice? According to a book I have been reading all furred animals have blood-sucking fleas and birds have lice which live largely on feather scale. It says wild rabbits have fleas which can live for a short time on dogs and cats. I have carefully examined our chins but can find no parasites.

I don't know how fertile the eggs are under the broody, but shall test them soon. I have been wondering about your Rhode Island cockerel from Kent. He seems very lazy, and never seems to take much notice of his dozen wives—they court him rather than the other way round. I have twice found him fast asleep in the middle of the day when he ought to be crowing and showing off his fine hackles to the ladies.

You see, I have nothing exciting to write about. Do tell me how exactly you intend building the rabbitry, modern style, I expect, each hutch with a floor of inch mesh netting, so their pellets and urine will fall through to avoid soiling their fur. This is especially good, the book says, for rabbits bred for pelting.

With all the young bunnies growing so fast and eating so much, I have had to buy a large sack of mangolds, having almost run out of wild greenstuff in the lanes, and my stock of garden cabbages looking like skeletons from daily cutting!

You are dreadful about my cakes, I doubt if I shall send any more. They must be several days old before they reach you, and then you write of eating one many days later. They must get heavier, staler and drier than ever!

I'm very excited about seeds and cuttings and young plants you are taking to the island. Do you like shallots? I thought you hated onions in any shape or form. Still I suppose I can pickle them, and when Papa comes to see us he can eat them, he loves oniony food and will be able to eat them with no thought of the morrow and his patients!

Oh Ronald, I'm glad I'm not going to marry a poultry farmer! I dressed those cockerels and made an unholy mess of them and Myself! I thought of Enid's dexterity, and tried to remember how she eviscerated a chicken with speed and ease, but I'm so slow compared to your sister. I can laugh at it now, but I began all wrong. Mama couldn't help pluck the brutes because of her asthmatic cough. I became quite scratchy with the odd louse that invaded my bare arms, and I had to scald them in a big basin of water I had put on the scullery table. While pulling the guts out I must have nudged the basin too close to the edge of the table, when hey presto it turned completely upside down on the new cord mat Mama had lately put there (to smarten up the place for a prospective buyer). Blood, entrails and water everywhere! You have got a muddleheaded wife no mistake, but you can't say I haven't warned you!

Tuesday, 14 February, 1928

There, is that sufficiently dated for my most imperious, capable, courageous handsome husband-to-be? I can't think of any more laudacious(?) adjectives, or I would throw them in too. I've just imbibed two full glasses of champagne and don't seem to be able to write coherently. Amongst other things we toasted Ronald Islandman. The champagne was for Mama, to buck her up; as she could not drink the whole bottle herself, (and it goes flat very quickly), Papa and I had to help drink up every last drop.

And what did we talk about in our slightly inebriated mood? Of many things, of cabbages (for rabbits) and kings (who have islands) and whether the weather will permit you to fly to us on wings of your now licensed steed?

Papa keeps saying he must spend his next holiday with you, helping repair the house enough for us to live in as man and wife. It would be glorious to see you again, if only a brief inspection to reassure us that you are thriving as your letters indicate—you may be worn to a skeleton on account of your strenuous life?

I have told my parents I am definitely coming to the island for Easter week-end, come what may, and Papa agrees. He intends to escort me. Good Friday is April 6th—take heed!

Laudatory was the word I wanted. I knew there was one but couldn't think of it, probably the result of the champagne.

I don't really like champagne, it exhilarates but in the end leaves me with a muzzy feeling. I think the sight of Lewis Carroll's boiling sea is worth all the champagne in the world . . .

I'd have loved to have seen you enthroned in the debris of your mainland palace!

I'm sending you some seeds for the Island. Don't be cross—you don't have to plant them if you're too busy. They are mostly beans and peas, which are said to be equal in nourishment to meat (I don't forget your Mother has told me that as a youth you were never keen on meat). Also some carrots, chicory and sea-kale for the rabbits. I have long ago put in brassicas like broccoli, kohlrabi and brussel sprouts, so will be able to bring strong plants with me at Easter.

Oh Joy—I'll be able to plant them myself!

Let me know about mating Liddy again. My text book says one

should give weaner rabbits bread and milk until they are able to graze properly. I have done so, but am glad the little wretches (darlings really) won't touch the stuff. I suppose drinking out of a bowl is so different from suckling; I am not wasting any more on them. With only one cow left, we need her milk for the house.

It's well past midnight. Goodnight Sir.

Martynshaven
14th Feb. a.m.

Hullo my dear,

Here's a matchbox riddle for you: Why are you never lonely on an island? Answer: Because there's always a little cove and a big swell running up the beach! Inspired by today's weather—a huge swell running up the little cove of Martynshaven. Too rough for crossing to Skokholm. We have concentrated on digging out a foundation for the new winch, to be bolted to a stout crossbar buried two feet under a block of stone, to resist the strain of pulling up a laden boat.

As we worked at this, on the east side of the lane immediately below the old *Primrose*'s berth, Sturt of Skomer, landing with his men and rabbit catch, came aggressively up to warn me that he would be obliged to take legal advice if I planted my winch there—the roadway was part of his freehold property etc.! I was determined to remain unruffled by this reputedly unhappy man and carried on with measuring the hole we had dug in the roadway. He went off to start his car in the nearby shed, but presently returned to watch us at work. I gathered that his car would not start, for one of his men was tinkering with the engine. As he stood silent and glowering at us, I said to Jack: 'Time for a cup of tea, Jack?' He immediately went up to the Hut to make one, grinning broadly.

I invited S. to join us for a cup of tea, adding that I wanted him to see the new hut; I then told him that the site I had chosen for my winch belonged from time immemorial to the tenant of Skokholm, handed on to me by the late tenant Bulldog Edwards of Orlandon. He hesitated, but seeing that his car was still not started by his grinning minion (by name Tommy Codd the Chapel) S. graciously walked up to tea in my rather untidy hut, where he quite thawed out as we talked most agreeably of our respective islands, and of his (very superficial) knowledge of the birds and history of Skomer. And as he has never set foot on Skokholm, I invited him and his family to call there after we are married.

He had completely forgotten a visit your father and I made to Skomer—I see by my diary of 1926 it was the last weekend in May, when (I quote) 'Mr Sturt and his lively and rather lovely young daughter Betty* saw us off at Skomer North Haven in a fisherman's boat we had hired for 15s there and back.'

Replying to your recent queries:

The stove in the Hut is the double-burner Valor Perfection, but it is too warm even with one burner, so I have taken it back to the island in exchange for a single burner Primus, sufficient for the Hut.

Certainly mate Liddy as soon as her young cease suckling. Cessation of suckling induces heat it is believed; does with very young babies will mate within a few days of removal of suckling offspring. At this time of year the more they produce litters to weaning age the more profitable they are. The adults cease to breed once they start moulting, late in summer—at least that is the case in wild rabbits. Artificially bred domestic rabbits can behave artificially, by breeding out of season. The young litters will grow up together happily, provided they have enough food. In fact they need company to play with, as an intensely sociable species normally living together underground.

Yes, I plan to build the rabbitry block on the modern wire-tray floor system. Although I had at first thought of Morant hutches in open wire-netted pens at grass, but decided Skokholm meadow would look too much like a poultry farm with such pens and houses dotted over the landscape. In theory perhaps ideal, in practice ugly

* [The lively young daughter was to rebel against going to boarding school later, and was to marry Reuben Codd. The happy pair settled at first in the old gamekeeper's lodge near Martynshaven, and their son Geoffrey became R.M.L.'s godson. Mrs Sturt was troubled by tuberculosis and mental problems; she is reputed to have taken to the grand piano and billiard table on Skomer with an axe before being put into an asylum where she died.]

and messy and moreover the young weaners would be exposed to the aerial attacks of predator birds, and winter gales would be likely to blow Morant hutches over.

Altogether after nearly four months of trapping and studying the rabbit situation on the Island I am forced to admit that the wild ones have won the first round. We shall never exterminate the last individual without a huge investment of manpower to trap, snare, net and dig out as well as poison-gas them, quite beyond our means at present.

The alternative as I see it now is to try to achieve our chinchilla experiment for fur production by more natural means, as we have tentatively agreed, that is by enclosing a few acres of grass from which we have excluded the wild population. To improve the herbage here by application of lime and basic slag; the wild clover is already present.

You are dying to have details of Hut life? Here's an example:

6 am. Waiting by lamplight for Jack and darning two rents in my greatcoat.

Mealtimes. I have bread and butter with jam or cheese, washed down with tea. When available a dutiful slice of the Queen's cake. Sometimes a tin of sardines, or some tinned bullybeef. A Milford kipper, boiled, is a luxury. At present no baking, I have only saucepan and frypan available. Now and then Jack and I walk to the Deer Park to spy out the weather and say 'Shall us?' 'Let's not—tis no shape for ferrying a cargo of timber.' So Jack gets on with his task of building a stone bank around the ramparts of the hut, and I to complete the interior of the Hut roof. I now sleep in the double tier bunk, and have fashioned six large drawers to fit under the bottom bunk, handy for storing clothes. Also in process of building a table fixed to the wall under the double window.

Night time. The wind whistles and the surf rattles on the pebbles as darkness descends. Owls cry from holes in the Deer Park escarpment at eye level with the Hut, and I am lulled to sleep. The book drops from my hand, I douse the lamp.

At dawn the next day the call of the gulls and mewing of buzzards wakes me. I leap to the window to study the weather. I make tea and scribble in my diary or a letter to you the events of yesterday while my brain is alert. For I am extremely forgetful by the evening.*

I must now drive up to the post, which is also the one grocer's shop and buy enough provisions for the next few days. So with vast quantities of love and kisses to you, and respectful salaams and good wishes to the invalid Lady, Yours R.

Tyr Bont
15 February, 1928

Dear Ron,

I wish I could vary the way of addressing you. I know you don't like the demeaning diminutive (above). But tit-for-tat I dislike the name Doris. I have always been called DO (not Doe, teasing man). I don't fancy you screaming out DORIS when you are looking for me on the island. If you do I shall shout back HUSBAND. Something dear to the heart of a spinster—this spinster who looks forward to being husbanded and cherished.

Just now I feel inclined to address you—My Dear Islandman, How is your kingdom thriving, ashore and islandwise?

Have you set up the new winch? Have you started the rabbitry? In default of having anything worth writing about happening to me, I am dying to learn every little and big detail of your more exciting life and adventures one hundred miles away from this existence.

I've written to Enid today. She writes that she is now enjoying life in London, though it's a great change from looking after Ronald. She hints that she would like to join Papa and me at Easter, and perhaps stay on afterwards helping to get the house ready for my arrival as your wife. There's no one I would like more to precede me than your marvellously kind sister! But I have told her that on no account is she to spoil you. She is a very dear person, but I shall be jealous all the same.

Muriel commissioned me to paint two daubs for a play our local

* [Always the morning was my father's work time when his best writing was done. This proved very difficult in later years when he had to collaborate with another writer who preferred to work in the evenings!]

arts club are putting on. As she gave me only a few hours to do them in, I enlisted the help of Charles who earlier told me he had won a prize at school for painting a local landscape. I suggested he should do one and I the other. Charles chose to do a sunrise when I told him I intended to paint a sunset. In great haste we knocked up both, mine I think more execrable than his. Such is life in our sleepy little village.

Yesterday was St Valentine's Day, I forgot all about it until Mama reminded me just now.

According to my dictionary St. Valentine's Day 'celebrates the day on which birds were supposed to pair and sweethearts chose their mate'. A valentine is an amatory letter or picture sent to a person of the opposite sex and decorated with cherubs or pierced hearts!

As you have chosen your mate, and I have chosen mine, I send you my belated valentine suitably embellished by

Your most loving wife-to-be.

Good bye
Very much love
from Do

Martynshaven
17 February, 1928

Dearest Doris in Wonderland,

Skokholm through the Looking Glass. The King sat on a promontory and surveyed the Chess Board of farm fields with their green and brown squares, the white clouds and turquoise sea, and the far away red island where his crown rested. The problem was to move the King to the red square. We have not solved it as long as the SW gales blow. After raining for twelve hours it has come on to blow harder than ever, so that the streams falling over the west-facing cliffs are flying straight up into the sky.

Have been thoroughly lazy in consequence, mooching about the Hut, re-reading your letters, eating enormously, polishing the stewpan and teapot, and going for predatory rambles in search of butter and bread in fine intervals, listing the birds along the lanes. The westerly gales hold up migration, but numbers of small birds are detained in the shelter of the hedgebanks, now crowned with gorse in full flower above masses of the white-blossomed scurvy-grass, violets peeping out here and there. Corn buntings and stonechats have taken up territories along this switchback lane, but while it blows they skulk out of the wind.

On days like these when I am weatherbound ashore I like to walk around the coast of the Deer Park headland, looking out for jetsam of planks and fishing ropes and buoys etc which are tossed ashore. A time to study the striving tide-races of Jack Sound ever changing by the half hour, and marked by the speed with which swimming sea-birds are swept along north or south, as they seek fish, in competition with the grey seals.

The seals lurk in the eddies around Tuskar Rock and the Haze. I have learned from Jack that the seals are the best guide to where you may catch fish, just now chiefly pollack. These fish are doing the same, lurking in the eddy made by the rushing tidal current through the narrows, watching for small fry.

I have invested in a rod and sea-line and caught enough pollack to feed myself (to be precise six) for the occasional supper. Pollack is not an exciting fish to eat but it is very satisfying if you are as hungry as I am.

Glad to hear about the seeds, as you are such an authority on them. Easter is surely the ideal time to sow them? By which date I intend to have the rabbit garden ready for your transplants.

On the way home from Milford where we had been buying winch wire, Jack guided me to Sandy Haven, where an old sea-captain lives, oddly enough a distant relative of my Mother. This gentleman, by name Captain Beer, is a builder of small schooners and ketches in which Jack had been first apprenticed as a deckhand.

One of my problems in setting up a home and chinchilla scheme on Skokholm is to obtain transport of bulky material, including coal for the winter, to the Island. I had interviewed the Trinity House contractor (living near Milford) who does the monthly Lighthouse Relief in his sea-going tug, but he had asked an astronomical sum for ferrying a load to Skokholm, nor could he use Relief Days to do so more cheaply; Trinity House forbids such use of contracted time, as any delay in relieving the three lighthouses in winter is critical.

Remembering that Captain Beer kept his ketch *The Cristal* at Sandy Haven, Jack suggested I might hire this cheaply. There she lay, on the mud alongside the private quay Beer's father had built. And upstream were two small schooners virtually derelict, in one of which Jack had sailed as an apprentice. Jack was shocked at the deterioration of these once fine ships: but there is little business now for sailing vessels.

Captain Beer was not at home, but his amiable wife Lilian was in her kitchen giving her newborn son Ralph a bath by the fire. She welcomed Jack as an old friend and said she remembered my mother visiting Sandy Haven as a young woman. She was delighted to meet Emily Mathias's son, and handing me the naked Ralph in a towel asked me to finish drying him while she made us tea!

She said she thought her husband would be pleased to take a cargo of timber, furniture, coal etc over to Skokholm, but first of all he had to fit a new engine in the ketch—a matter of a month or two's work.

As we drove home Jack expressed his forebodings, that Beer junior was not half or quarter the man his father had been; ''E 'as bin messing about in that ole ketch for two years to me knowledge, she leaks like a sieve at every 'igh flood tide. Did you see 'ow that engine be still in the crate tied on deck? 'Cos the old 'ull be full of water.' He explained that Beer's father had bossed his son 'around cruel' until he became sick of going to sea. Now he makes his living carting anthracite from the Cleddau Collieries to local villages by road.

We passed onwards for Marloes. In the hamlet of St Ishmaels I stopped for petrol. A filthy looking lorry passed us there, its tyres bound up with old bits of rope holding them to the wheels. The garage proprietor said the lorry belonged to Beer of Sandy Haven!

Saturday night, 18 February, 1928

This is a much travelled letter. It has been to Skokholm and back in my canvas holdall, hence its crumpled state. The wind went down at dusk on Friday night. Jack had said, 'No sailing in the dark'. Whereupon I swore several oaths to myself, thinking that if this goes on we'll never get to Tir Nan Og—who's master anyway? So aloud I said 'There's a fair wind tonight, and that will have calmed the sea in Skokholm Haven by now.'

And thus it came to pass, as the darkness crept from the land over the sea, that we set sail to the dark red shores of our Island before a fast fair wind. South Haven was perfectly tranquil. Dicky was surprised to see us as he sat by the fire mending his clothes by lamplight. He reported the kitten Peter dead of a chill and the back of the house roof blown off several nights ago.

Now when I woke this morning the sun was already shining and there was not a breath of wind, so that it was even more marvellous to be alive. The whole Island was full of the cries and flight of birds, but especially the singing of larks in the sky, and of robin and dunnock in the garden. The raven croaked his delight and soared over Spy Rock when I raised the flag there. The Welsh Dragon barely flapped so slight was the South breeze. On that breeze we crossed back with a cargo of 170 rabbits, and just missed the dealer, due to a contrary tide off Crab Stones, but the rabbits have kept well and will probably all be accepted tomorrow.

Answer please to query: what colour do I paint the Hut outside? And also the matchboarding inside. (Or do I varnish or Solignum the latter—supposing I find time to do so one day when marooned ashore?) Red is our Skokholm colour, and Martynshaven just now is russet with dead bracken, golden with new-flowering gorse . . .

The pair of stonechats has reappeared, clacking on tall gorse below the Hut, and I can hear a cock corn-bunting singing his little wheezy bit-o-bread-please invitation to his lady friends in the still warm air.

Tyr Bont
Friday night, 17 February, 1928

Dear Islandman,

Surely the weather is about to change? All day it's been gusty with the wind in the old prevailing quarter, calming at sunset. Now it's quiet, the clouds rolled away and the sky brilliant with stars. I noticed this morning a very thin crescent moon when I went out just before sunrise—a nice change after days of cloud and rain.

The sallow catkins are out everywhere, shining golden in the lurid sunlight we've had today. I found at least six primroses in full flower but their petals short and crumpled looking, yet with a real scent of spring. I shall be glad when this old month of February will be gone; it has seemed an eternity despite being the shortest month of the year.

I see from your last letter you ate 'a dutiful slice' of my cake. Pray throw it in the sea if it is only out of a sense of duty you eat it. It may fatten a few eligugs, or more likely kill them off.

The lords-and-ladies in the hedges are looking so handsome and springified I wish sometimes that the leaves were good for rabbits to eat, so I could plant arum as a crop, but they are said to be poisonous. Yet it would be a shame to pick them just now, they look so strong and handsome—like a certain islander who writes me, now and then, long descriptive letters of his exciting life making me as green as the arum leaves with envy.

Goodnight. There's nothing interesting in this letter but I shall post it tomorrow, out of my sight, as I'm ashamed of it.

Tyr Bont
19 February

Dear Islandman,

Thought I'd try a sponge, but not as good as Mama makes. It's a queer shape because I had only this oblong biscuit tin.

I am very sorry to report that one of Ann's children died today. Can't think why—not a mark on her, and she had seemed so healthy, frisking about with the rest of the family not yet weaned. So now my total of rabbits is 36. I hope they are not going to start fading away like the ten little nigger boys.

You are a nice but very naughty fellow! But I must hurriedly thank you for the splendid surprise present you sent me from Burma, it was awfully kind of Ken to post them direct. Please tell him from me how much I appreciate his choice of fine embroidered table linen, for which the Burmese are justly famous. All the same you are to be reprimanded for once more breaking our no-presents rule of saving for the future. Cake and rabbits are lawful, but not expensive presents from the Orient. Nevertheless I love you for the thought, and have put the gift in my (empty) bottom drawer. With fond XXX to the giver!

Great haste to post
Ever your Do.

Martynshaven
22 February, 1928

Dear Do,

I've just written you another wandering senseless letter and destroyed it.

Thank you sweet confectioner, for the delicious sponge cake, with the little flag in it to prove YOU (not your Mama) made it. I thought I told you not to send me food? So I will retaliate with a pair of fat rabbits. I should have sent more, only they are often so bedraggled: we've been lucky with the present dealer, for he took the last lot—some were nine days caught!

Did you pray for this lovely weather? For more than a week we have had calm, spring-like days, so that in three crossings, ending today, we have ferried over all the bought timber and safely housed it in the long-suffering barn without having any rain or salt-water upon it. I have only to collect a few more miscellaneous items before starting on the rabbitry. There are so many things to be done before July, which all the same makes me very happy. But forgive me if I do not write so often.

Today we had to row several miles in Jack's heavy-laden *Foxtrot*, crossing in a windless fog so dense it exaggerated the cliffs and tidal rocks which suddenly loomed up enormous within a few yards. It was my first experience of a *dense* fog at sea, but Jack turned not a hair. From a hidden waistcoat pocket under his jersey he produced a much treasured compass. With this indispensable aid, plus a reading of the tidal races, we made a perfect slant for home, not unaided by the Skokholm Lighthouse foghorn growing louder and louder until we made landfall at the Stack . . .

There, I've just nodded off to sleep . . .

[Undated]

Dearest Ronald,

Thank you for the rabbits just received—I accept the gifts of the Gods and am thankful. Papa loves a fat rabbit, but skilfully avoids skinning one. I practised on these right away. I can't boast I did so very expertly; the poor bunnies seemed to prefer to come to pieces rather than part with their fur coats.

I'm really writing to tell you some bad news. I'm awfully sorry to trouble you when I know you are so busy, but that stock cockerel you obtained from Kent seems to have gone funny in the head. I noticed that he never tried to perch at night, but simply squatted to sleep under the perches. I did once try to place him on the perches when locking up the fowl house at night, but he flopped off, and then I supposed that it was the new modern way—to have no perches in this Kent establishment famed for its pedigree stock?

But now he is acting very oddly. When you come near he

staggers away awkwardly, crab-fashion, twisting his head over his back; Charles has seen him fall completely over.

I shall write and complain to Cooks and ask for a replacement. Do you think it is due to any mismanagement by me? When he arrived I put him straight into the pen with a dozen breeding hens. Perhaps twelve wives so suddenly are an embarrassment for a young pedigree male Rhode Islander? I'm so sorry I did not notice his odd behaviour at once. But this morning he seems even more of a lunatic bird!

Your sorrowful partner D.

P.S. Talking of bathing babies, I've just bathed Mary in front of the kitchen fire. Vi is up here, and gone to a theatre. As Papa has been painting the bathroom, I have had to take my daily dip in this child's tin bath. Good practice for Skokholm? I don't fit the bath as well as Mary does.

Martynshaven
23 February, 1928

Dearest Do,

Will you please try whole black oats instead of clipped white oats on some of the chinchillas? Just to see if they will eat them freely. White oats are not grown on local farms here, where black oats are plentiful and cheap.

In answer to your queries tell Papa that his winch is now firmly planted beside old scrapped *Primrose*, fastened down with two 30 inch long blacksmith-made iron bolts attached to a hickory board (picked up as jetsam on the beach) buried in the roadway; it will take an earthquake to move it! All devised by the experienced Jack who incidentally found that hickory plank and trimmed it to size. Jack is handy at any such work, and seems to know his timbers. His fine hand-carved tiller on *Foxtrot*'s rudder he made himself, again out of hickory washed up on this coast. It is an American tree, and Jack says it is popularly believed the wood drifts to these shores on the Gulf Stream?

We are now organised to tackle the rabbitry; we shall need

Charles as soon as you can release him. We shall put Dick ashore some time next week, although I shall miss the revenue from rabbit sales. He is now catching much fewer, about 15 daily. So please look out for a telegram from me. I am sending a note to his mother saying these arrangements are in hand, and he is to be guided by Miss Shellard in making his departure.

I am hoping to have time today to tidy up the inside of the hut. I have begun on a food cupboard with mouse-proof doors.

The front door, by the way, opens outwards—when closed is thereby rain and windproof. With a southerly wind we are very snug here, almost too warm. Jack arrives to work looking quite blue, but soon picks up in our little riviera.

The weather has been so ideal that I ordered enough timber and corrugated sheeting to put a roof on the old building next to the barn. Have had my eye on that largish building as a place to store timber etc while we are living in the barn. Later it will be ideal as a cottage for any men we have to employ.

Now I am alone in the hut wondering if you'll approve this really humble little dwelling. I have grown fond of it, the first complete roof over my head I have ever built with my own hands. But it's full of imperfections. I admit that but for my wonderful partner Jack Edwards, so humble, smiling and efficient, the Hut would hardly have been achieved by now. He has gone home by the timber lorry instead of walking his usual 2½ miles to the village.

You ask about birds and flowers in the spring which has at last arrived on the Island. I have had little time to make notes in my diary but here are the salient ones which may interest you:

20 February

Herring gulls sit in pairs along the cliff-top, some in niches below, and some sit paired beside a few inland outcrops of rock. A handy rock seems to suffice for their courtship and nest site. They cackle all day long when it is reasonably calm, bowing to each other, and often a third gull arrives when there is a confrontation, and the intruder driven off.

I try to make a habit of jotting down every bird I see (that can be identified) in a ruled exercise book, just as I used to at my farm. I hope it adds up in the end to what may be significant to an ornithologist. You shall see it when you come, and you shall keep the floral phenological calendar please, since you are a so much better botanist.

The lighthouse goats have been kidding, so the keepers drop by with what milk we require, no charge. They report that our nanny Matilda has had a love affair with their hirsute old billy, so with luck she will be in milk by early July.

And so to bed—in the top bunk which has the better view of the dawn over St Bride's Bay.

Ever your R.

Tyr Bont
[Undated]

Cruel Wretch!

I had no time to be cross with you this morning, I went to town with Mama (her first day out—not very wise as there was a cold east wind). How dare you destroy a nice meandering letter to me? I demand you rewrite it . . .

I won't give a long account of how I rode home from Whitchurch on a most gorgeous calm evening after lacrosse . . . or how I later fell into the pond and how we went to a Shaw play in Cardiff. You will say 'Thank goodness I haven't a long epistle of execrable writing to wade through when I am so busy!'

To answer your query, I think perhaps medium dark green is the best colour for corrugated iron—it will blend better with the summer bracken background. Don't varnish the wood inside, just leave it until I come and we can decide together. One can get Solignum stain in several colours I believe, including transparent; the main thing is to keep woodworm at bay.

Goodnight. I have kissed myself for you, forgiving you for your sins, but it doesn't feel in the least like the real thing. Your D.

Saturday, 25 February

What sort of roofing will you put on the Island house, when you get around to repairing it? You needn't be so beastly joyful over going to Skokholm and not being able to post me your news. I shall probably be so busy soon that I shan't have time to write more than once a fortnight!

Today's little problem. How long can you keep young bucks and does together happily (in a platonic friendship)? I have twelve of various ages together grazing in one run about 5 x 3ft. Papa says they are too crowded, but I move the pen to fresh grass twice a day, and so far they haven't quarrelled, but frisk about, graze or snooze.

Papa says he may not be able to spare the time to go to the island this Easter. In that case I told him firmly, I will go on my own, and he can jolly well look after the rabbits and hens himself, as Charles will be with you!

In any case I think Charles must take some of the weaned chinchillas down to the Island with him. When an orange-box is lined with hay it will take 4 to each compartment—12 in all. Charles will travel down by passenger train and ask the guard's permission to keep his eye on the rabbits in the parcels van. That at any rate is our present plan—he's wildly excited.

By the way, I despair over our chickens. The first eggs under a broody were supposed to be fertilised by the unfortunate Kent cock, the broody lost her broodiness after a week, and deserted her clutch. I have now got another sitting on a fresh clutch sired by the replacement RIR cock, who is young and suitably amorous. Charles put the lunatic cock out of its misery for me.

I'm tired. Goodnight.
Your D.

Martynshaven
Friday, 24 February

Dear Do,

The wind was too strong from S.E. to risk a heavy cargo of sheet iron and timber. So we stayed ashore, finishing off some indoor carpentry.

While we were eating our modest lunch, we were interested to see what Jack called a topsail schooner tacking past Martynshaven close-hauled and heeling against the S.E. gale. She looked rather splendid, with two square rigged topsails furled, her big white mainsail reefed and her red mizzen sail likewise shortened. Jack thought she was running for shelter in the corner of the bay a few miles eastwards, known as Musselwick Mouth.

I write this alone in the Hut. Fortunately the wind has nearly gone and a thick mist is blotting out the whole bay. We shall cross early tomorrow, so I'll leave this brief letter for the postman to collect—from our brand new letter box which I finished and put up today!

Goodnight and happy dreams, but don't expect a letter for at least a week after this one.

Ever your loving R.

PART 7

February to March 1928

A wrecking operation

'Alice'

Skokholm
Marloes
Milford Haven
Pembs.
Sunday, 26 February, 1928

Dearest Doris,

How do you like the title now? All printed in Skokholm red? Extravagance? Not a bit! Just a present from Dad's printers. Cost him nothing, he says! Yesterday was a red letter day in more ways than one. I hardly know where to begin to tell you of our great good fortune at this moment—and I have precious little time either! For we are in the middle of a strenuous wrecking operation!

The wind switched to SW and we managed to load about half the cargo when we pushed off before noon. It was rather a head wind for Skokholm, but *Foxtrot* sails well and we tacked down in 1½ hours, taking advantage of the south-going current.

Now as we downed sail and took to the big sweeps to gain the landing steps, Jack casually mentioned the rumour that the schooner we'd seen on Friday had gone ashore on Skokholm. But we did not look out more than usual, not believing there could be a wreck anywhere in such moderate weather. However, just as I was again feeling that great satisfaction I always enjoy on returning to Skokholm, Jack cried out: 'There! There she is, sir! Fast in the clift!'

Sure enough there she lay, immovable with all her sails still spread in what we call Razorbill Cove, just beyond the Ebbing Stone south of the landing steps! Just visible, her topmasts peeping above the cliff! We hurriedly moored the *Foxtrot* and ran to her. Evidently she had come ashore on this south-east corner of the island while the south-east gale had been blowing *in the night*, but now the cove was windless with the shift of the wind to the west. She must have struck with some force, for her bowsprit was smashed against the cliff on the south side, and her rudder unshipped by the large boulders under the cliff on the north side. Yet all her sails were still spread, except the jib and stay-sail, hanging in shreds above the broken bowsprit!

When Jack and I scrambled down the cliff it seemed all Jack's inherited love of wrecking came to the fore. He was first to leap aboard, I was close behind, I felt an enormous surge of excitement.*

There was no sign of her crew, only a great hole in her bottom through which the sea was washing lumps of her cargo—coal, glistening coal! She had been fully laden. But now it was near low tide and the ship at rest, her masts erect and her sails pressing her to the cliffs in the centre of the cove. She had struck at the top of a spring tide. The hatches to the poop and fo'c'sle cabins were wide open, and looking down we could see only a jumble of sea-washed boards, and below that a wash line where the coal had tide-marked the interior. The hatch above the main hold was still battened down.

The name on the schooner's bow and stern is *Alice Williams* and as we were soon to learn she was built in 1854 at Llanelly. A plate above the companion way to the skipper's cabin showed that her port of registry was Falmouth, and among the disordered papers floating around was one showing her cargo to be '100 tons of First Class coal loaded in the Mersey'.

We could not do much immediately, as we had to hurry back to unload our cargo, and haul *Foxtrot* up to the winch. Thence to the house to find Dick making breakfast and very surprised to hear of the wreck! At the lighthouse, I got some enlightenment.

It seems the *Alice Williams* had been abandoned in the night, close to St Ann's Head, when, according to the crew, she had struck a rock in dense fog. Flares and rockets had been fired from aboard, but had not been seen because of the mist. She must have drifted about all night without sinking, although her captain had reported her sinking rapidly when they rowed away in the ship's boat to the safety of Milford Haven.

By coincidence the Trinity House supply ship had been working the area between St Ann's Head and the St Govan's lightship, and had noticed the schooner drifting about, spoken to her in vain, then

* [Father always swore 'the salt in his veins was due to his seafaring ancestry. He was raised on his mother's tales about her father, Captain David Mathias, (after whom R.M.L. was given his middle name) who sailed an ocean-going barque on the tea and teak trade with India. When he lost his only son at sea, his wife made him come ashore, where it is said he was 'as miserable as an albatross tied by one leg to the land'. They lived in Prospect House, Milford, which looked down on the Haven, constantly reminding him of his seagoing days.]

tried to put a couple of sailors aboard. But with a swell still running had been unable to succour her before she 'stood into danger' and went ashore on the island!

St Ann's lighthouse had ordered our Skokholm P.K. to ascertain if anyone was still aboard the *Alice Williams*, send details of the ship's name and papers, to keep a watch on the wreck and contact them at any sign of her being washed away to sea and so become a 'danger to navigation'.

Well, I can say right away the *Alice Williams* is in her last berth, with her hull firmly embedded in the boulders of Razorbill Cove and her anchors and chains tumbled and tangled among the rocks.

We spent the rest of the daylight in some mild wrecking, carrying away a few useful items, a compass (glass cracked) and some kitchen utensils from the cook's galley. But as the tide was now beginning to rock her, there was some danger in getting aboard. We had to leave her as darkness fell, but not before we rescued and hauled ashore her battered figurehead. At high water she seemed to emerge from the rocks, this handsome old fashioned wooden lady, rudely knocked from her perch under the bowsprit, and swum to sanctuary!

She wasn't much interested in being rescued when we threw down a grapple, but at last I hooked a fluke in the pigtail coil of her wooden hair, and with great care Jack and I put her well above the tide line. And there she is perched, salt tears in her eyes, a big bruise to one cheek and one arm quite missing!

Jack, with his experience of wrecks, warned me that until you had the owner's permission to pillage a ship, anything you removed from a wreck was considered theft. The proper course of action was to go ashore at once, discover who owned the wreck and offer to buy it. He cautioned me: 'But not thee pay more than a quid or two!' She's an old ship, he'd seen her trading along this coast years ago. But without engines today she won't be worth trying to float off, and he said that I would do well to ring up Lloyd's underwriter at Milford Haven soon as possible.

This sound advice made me decide to do this so we made a full survey of the situation of the wreck today. With Jack's help I tried to assess what the wreck signified to our future—yours and mine. I was tremendously excited of course, for she is a great prize; if I can only get ashore enough of her fine timbers, oak frames, pine planking and masts, metal fittings and stanchions etc. for the rebuilding of the house. Jack said her large white mainsail was brand new and worth a few hundred quid, and advised us to get it ashore before it was blown to pieces by the next gale. Luckily it was dead calm in the cove, so Jack at once proceeded to rig the gear to haul that sail ashore! First we had to drop the sail to the deck. This done, to the manner born, Jack swarmed up the ratlines, then out by the footrope along the topsail yards, fortunately still braced by halyards to the bulwarks.

He now hooked a large snatch-block to the end of the lower topsail yard which leaned closest to the landside, and reeved the halyard through. It was possible to haul both the mainsail and the good red mizzen sail ashore, having first cut them free of boltropes and their other fastenings to gaff, mast and boom. I used the ship's deck winch to hoist them to the block on the yard arm, and then, using a rope fastened to the bottom of the suspended sail, Jack assisted by Dick and a lighthousekeeper heaved the great canvas foot by foot ashore.

It was exhausting work, but very exciting. We landed both sails as well as a few baskets of coal by the same method—a trial run for getting more, having opened the main hatch to get at the coal. Dick refused to risk his legs in climbing down, but presently went off with a sack of coal for the evening fire, carrying a lump of salt beef from the ship's pickle chest, a handsome brass-bound barrel tethered to the foot of the mainmast.

When I told Dick I intended to go ashore tomorrow and engage more help to strip the wreck, he decided to come too! I was glad to tell him to pull up all his traps, and store them away.

We dined on rather tough boiled salt beef and rabbits—a farewell party for Dick!

Back at Martynshaven.

No time for more.

Love Ronald.

Ronald's diary:

Monday, 27 February

Up betimes to get ashore by early tide with Dick and the last load of rabbits. At the Post Office sent a telegram for Charles to come. Was about to ring up the underwriter at Milford when Edwards the Post told me he had just been rung up by Kelway of Lloyds who wanted to know the exact position and condition of the *Alice Williams*.

In the ensuing phone talk with Kelway I discovered—a remarkable coincidence—that he knew Mother as a young woman in Milford Haven . . .

He seems a dry old stick but kindly. He wanted full particulars of the wreck, he told me to salve all I could, and to make a deal with him for what I could get ashore worth saving! He surmised that she would not be worth much, (from what the Captain told him).

'. . . Probably a put up job, judging by the fact they hit a rock outside St Anne's Head and had to abandon ship. A likely story considering how calm it was, but nice and convenient for them to row to safety! However, he had to wait until they claim insurance; Lloyds would doubtless pay up in the end . . .'

Jack said he would try to raise some help in Marloes village to come to the island and we could pay their wages in coal!

Tuesday, 28 February

Jack reports that no fishermen are willing to come to the Island to work on the wreck. He says they are too busy making their lobster pots, and anyway the wreck has probably broken up already. But as the A.W. struck at high water of a high spring tide, she'll almost certainly last over the present neaps.

Fetched Charles from H'west station. He had brought four chinchilla bucks with him—which I did not really want, as we have no hutch accommodation for them yet. We had to settle down for the night in the Hut, allowing the chin. bucks the freedom of the store-room.

Wednesday, 29 February

Strong sou'easter blowing. But having unfastened the winch in

Martynshaven and loaded a full cargo of wood, corr. sheets and stores, we rather unwisely launched *Foxtrot*. An unfortunate trip for Charles's initiation! Smooth as we rowed out as far as the Anvil Rock below Jack Sound. But on setting sail the wind increased to half a gale, and blew us out into Broad Sound. In a very few minutes we found it impossible to gain a true course for Skokholm in the heavily laden boat, by rowing or sailing. We were drifting rapidly back towards Midland. There was no alternative but to run for it through Little Sound, where the south stream and the wind were roaring down against us.

Little by little the gallant *Foxtrot* gained north thanks to Jack's skilful steering and taking advantage of the few eddies. I broke two sweeps so we were left with only one whole oar. But the *Foxtrot* had gained through, and Jack sailed her on to Skomer North Haven where, out of dire necessity, I borrowed an oar from the boat shed there.

It was a long stiff pull to get back to Martynshaven, creeping along the cliffs, and getting there by dusk. Charles stuck it manfully, but was several times sick, and very cold. But revived in the warmth of the Hut.

Thursday, 1 March 1928

A lovely dead calm day. Went oar hunting in the car—to Captain Beer. The hoary-headed skipper was excited when I told him of the *Alice Williams*—so at once he gave me two (rather short) oars, and on the spur of the moment offered to come to help with stripping the old schooner, thinking he could save some gear to use in his own vessels.

This time the four of us plus chin. rabbits rowed down to Skokholm in a calm and favourable tide.

Friday, 2 March

All day at the wreck, fixing my winch at the top of the cliff, and by way of the block at the end of the *A.W.*'s mainyard, hauling ashore the spars, spare sails and other useful gear, and stacking it on ledges further up the cliff, the ship's deck winch lifting the items clear of the bulwarks and rigging.

We ate prodigiously this evening, Capt. Beer amusing us with his incessant seafaring yarns. He also gave useful advice that I should offer virtually nothing for the wreck, since she was worth nothing to the insurers, and he intends to pay nothing for the spars etc. which he had got today.

'Offer them a quid, take it or leave it, just to make it legal.' I have discovered Lloyds could pay only salvage wages and claim everything we've rescued so far, so I have decided to go ashore soon and make them an offer.

4 March

Run out of provisions. Went ashore in dense fog. Spent night at Sandy Haven and then went to see agent and offered 5 pounds for the wreck.

Tuesday, 6 March

Still thick fog which means a calm sea. Up betimes, leaving Sandy Haven in my car with Charles, Captain Beer, and his labourer Tom. At Marloes where we loaded provisions, Jack had enlisted his uncle the mason—with promises of coal. So we were six in the *Foxtrot*, plus the last of the matchboards for the rabbitry. The fog lifted as we rowed down over a flat sea. After a feed in the old house, we began work on the wreck, spending some time in fixing more firmly the tackle for hauling up by the two winches, and a place to stack the coal conveniently for the house or for loading again in a boat at high tide for transport elsewhere.

As from Skokholm
March 5th

Dear Doris,

Just this short note to say that Charles has safely arrived here, and is wildly excited to be on the Island and taking a useful part in the salvage operations on the *Alice Williams*. The weather remains marvellously calm, and our small crew of helpers is getting as much as possible ashore, especially timber useful for the rebuilding of the old farmhouse. And tons of coal!

I can scarcely believe my good fortune, for I finally bought the grand old schooner for 5 pounds from the underwriters!

No more now as we are just off to the Island, fully provisioned for at least a week's wrecking while she lasts over the neap tides—we hope!

In great haste, your R.

Tyr Bont
10th March

Dear Gilliatt,

I've been having such an emotional time lately that I simply could not write to you, but now I'm beginning to be afraid you may come ashore any time and be disappointed at not finding a letter from me (conceit!)

First of all I wanted to let everything go hang and rush down to help salve treasure trove! On more sober reflection I realised I could not possibly do so; and my feelings turned to impotent rage against all the dumb animals and humans dependent on me. Papa made it worse by declaring that he intended to go down for the weekend to help you. That was the last straw. I thought that if I couldn't go too I should probably shoot all the animals—yes, even your rabbits. You see I am not to be trusted with a revolver!

Perhaps you will now believe I am selfish? But it seemed utterly flat and dull just to continue with the usual mundane jobs when you were having high adventure out of a book. I was desperately longing to come, and you can imagine how much sicker and jealous I was with the knowledge that Charles was joining you!

I'm longing to hear more of your wrecking news. Its quite *incredible* that you have bought a whole topsail schooner for a 5 pound note! Must be a snag somewhere, Papa says.

As usual Mama took the news calmly and has told Papa that it is quite ridiculous that an old man should go down in mid winter (!) and risk his rheumaticky limbs in a wild wrecking adventure. This made Papa reluctantly change his mind, his principal excuse being that even if he got as far as Martynshaven how was he to be sure he could get across—you would all be busy on the island? He consoled me with the promise that come what may he would take me to spend the Easter holidays on the beloved Island.

It was a perfectly gorgeous evening as I came back alone across the fields, from walking Muriel home—she came to hear about the *A.W.*! The lapwings were restlessly crying over the river meadows, as you say they do by night with you. And there was another link—I disturbed the little owl in a holly bush. It had such a croony small voice, and I listened to it a long time until it broke out into its typical little owl cry, as if calling up its mate, or challenging a rival. I tried to imitate it, but it was not in the least deceived, because it immediately shut up and wouldn't talk anymore—until I walked on, whereupon it sent a derisive squawk after me.

Later I heard two little owls talking to each other in the same gentle crooning voice of love—in fact it was a night for lovers, for I ran into a pair of the human species, by the Drawlands kissing gate.

I'm afraid I've nothing more exciting to write about, except that I counted 42 wild geese on Monday, flying high in a great V. Such a gaggle and chatter they kept up—I heard them for minutes before I could spot their formation in the sky.

Things are looking more rosy here today. We have sold the last cow; soon I won't know what to do with myself, except that Mama, feeling much better, proposes to go shopping in London as she considers I have virtually nothing to get married in!

Did I tell you we went to the Opera twice last week? I wish you had been here so I could have taken you as well . . . And I may add here that you are not to buy a gramophone—in case you have thought—for the island. Mama says she is giving me one for my birthday, when I told her rather secretly that I was saving up to give you one for your July 12 present! So now I shall save to buy records—of the music and songs I know you love best; my savings now are almost nil.

Enclosed please find some seeds. The Peter Pan peas ought to go in first, they grow so quickly in the spring. As I know you love parsnips I have put in some for you to sow now; they are slow-growing but fine for winter harvesting. Never mind if you're too busy. I think I asked you not to sow any brassicas. I have rows of them well up already and will bring transplants when I come. Easter—roll on Easter—exactly one month away!

Goodnight, I shall post this letter tomorrow, hoping for further news of your miraculous adventure with *Alice*—I'm longing to see the wooden lady, so take great care of her. And with love to her I shall sleep and dream about you both!

P.S. Supposing the weather's too rough for you to cross and pick me up, make sure you put up the Welsh Dragon flag the moment you are able to launch the *Storm Petrel* to fetch us. I have at last finished the Three Petrels Rampant flag, so we will have the honour of raising it together on Spy Rock for the first time. And Papa says he will bring champagne!

Ever and ever your faraway sweetheart D.

P.P.S. Tell me where I can find the key to the Hut, in case it's too rough for you to meet us.

Skokholm
9 March, 1928

Dear Do,

If you had come down to help with the wrecking, you would not have enjoyed such rough company as six noisy, unwashed men working all day on the cliff, and by night sleeping all over the place. (Where indeed would you have slept?) With six of us, in just under a week, we have winched ashore at least 25 tons of coal, stacking this carefully on the ledges of what we now call Wreck Cove, by building an outer dry wall of the larger lumps—this was the mason's task!

There's been no time to write each evening after our one big meal of the day, mostly potatoes and generous helpings from the salt pickle chest of the *Alice Williams*. This meat is chiefly beef, with one or two lumps of pork. I appointed Charles as chief cook and bottlewasher, with the duty of debrining enough meat for our supper, and boiling it in the ship's big stewpan; the Cap'n and the mason each brought a shoulder of home-smoked bacon which made good lunches.

Charles and I sleep comfortably enough on ships' cots we have hung in the barn; the other four we leave to their own devices in the living room and the one habitable bedroom.

We have been a great crew, skeletonising the old ship with the enthusiasm of the innately greedy wreckers that all men are at heart. But that enthusiasm has waned gradually and it became clear to me that the mainland half of us—Beer, his labourer Tom and mason Edwards—are ready to be returned home.

We have got ashore, beside the coal, so many useful items such as her 200 gallon water tank, (ideal for collecting roof water for domestic purposes,) all her sails and their halyards, tow ropes and hand lines, blocks, lines and small gear. The ship's galley—a separate wooden cabin on the mid-deck—was difficult to hoist out, so it was swung overboard and towed by the *Foxtrot* to the landing steps, and with much labour, helped by the two lighthousekeepers off duty, was levered and turned end over end in one piece up the slipway to the lighthouse tram-line whence the donkey pulled it as far as the foot of the meadow.

The same fate was served out to the 'Little House on the Poop', more vulgarly known as the Thunder-box. Seamen call it (very strangely) the Heads, but in fact it sits at the stern of the schooner! In striking the rocks, and settling down, the big rudder post was forced up and the 2-inch square axle of the wheel was snapped off about two ft. from its junction. It was easy to unfasten the bolts and bring this handsome wheel ashore, where at present it lies beside Alice herself, perched at the top of the cliff!

This thunderbox is really a decorative structure, beautifully carved with ornamental bosses and a small window looking forwards upon the Helmsman. Inside it has shelves for brooms and lamps and a box full of signal flags; (like the lav. at Vi's farm, this ship's latrine hung over the water.). A notice says, 'Do not use except at sea!'

Charles's chinchillas escaped from the yard and were observed frolicking in the sunshine. Three were seen mixing with wild rabbits quite happily, but later one was found dead bitten through the paw. An altercation with a shearwater perhaps?

We are going ashore tomorrow with the men. I do apologise for my lack of correspondence of late, so much to do.

Ever your loving R.

Skokholm
Sunday, 11 March, 1928

Dear Lady Faraway,

It's a dead calm night, so windless that the throb of a trawler's engine far out in the fairway by St Anne's Head four miles away can be heard. The shearwaters are screaming in hundreds about the home meadow tonight, and one or two have landed on the roof of the old house, and slithered down to their burrows in the peaty soil of the knoll behind.

Skokholm spring nights might be noisy, but are utterly peaceful too. For at last Jack, Charles and I are thankfully alone here.

Wednesday

This morning the *Alice Williams* still stood with her masts proudly erect when I went to look at her and carry back some useful items stored on the cliff (a chore we all follow if we go her way). But after lunch with the wind increasing, she had completely broken up, and lay in fragments submerged by the breakers of the east wind!

We spent the rest of the day pulling up and putting away planks and useful wreckage onto ledges in the sloping cliff, above all tides. Fortunately my Martynshaven winch is still in situ on the cliff top to help lug up the larger timbers.

A later S.E. wind drove the wreckage into South Haven where we rescued spars and deck beams etc. of oak and teak which luckily we could haul up with the *S.P.*'s winch. Two young lightkeepers joined us, asking permission to collect firewood and small items to take home on their next relief.

Less windy in evening. At dusk more oystercatchers came inland with their piping duets and trios in the meadow and upon the rocky knolls, performing their characteristic spring ecstacies of courtship and rivalry. At midnight they were joined by thousands of incoming shearwaters flying and crying over the whole island. Such is our now fearful and fascinating lullaby to put weary islanders to sleep.

Friday

Still a S.E.'er so that we spent the high water hours saving more useful timber. The new principal keeper appeared, as if to help, but was very aggressive, claiming equal rights to take any timber that he could salvage. I had to tell him I had bought the wreck, but he marched off angrily, taking with him a useful length of the polished taffrail.

Saturday, 17 March

A rough day with squally showers, spent largely in the barn with John, who is building a masterpiece of a fireplace against the end wall using red sandstone slabs as broad hobstones each side of the iron grate. As a breastpiece above we are building in the ornamental top of the ship's winch; I plan to use the big brassbound wheel which will turn, (its axle hidden within the chimney), to wind a chain to lift or lower cooking pots over the fire. I have built two rough settles, one each side of the fireplace covering the space between this and the walls. The matchboard back and shelves overhead hide the unplastered wall behind. We nailed *Alice*'s nameplate on one of the roof-beams, and decorated the walls with the port and starboard lanterns, two of her inscribed lifebelts and her beautifully chequered bowsprit bargeboards.

I have told the Principal Keeper that if he did not apologise and return that length of taffrail (which I really need for the repair of the house) I would have to report his behaviour to Trinity House and request his transfer elsewhere! I hated to do this, but when after dark he came to the door of the house with that length of taffrail I was pleased. He also brought a message for me which had been relayed by Morse lantern from the coastguard at St Anne's head. It read: 'Lockley, Skokholm, offer accepted re wrecked *Alice Williams,* Kelway.'

I invited him to share our pot of tea, while I composed a brief reply which he said he would transmit back to St Anne's. Thank goodness he appeared to be agreeable, and had seemingly swallowed his pride or bad temper. My reply to Kelway read—'acceptance of offer acknowledged—wrecked schooner totally destroyed in gale March 14'.

Sunday, March 18

Made six loaves of bread, strolled with Charles around the cliffs, looking for nests of buzzards and raven. The latter have a brood of five scrawny offspring in a quite accessible ledge in Mad Bay. When I climbed down the hideous squabs opened enormously expanding bills. No sign of the buzzards, but a peregrine flew up from the south cliffs. Lapwings were winnowing over the central bog, tumbling in the south air as if nesting, or at least courting. Ducks flew off the north pond, frogspawn appears to be hatching. Showed Charles some tiny palmated newts living under damp stones by day. First wheatear seen.

Monday and Tuesday

The S.E. wind came to a gale today, forcing us to work indoors. Pleasantly enough on further titivation of the barn, which is now named 'The Wheelhouse'. Hauled forth an old cupboard-bed which had been abandoned by Bulldog Edwards but proved to be fairly sound. After scouring it out with caustic soda and hot water, I started to turn it into a food cupboard if I can make it mouseproof.

Did you know that the old cupboard-bed—typical *lit-armoire* of the Breton-Welsh people, according to a book I have read, was used to ensure privacy for husband and wife at night in one-roomed peasant homes, or even for the interesting custom of 'bundling' (courting couples were allowed to get together for a few evening hours inside a cupboard-bed but their legs were tightly bound by the parents so that copulation was impossible!)

Jack has a feverish cold and more wheatears have arrived.

Thursday, 22 March

Stained some of the new woodwork in the Wheelhouse with tar from the wreck. We tried a ship's kettle of water for tea on the chain above a fire of driftwood debris. The fire worked well, disclosing sundry holes in the chimney breastpiece through which smoke belched, indicating places which John proceeded to cement over. I have also had to touch up holes in the walls with plaster made from the sandy loam from South Field mixed with lime.

Hundreds of starlings feeding in the home meadow with a few rooks, chaffinches, pipits and the first corn bunting. Carried on staining of shelves etc. After lunch today we found a big length of *A.W.* mast floating close to the landing steps. In tying this to a ring-bolt I stepped neatly up to my shoulders in the sea, but I managed to secure it.

Friday, 23 March

High time we came ashore, to get provisions for man and rabbits; (I expect the rabbits from Tyr Bont to arrive soon). The clutch of my car defied all attempts to get the engine in gear, and after struggling with it for two hours I gave up in disgust and returned to sleep at Martynshaven, where I helped Jack and several fishermen pull out all boats there safe above today's tide, said to be the highest spring tide of the year.

Must haste to post.

Love R.

Dear Doris,

We left at 11.00 on Saturday with two weeks stores; a full cartload containing 4 cwt of potatoes, 1 cwt each of swedes, mangolds, black oats, hay and some seed potatoes. A bit dubious about getting across with a heavy groundswell and headwind, and strong spring tide; we thought twice about going through Jack Sound. We had to row all the way and poor Charles had *mal-de-mer* badly. The tide was so far out in South Haven, beyond reach of the lowest landing steps. I rashly decided we could unload on the boulders and pebbles; result, the groundswell rushed in and thoroughly wetted our large cargo.

We spent Sunday spreading out the cargo to dry in the sun, made cake, cooked a fine dinner, put up an old mast as a clothes line post, and rigged up a line for washing. In the afternoon walked about most happily, observing a peregrine falcon and a buzzard. A visit to Wreck Cove at low water procured some small useful items from the boulders there—a kedge, sundry irons and belaying pins, and a missing part of the ship's winch. Went to the lighthouse for milk and a friendly chat (I wonder how much useful gear the keepers obtained from the wreck? Doubtless packed away in their kit-bags for the next Relief)!

Such a lovely day, herring gulls on the cliffs and black-backed gulls on the bog all intent on courting and bickering over nesting sites, resenting my presence with great clamour. The young ravens are growing apace in Mad Bay. At dusk we replaced the dried out cargo in sacks, covering these with corrugated iron.

Very pleased to hear a chiffchaff singing from the heather near Spy Rock. Wheatears abound but was too busy to go gazing at birds. Put glass into Wheelhouse windows, adjusted front door improvised from the cabin door of the wreck—with the original plaque 'Master' nailed thereon! And whitewashed exterior walls. Jack carried on with the chimney piece, which now assumes a ponderous appearance!

After much cogitation and mind changing I have started the rabbitry; each hutch to face south with an inner room for nesting and resting at the back (with an inspection door facing north). It was delightful working in the shelter of the yard, with a bumble bee queen visiting a mousehole under some nettles. Primroses are in flower in South Haven; the wild rabbits never eat them.

Jack has finished the fireplace!

Thought I might be going ashore but too busy building the rabbitry and polishing up for your arrival, you will have to read this when I see you . . .

Tyr Bont, St Mellons
17 March, 1928

Dear Islandman,

Are you ever coming over to the mainland again?

How has the weather been with you? At least we have not had much wind—which must please you, but I didn't much like being plunged into winter again, all the fowl's drinking water tins a solid lump of ice, and the poor brave daffodils with their heads bowed in sorrow in the snow. I have been trying to force on more seedlings for the rabbitry gardens—to bring with me at Easter.

I have nothing exciting to write to you about. Our local hedger Lewis Rowland is laying our woodside hedge. He asked after my 'young man' and was deeply interested in the wreck . . . What a charming old fellow he is. Told me he had found an old 'Roman spear' in the rotten heart of a dead tree. Lewis paced off our hedge very meticulously, at every 22 paces he gave me a little hazel stick to put in the ground, saying it marked four perches (by which he charges). The poor fellow was quite scratched and bloody each evening when he finished work. Told me the hedge had 'gone truly shameful, truly shameful!'

I'm here all on my own. Mama has gone to stay in Plymouth to console Auntie Minnie (whose husband has died).

None of us really liked poor old Uncle, but he must have had his good points and Auntie must have loved him or she wouldn't have married him!! I remember walking with him from Caerphilly to home. Because I took him a roundabout way he would not believe he was not lost and kept asking passers-by the way!*

I am sure Skokholm is full of interesting sea-birds and migrants by now. Have you heard the chiffchaff yet? I wonder what you are up to at this moment? Has the wreck disappeared?

How much are you able to save? How does Charles like Island life? He came just in time for all the fun—lucky lad.

Good Friday is only a fortnight away. I have marked it on my calendar with a ring around the GOOD, and keep looking at it, trying to make it a week instead of a fortnight. I hope to bring you some soft fruit bushes—black and red currant and gooseberry, but I shan't dig them until the day the lorry is ready. I hope the gods of the island will be good to them, and shall have a plentitude of rain to give them a fair start on Tir Nan Og. There is a newspaper forecast of a series of depressions for the Easter holidays!

I now have 15 young weaner rabbits in a hutch with a run 6 x 3ft or thereabouts. Papa frightens me by talking of the danger of disease through overcrowding. But I clean them out daily and move the run

* [My Mother had a very poor sense of direction so one can hardly blame him.]

twice. Suddenly like the twelve little nigger boys they began dwindling; but I found a hole in the netting run, evidently made by a rat or a stoat which had gnawed the wooden selvedge. I am thankful whatever it was carried off two of the light-furred sort. Now I've strengthened the run, and am putting Punch in his kennel close by to scare off night raiders. Will the lighter weaners moult out darker? It doesn't say anything about moulting in my rabbit keeper's manual. Eye-colour is another interesting difference. The king buck has handsome grey eyes, but not all of his progeny seem to have inherited this grey colour . . .

I'm finishing this off in bed, as I have a feeling that you must be coming over soon, though I've been having that feeling for more than a week, with no resulting letter, alas.

It's after midnight, so *au revoir,* with love from Do.

PART 8

April 1928

The Easter visit

Puffins—from Do's sketch book

[At this stage there were no letters and even R.M.L.'s diary notes are scanty. Perhaps panic had set in with the arrival of the family imminent?]

Excerpts from Ronald's diary from that period:

Monday, 2 April

Building the rabbitry. A perfectly calm day, not the smallest ripple of white on the rocks. Scores of razorbills and a few guillemots were swimming inshore, and some began flying prospectively along the cliffs. A meadow pipit and a pair of pied wagtails were carrying nesting material . . . I traced the latter to their nest in the wall of one of the roofless farm buildings. It is as yet unlined. Watched a confrontation above Mad Bay, with the ravens attacking a buzzard which they drove fiercely towards the Neck, the hawk hard put to escape their furious swoopings.

Tuesday, 3 April

Continued strenuous preparations for the VISITORS. Much polishing and cleaning of the wheelhouse etc. Finished rabbitry, 52 compartments, now only needs a coat of preservative, and canvas cover for the roof. A chiffchaff frequently answered our hammering, singing from the tall nettles by the wheelhouse door.

After our midday snack the stoic Jack called our attention to the first PUFFINS, seated by their burrows about South Haven and the Neck. He was quite excited, shouting 'Mr Lockley! Puffins, sir!'

Thursday

A wet misty day. We rolled the ship's deck house head over heels across the meadow and placed it behind the fold with buckets and basins (from the *A.W.*) as a place to wash clothes. White-washed the interior of the wheelhouse. We should move in there by Sunday; so we have made frames on which to sew canvas to make temporary cots on which to sleep while the house is being finished. We have had some trouble with the Wheelhouse fireplace, which does not draw in calm weather, a misfortune aggravated by having to use the *A.W.* coal, which burns fiercely, quickly and sootily!

Sunday, 1 April, 1928

Having said we were going to move into the Wheelhouse today I got up early to make cake and bread before breakfast, and proceeded to the barn. Disgusted to find the fire smokier than ever, some smoke even issuing from various joints in Jack's new stonework. So passed the day plastering up the said vents! and feeling disgruntled because the fireplace has to be screened low to keep the smoke and soot from belching out.

Good Friday, 6 April

Up betimes to cross on a windless sea, with hundreds of puffins in South Haven. At Martynshaven walked up to the village eager to get provender and news—Do and Mr S. arrived late at 9 pm, having had sundry mishaps in their car. They brought 32 chinchillas. Do slept at Trehill, Mr S. in his car, Charles and I in the hut.

Saturday, 7 April

An ominous circle round the moon last night and one around the sun this morning foretold foul weather, and when a sou'east breeze sprang up I began to think we might not cross. But at 11 am we five set forth with a cargo of bedding, food, rabbits, mangolds, and a bag of phosphate, in Jack's boat, arriving in comparative calm after a choppy sail down to Gateholm to gain our easting.

The rabbits were at once installed in the hutches. And so to dinner in the Wheelhouse, the first 'in state' meal ever held there, and Doris the first lady to dine therein.

The rest of the day was holiday. So was, more or less, Sunday.

Doris and Mr. S. stayed until 12th April, frequently making excursions to examine the wonders of the Island. We pulled down the wall between the little kitchen and the roofless south corner bedroom, as we intend to have a larger kitchen. This division wall proved to be hollow, and contained a fireplace and blocked up chimney, which we removed altogether.

Do slept in my little room in the house, the rest of us in the wheelhouse.

Everyone took turns in the garden for the rabbits, enthusiastically planting out Do's forage seedlings; two thirds of the garden is now green with early potatoes, peas, beans, carrots, parsnips, shallots, rhubarb, currants and gooseberries, etc. Willow-warblers arrived in strength on the 10th after a big swallow migration on the 9th. We climbed down to photograph the raven's nest . . .

Thirteen surplus chinchilla bucks of tender age were set free on the Neck and seemed to settle down to a free life easily. The 78 years old lady Alice Williams was given a new nose and arm, and made beautiful with rosy cheeks, black hair , blue eyes, and around her throat a silver cross. Carpentry by Papa and cosmetics by Doris, and planted in situ by Ronald and Jack, wedged at the correct angle in the red rocks above the South Haven entrance, as a permanent anchor-mark for visiting vessels.

On Wednesday we bathed in South Haven. Thursday, the day of departure. At 6.30am, when Do and I hoisted the new *Storm Petrel* flag on Spy Rock, it drooped lifeless in the still air. It was so calm that we had to row the *Foxtrot* all the way to Martynshaven, Do taking turn at those heavy sweeps, aided by a favourable tide. Charles stayed behind—for the first time alone.

We four—Jack included—lunched in the Hut. We then launched down *Storm Petrel* from her winter berth, and hauled up *Foxtrot* in her place, before Jack and I set off for Skokholm, Doris and her father waving to us from Deer Park Headland.

Friday, 13 April

Traditionally the unlucky Friday, and it certainly turned out windy and disagreeably cold. Jack kept warm digging in the rabbit garden, Charles cleaned out the whole rabbitry and put in new hay. I baked five loaves and cleared up after the visitors.

Tyr Bont
April 5th

Dear and Trusty Knight,

Will you kindly await our arrival tomorrow? Herewith the token—take great care of it. We intend bringing 32 rabbits. Two families are too young to be moved. Heaven knows when we shall arrive, as early as I can get Papa moving. Be patient and don't fly away home if there is a favourable tide.

I don't want to be abandoned weeping on the shore! Great haste—Your Do.*

Tyr Bont, St Mellons
16 April, 1928

Dearest Ronald,

In bed, nearly midnight. At last I can visualize you, asleep in the Wheelhouse, or have you taken to the guest room in the house in the absence of the undersigned?

How splendid the *Alice Williams* wheel looked in THE WHEELHOUSE—in big capitals! Thank you for receiving us so royally—nicely deceivingly too, after all your pretence of having nothing ready on our Dream Island! Words utterly fail me. My heart is too full of love for YOU.

As Papa and I watched you from the Deer Park Cliff go back to the Island I had the most happy yet desolate feeling that I should never marry Island man, that I should always be the one to be left behind, as you sailed away to the land of your desire.

How frightfully morbid I am tonight. Just reaction and the lateness of the hour and the coldness of the weather here at present. I've been trying to garden today, but find it totally different from gardening in Skokholm's friable red sandstone soil. I cannot get our clay soil into a fit state for sowing; the wind has dried its wetness into clods of iron.

I've been extracting raspberry suckers out of the soft fruit bed, it struck me that they ought to grow well at Skokholm—anyway I am going to keep a few suckers and some strawberry runners ready, I hope, to bring down in July.

I am sending you by the first post some savoy plants that I bought in Cardigan on our way home from Rhydygath. Martin did

* [This letter did not arrive before the sender. The token was a small piece of red rock which Ronald had sent Doris soon after settling on the Island in November, as a token of 'faith'.]

not think much of them, said they were too lanky for the time of year, but I thought they would do for the chinchillas, even if they run to seed prematurely.

Sorry to be piling work on you. Just remembered that this is supposed to be my bread and butter thankyou letter—so I hope His Gracious Majesty will accept our warmest thanks for extending his splendid welcome to his humble and admiring subject. Papa of course sends his thanks and best wishes too.

Ever your loving partner D.E.S.

Tyr Bont
17 April, 1928

I knew there was something else I ought to have asked in my letter but I only remembered after I posted the savoy plants. Martin wondered if you had a piece of small canvas from the wreck big enough to cover some of his farm machinery—he said he'll be pleased to buy it from you, assuming it would be *cheap*. Cheap underlined! Anyway I said I'd let you know.

Oh when are we going to have some settled warm weather! Rhyd-y-gath was white with snow on Sunday. I've had several pieces of advice on how to cure smoking chimneys. Vi said her smokey chimney in the living room was cured by lowering the lintel above the hearth with a sliding hood . . .

Wednesday night

I wonder if you've been over to the mainland today? Here it has been blowing a bit from S.W., and generally cold and squally. However I heard the cuckoo today, and bees were buzzing industriously in quite a summery fashion, so I'm living in hope of greater warmth.

I went to a local lecture on the Faeroe Islands with Eunice last evening. It was most interesting—I tried to picture you and me living in that somewhat grim environment of mist and sheer cliffs. We ought to go there one day?*

* [Many years later they did.]

I had to tell Eunice (strict vegetarian), to shut up because she kept groaning in my ear when we were shown slides of puffin netting (with a thing which looked like a lacrosse stick!) and whale catching. It was very bloody, but as the lecturer explained, the Faroese had virtually no other source of protein to live on—no corn grows there.

So do not worry about me being tender-hearted. It would be fun to try and be self supporting.

A pity Skokholm has no eider ducks—the idea of home made eiderdowns rather appeals to me.

So that answers some of the absurd questions my nervous Islandman asked me on the Island, such as are you sure I still want to come now that I have had a taste of the rough seas on his wild island? Don't I prefer to remain civilised and sophisticated on the mainland to having a selfish husband who prefers to talk of birds but not to sing, or even look ornamental? Too late you ask, there's no turning back, no escape! I still sign myself,

Yours Forever—as I long to be, and shall be on July 12th,

Ever so much love from a tenacious Do.

Part 9

April to June 1928

Tackling the farmhouse

Shearwater

Skokholm
17 April

How fares the islandlady? Whose soul saw not the castles she had built at home all ready to transplant to Tir nan Og, but the dull dirty grey ruins untouched and untended. But she turned to the birds and wild flowers and went back to her dreams again, and even laughed and was glad and sometime kissed her mate. And when the sun burned down more warmly (less coldly perhaps?) she swam in the sea, diving after the laughing puffins. And even sighed heavily because the days flew too fast, and she had to leave it all too soon. And so she promised to return and live with her man and be happy ever after.

18th Ashore: and no letter from you. Only dark silence, and I wondering what you are doing and thinking.

Kath's birthday today—she is 28! She has arrived and met me on the beach at Martynshaven after we finally got the motor to go.

In haste and undying love.

Ronald

Tyr Bont
21 April, 1928

Beloved,

I believe you are growing up. Don't entirely grow up or you will leave me far behind. What is it? Are the cares and worries of approaching matrimony weighing too heavily on you?

Let me know when you are taking up the kitchen floor because before putting on the final surface I shall have to decide on its colour—a wife's privilege, since she will have to live most with it. But I am secretly hoping you won't be able to do more than put a waterproof roof on the house before July 12, so I can help you then—it will be *such fun*.

I'm sending you a few essential items bought at Woolworths that I thought might be useful. Please don't be angry. Of course I would much rather make do with your—or John's—pegs, only I noticed that you bachelors had *none*!

I'm sure you will be charmed to hear that I have only four laying hens for you? But out of two sittings hatched while I was away, seven hatchlings died from starvation because Walter the gardener, in spite of my minute instructions, kept the broody hens shut up from Good Friday until the following Thursday! The stupid man had not noticed the eggs had hatched—that was his excuse, but I am sure that he had completely forgotten the broodies existed, tucked away as they were in the potting shed.

The present poultry population is now four hens, the young cockerel (and very noisy he is) and six chicks which by a miracle have survived Walter's shameful neglect. I hope these will suffice.

I'm most anxious to know whether Beatrice has had her family, and if so how many? My 15 weaners here are still intact and getting very frisky. No light coloured throw-backs in this lot.

I've been busy sowing more seeds— spring and winter greens. If half of them come up there'll be plenty for transplanting in the island garden. It's the last time I'll be sowing seeds at Tyr Bont—hooray!

Muriel came to tea yesterday, tremendously interested to hear all the plans. She tried to convince me that it was a mistake not to have the cooking arrangements in the living room, which Eunice has on her farm in Germany. It is all very well when you are only two—well I remember one Christmas when we had breakfast in the kitchen, Vi and family were here, and at the same time Papa shaving over the kitchen sink because it was so much warmer than the bedroom! Mama fussed and Mary would stand on the fender, looking hungrily into the frying pan—I was in constant terror that she would topple over onto the hot stove. There was no room to move so I said I vote for a separate kitchen every time.

I wonder very much if Kathleen has arrived. I find I am terribly jealous—jealous that she is there and I am not. I'm green with envy. Do you know that once or twice I have woken in the middle of the night fancying I had been startled by the cry of your cocklollies.* Devil cries as of lost souls in torment! They gave me an awesome uncanny feeling inside when I first heard them.

* [Pembrokeshire word for Shearwaters.]

Did you catch another lobster in the pot we set on leaving? My head is full of happy memories as I write, and just now I am pretending to be arm in arm with you walking over the big clumps of molinia grass on the BOG.

I think Spy Rock will be my favourite place for thinking and seeing, when I am alone . . .

But just now I am awfully sleepy, must say goodnight . . .

P.S. Next morning! Papa says mind you get the boat engine going in good time for July. He suggests that you have the magneto properly overhauled—remagnetised he said. He had just had his car done and it goes so much better for it.

By the way if you should happen to see your local parson you might ask him about getting married *on Skokholm*. My idea, keep it secret but I think it would be the nicest way, don't you?

P.P.S. Even as I was boasting that I still had 15 healthy rabbits, I found one this morning dying. So now they have six each. So sorry.

Tell me about Beatrice when you write next to your anxious partner D.

Ronald's diary:

Monday, 16 April

Began a second rabbitry consisting of 36 breeding hutches. I decided and Jack agreed that we should burn off the useless thick old, mostly dead, heather in the centre of the North Field, thereby encouraging a stronger growth of grass and wild clover. It made a splendid fire, covering several acres of otherwise useless ground, with no loss of wildlife. There are no rabbit holes on this flat level surface close to the base rock, and only a few rabbits bolted from their heather hide-outs.

I wonder if Kathleen had seen the blaze from the mainland—she was due at Trehill. We were busy launching the *Storm Petrel*, and putting out summer moorings for her—the *A.W.* Kedge with a chain and float to haul her beyond low water on an endless rope. Sundry chores, letter writing. Ashore in late afternoon. Unfastened the winch in Wreck Cove to return to Martynshaven. Kath was on the beach to meet us. (She and her lacrosse friends are here to collaborate on a booklet about 'how to play lacrosse' and have a short holiday).

20 April

Dear Islandlady,

Thanks for your sweet letters, which I read in the morning sun yesterday outside the hut. Very warm, two lizards crept forth to bask on the exposed rock below. To reply to your queries:

I'll try the patent chimney design you suggest. Martin can have any spare canvas he wants if he gives me the measurements, I can store it for him here.

No, we had no snow here—it's just been cold but most days sunny. The savoy plants look a little bedraggled but will be planted.

But much regret to report that three chinchillas died in the hutches—all of course does—the day after you left. I can only suppose they suffered delayed shock from the long journey, but the other hutched ones look very fit and lively. Beatrice's litter turned out to be *only one*, a great fat thing, growing apace, sex not yet determined but probably a buck from the squat look of the infant's head. I hope to have another stack of 36 hutches built soon. Shall then stop, and concentrate on tearing the roof off the house! The new hutches will be similar to the first lot but instead of a solid partition, just a movable one with an open hole for the mother to enter her nursery, and removable for rabbits who won't need a private boudoir. That's my latest plan.

Molinia makes ideal litter, the rabbits revel and burrow into its soft dead stems, and nibble any green growing ones. We fill each hutch with it, so the pregnant does have plenty of amusement carrying mouthfuls to the nursery in good time before parturition.

Have you had the films we took developed? And can you be wifely and send me two fresh films, and one 2¼ A Ensign film for Charles's camera? Thanks.

On Thursday we took Kath and her friends to Skokholm for the day. A fresh wind developed from north, but Jack and I sailed around through Jack Sound to calmer water under Renny's Slip to pick up the three ladies. We had a glorious sail down to South Haven, dolphins several times leaping at our bow. It was Kath's first visit, and all were enraptured by the Island. We lunched in the Wheelhouse, where the new windows provided the usual cinema glimpse of the wild inhabitants. The wild rabbits—one is all black—the chinchilla bucks living free, the noisy courting oystercatchers, the little green-yellow migrant warblers and one fine cuckoo which uttered his masculine cuckoo call . . .

Charles, having slept alone in charge of the livestock last night, came for the return jaunt to the mainland, taking tiller and sheet proudly and well. We landed the sunburned ladies upon the pebbly cove of Horse Neck, under Gateholm (here the Marloes fishermen, if unable to get through Jack Sound, sometimes land their boats, hauling them up by way of some ringbolts they have fastened there for emergencies.)

Continued 25 April

Ain't it marvellous? Guess? The peas are shooting up! I walk round the garden first thing after breakfast and survey them with enormous pride. Kath came back here for a few days. Wish you had been here too, dear heart.

Never mind about the chickens, half a dozen hens and one male will suffice—you know I dislike chickens from having been obliged to get a living from them for five years since leaving school!

We went in Pat's car to see Miss Bland of Dale Fort who offered me young chinchillas at around 5s each (she can spare nineteen!) Also 11 young goats (nanny kids 12s 6d, billies 8s 6d). So think I must purchase the chins, and perhaps two lady goats. If I can get all her young does at this rate—she claims they are all pedigree registered or will be, then our problem of quick stocking will be solved.

We are now stripping the walls inside the old house. I am sure my artist bride-to-be will want to choose the colours for the interior—I remember you said I should not have covered the big red slabs of the Wheelhouse floor with canvas—the red sandstone slabs are beautiful and easier to clean. Well, dear discerning lady, I find the floors in the old house are just a thick debris of miscellaneous stones and rubbish, what wood is left is rotten, and will have to be burned. Better let me know what colour you desire for the floors of your future abode, although I doubt we shall get as far as decorating the interior.

With heaps of love and kisses, your R.

P.S. Dear White-bearded Codd senior of East Hook told me that he wished to make us a wedding present of two white doves! He breeds fancy pigeons on a small scale. Of course I could not resist when he showed me two fantailed beauties not long out of their mother's care. I shall have to make a traditional dovecote to hang at the mast?

Tyr Bont
24 April, 1928

Dear Islandman,

I may not write every day, but I need to communicate with you *silently* every day, dreaming about the days to come.

Here there is absolutely nothing of interest to write to you about. Only mundane things like planting potatoes, which I have been doing all this afternoon, and I've managed only seven rows. I stop and stare and dream about island life—most unsettling—and I can hear you saying 'Jolly Slow!' But really planting things here and at Skokholm are totally different exercises, this soil is just awful.

I've been burning all the hedge clippings and digging the ashes into the garden, trying to lighten the soil. But by the time I've wheeled barrow loads of ashes and compost up to the potato plot, spread out and planted, I could have planted half a dozen at Skokholm.

It's a terrible temptation to stop half way up to the fields and read your letter again. Bucks me up no end.

I thought when Papa engaged this new man Walter, and with practically no farm animals to look after, I would be a lady of leisure, but vain hopes, there always seems to be a thousand petty jobs to do if we are to get the place fit for sale. Mama urges me on, even to plant potatoes for a prospective buyer, but it gets rid of the weeds. Mama is determined to live in a flat, Papa grumbles and does very little, works hard at his surgery of course to get enough money to retire comfortably . . .

This week Walter is harrowing and rolling the fields, and a fearful time he has had with my horse Bright, who has got completely out of hand during her winter idleness . . . There was I, dressed up to go to town, with one eye on Walter struggling to harness Bright to the roller. She kept waltzing around, getting tangled up in the harness and chains until at last she tripped and fell heavily on top of the shafts. Of course I had to rush to the rescue, very frightened she had broken a leg. Between us we disentangled her and for a while she refused to stand up. However after a bit, the sly lady got up and behaved like a lamb! Nobody was much hurt. I had to change my skirt which had blood as well as mud on it—the blood was from Walter who had cut his arm in the struggle.

I don't know why I write all this trivia, it must make jolly uninteresting reading.

Goodnight, ever yours with x x x D.

At the Griffin Inn, Dale.
27 April, 1928

What ashore again, neglecting your island duties! Unfortunately if you want your house properly rebuilt I am obliged to get more material from the mainland tho' I'd prefer not to. Just now I have been ordering that material, paying bills, gathering 'hard' groceries (sugar, tea, coffee, soap, candles, paraffin, etc), and grain and roots for the rabbits.

I am scribbling this at the Griffin Inn. I asked the Dale vicar about marriage. He is a bit of a historian, and told me that 'holy matrimony' can only be celebrated in a church, chapel or registry office, and revealed the interesting fact that although Skomer Island is registered as part of Haverfordwest Borough for ecclesiastical purposes, Skokholm lies out in the cold, as a purely *civil* parish. Which explains why some time ago I received a notice, which somehow reached me in my mail, addressed to 'The chairman of the Rural parish of Skokholm in the County of Pembrokeshire'. It was a bureaucratic form of admonition that the said chairman had neglected (for several years) to fill in and return to the Statutory Office the records of parish meetings! When I told the Dale priest this, he laughed. 'What fun!' said he, 'I hope you'll fill up the form and record the observations of the local residents' but seriously as Skokholm seems to have no church at all, he thinks that I can adopt one nearby if I so wish, suggests that as Dale is the nearest church as the crow flies, I should apply here to be adopted officially. We left it rather in the air, since it is possible, he said, that there is a record somewhere in the past of the former farmers of the Island attending Marloes Church for their ceremonies.

Kathleen suggested that we could be married quietly in London, where mother's church is Fulham. Very quietly, only close relatives? I am quite scared about the ceremonial side and begin to tremble at the thought!

I took Kath and friend Pat to Skomer, where Sturt graciously granted us permission to explore and try to capture a semi-wild goat or two—he'd like to get rid of the billies, he said. But they were far too wild. I asked him if he wanted to sell any of the hundreds of slate tiles which have fallen from the numerous now roofless farm buildings, but he was quite offhand about this, saying that he intended one day to rebuild. He has put up a rather ugly steel verandah (rusting already) along the whole front of the large farmhouse, with an upper deck giving access to the first floor. I never have been invited inside the house, but it is common knowledge it contains a full-size billiard table and grand piano!

Their young daughter Betty, Jack says, refuses to stay in boarding school in H'west, escaping as soon as she is left there each term! We will in due course, I hope, pay the Sturts an inter-island visit.

Somehow I don't take to him very much, he is terribly formal, wears a collar and tie on the island as if he was still a business man—he seems fairly wealthy!

Keeps a motor yacht, but it has long been laid up on his landing beach—Jack says it has been holed, is quite unseaworthy and unsuitable for Skomer. I showed the girls the famous Wick which was alive with seabirds.

Just been out to examine the weather in Dale Roads. Its blowing even harder from NE, so no hope of returning today. Which reminds me, I can't find my watch, which I need for time and tides; and which I strongly suspect you stole away? Answer please.

Dad writes—a rare letter—to say he wants to come down and explore. He's never been except once to Pembrokeshire, long long ago when he was visiting Mother's parents. He's such a town bird that I am sure it will be a fleeting visit, but I'm putting him off for better weather nearer June. Also two applications from naturalists who want to come in May. Hang it, how can I get on with the work if we have interminable strings of curious visitors? I like having Kath, and she was useful, but it took up too much precious time when I was itching to start on the house. I have refused the naturalists, and probably shan't have time to answer further requests from idle holiday-makers.

The Dale vicar was very curious about YOU, chiefly I think because he was wondering if you would be able to face the isolation on our inaccessible island. He told me he had never been to Skokholm, nor had the owners—the Lloyd-Phillips of Dale Castle —to his knowledge ever visited it.

Later: P.S. Goodnight, it must be very late, but how can I know? I haven't a watch!

Standing outside the Hut for at least a moment. I can hear the little owl on the hill opposite calling a mournful goodnight, and there are faint bird cries from the clear sky above. This offshore wind is grand for blowing migrants across to Skokholm.

Love from Ronald.

Dear Thursday Bride-to-be,

All the flowers for our wedding are long planted on the Island by the God of Nature; and so many are in flower already: with handsome names—Ladies Fingers, Vernal Squill, Heartsease, Scarlet Pimpernel and Blue Pimpernel. Thrift begins to blaze, I haven't time to identify and record them all . . .

The white doves seem quite at home flying about the Wheelhouse yard. They are really pigeons with fantails, and I dare say could be used for sending messages back to the island in an emergency. The cock dove is already bowing and courting his lady.

We are very much amused by a young cock sparrow—its small black bib showing it was only a year old, which arrived in the Wheelhouse and cheeped forlornly all day, but got no reply except the few crumbs we threw it. It flew off about tea-time, heading straight into the sky in the direction of the mainland.

The bird-by-the-well-that-sings-day-and-night has come back! In the crevices of the hedge-walls and the rocks in South Haven I have heard the weird crooning purr of the returned storm petrels. I first caught that nostalgic sound when walking past the old limekiln above the landing- steps. It is full of narrow interstices between its perfectly shaped bowl. Bulldog Edwards told me it had been newly built by the landlord in the days of one Captain Harrison, who farmed Skokholm well in the last century, but left when he grew old and had only daughters to succeed him—one of them still lives in Marloes: Mrs Folland. Bulldog said he never burned lime in the kiln, it was too much trouble.

The razorbills are flying each day to their crannies in the cliffs, even to the wall of coal we built on the steep slopes of Wreck Cove. It was amusing to see them flighting above the coal, probably surprised to find their old nesting crannies hidden. Presently one or two landed at the top of the coal wall and now they seem to have accepted the situation, so it looks as though they will nest there!

Yesterday, the island was alive with migrating warblers, and hirundines, and so hot I walked about stripped to the waist. A bathe is now the order of the day, to wash off the grime of work, a plunge in the cool(cold) waters of South Haven. (Jack does not bathe—he has that peasant shyness about exposing his body, and at most will take off his shirt, but not his vest when it gets warm).

Sunday, 29 April

A day of comparative rest, I usually bake bread and soda cake, we wash clothes, and potter about, never really idle. A wild rabbit which lately invaded the garden and nibbled the cabbages was snared by Jack, so we had it roasted for dinner tonight. Even so we laid a roll of netting along the garden hedge to prevent further inroads.

It was such a lovely calm afternoon that we went for a sea cruise—Jack, Charles, a young lighthouse keeper (another Charlie) and I. We set three lobster pots, and later when Jack hauled them in he brought home a medium large lobster—there were also some small crabs which he threw away. Jack cooked the lobster in a bucket over the Wheelhouse fire, plunging it in boiling water for instant death, which he says is more humane; others say you should start off with fresh cold water—the idea being that this induces a trance in the fish so it feels no pain!

South Haven now surpasses any rock garden I have ever seen for its massed flowers, which include white scurvy grass and sea-campion, still plenty of vivid yellow primroses (one budding cowslip), rich blue of bluebells, lavender-coloured ground ivy and yellow celandines in full bloom and the dead stems of last year's bracken (this is now sprouting), and everywhere stray tufts of thrift almost to the water's edge. Immediately above the landing steps I found a hanging plant of samphire (*Crithmum Maritinum*), its fleshy leaves are quite a tonic but peppery to nibble—but I'll leave some for you to taste. And so goodnight from your peaceful clam bowery island,

Ever your R.

Tyr Bont
2 May, 1928

Good news about the peas—mine are far behind, but Skokholm is so much warmer.

Such riches! Mama and Muriel went to a Womans Institute sale, and Mama invested in two armchairs for us, a largish table—not very grand but it will be useful. Also a dinner wagon I did not particularly want, but as Mama said, it would be decidedly useful for meals by the fireside. And a mirror which tilts.

Seems to me we have already got enough to furnish the island house pretty fully. It was really sweet of Mama, she was so nervous I would reject the lot, partly because she knows I am not interested in domestic details and she is so emphatic about her own taste—late Victorian. She doesn't care for worm-eaten oak chests or old Windsor chairs, the sort of thing Papa loves and hides in his workshop, intending one day to restore them—one rainy day which never comes! The armchairs are slightly faded but look so comfortable, with fat broad arms on which you can put plates and saucers. I told Mama we would love them, which made her say she would make covers for them, if I'd choose the material.

Seems to me we shall need a large pantechnicon to transport everything down by July. If there's anything you particularly want, please let me know. The more we have the more economical it will be. What about more comfortable beds—I suppose we'll be inundated with guests in summer? But I can't picture a big old-fashioned Victorian bed in our little farmhouse loft. Let me have your views on this important part of our lives. After all people do spend one third of their existence sleeping . . .

Kathleen and Pat called to tea a few days ago and they said you were thinking of making a lavatory and bathroom out of that roofless lean-to by the porch. Don't be in a hurry, please. For the present, as we shall be (I hope) only two in the house at first, I'd be happy with a tin bath in front of the kitchen fire. It would save a lot of water carrying for one thing, and can be used for washing clothes in bad weather. I'm all for the simple life.

I'm dying for another letter from Skokholm, with every detail you can cram in for your lonely partner. Hope there'll be one tomorrow.

Thursday night, 3 May

Your letter today is almost obliterated, written in pencil and now being dragged out of my pocket so often. I'm glad you realise what you have to face in marrying me—the marriage ceremony, etc. Myself I am quite sick inside with excitement every time I think about it, and your promise that we shall sail away on our honeymoon to Grassholm. There is a raging wind from the north today that would blow us there this moment.

I'm afraid however Mama is right and I ought to be thinking more practically about the wedding ceremony. I do *not* want to be married in London; but if you and your family would like that best I suppose I shall have to agree. Vi suggests that we be married in her local church which would be more convenient for you and me. If we could get the parson out of bed at 8 am Vi would give us a wedding breakfast before we retreat south to the Island.

Papa suggests that, failing an anonymous (?) wedding at a Cardiff registry office, we get married at St Mellons church as early in the day as possible. He thinks no one need know, but Mama pointed out that you have to call the banns—Papa and I had both forgotten this! Mama agrees that St Mellons is the ideal place for us, easier for her to provide the wedding breakfast, to pay for this and to 'give me away'—I am very willing to be given away, of course, but shall dread the ceremony as much as you say you do. I'm sick to death of the subject—I thought just we two could get it over by ourselves without any fuss or publicity. Although Mama does not go regularly to church she is basically religious and conventional, and loves a wedding with all the trimmings. Papa as you know is a proper pagan, like me, a worshipper of the colours of the outdoor world he loves to paint.

So there it rests at the moment. Your mother will argree with mine I am sure!

Yours in trouble, D.

P.S. Papa has been house hunting in his desultory fashion near

Cardiff. He and Mama will never agree! He now says he won't sell Tyr Bont until he gets a big enough price to afford a house handy to Cardiff, but close to the sea! He fancies Penarth. I'm afraid my pending departure has thoroughly upset my parents!

Now Mama says she is taking me up to London next week, to do some shopping for my bottom drawer and to see your mother to discuss wedding arrangements. I have told her that I shan't stay more than three nights—too much to do here. She loves London so I shall try and persuade her to stay on for a bit, she needs a holiday.

Papa has been hanging paintings at the museum where he bumped into a chap from the Natural History department who asked if he could send a party to study the sea-birds at Skokholm in July. Papa quite firmly said NO, they would be interrupting the honeymoon of his daughter! This is just a warning in case the Museum writes formally to you!

Skokholm

Dear Doris, (which I call you when I'm cross)

Whether you deserve a letter is questionable, you must have more time than I to write. You don't reply to the questions I've asked about the rabbits. I am ready at any time to take all the rabbits remaining with you, when you are ready to send them. The driver of the mail bus from H'west station tells me he can deliver anything not too large to Marloes Post Office, from a cwt of corn to boxes with livestock. All you have to do is to give me a few days notice of the passenger train arriving at H'west and he will collect for me. And I can take delivery from Edwards the Post.

It would be so good if you and your Papa could come for Whitsun, I need his advice on the house repairs, he's so good at carpentry.

No, it's not been all that cold lately, just wet for a day after a month of hot weather. The cooking fire in the Wheelhouse makes it too hot even with the door open.

The birds have been marvellous. Last time we went through

Broad Sound a hundred thousand shearwaters appeared like magic from nowhere, and we sailed through a living carpet of silent birds, some settled on the sea, but rising voicelessly and sweeping in an endless wraith about us, like swallows, only they did not flap their wings, the wind was strong enough to keep them gliding, and our boat gliding with them. The sea and air from island to island was black and white with them. One great flock came up like a cloud of locusts from St Anne's Head, gradually drifting away towards Grassholm. A marvellous experience we shall enjoy together on summer nights, when these assemblies gather for a few hours (Jack says especially in misty weather) before they hurl themselves with screaming joy upon their nesting burrows.

On the island there are swarms of whitethroats, willow wrens, sedgewarblers, and one day I was delighted to see a HOOPOE, but it was very shy and kept away from me.

Continued: First Sunday in May.

The lime I ordered did not turn up when we went ashore for it and sundry other cargo on Thursday. It seems there is only one working lime-burning firm in Pembrokeshire where there used to be dozens. So I am getting it sent down next week on the same lorry from Fishguard with the windows and other planed timber for flooring, etc. Did I tell you Sturt wants all the slates fallen from his old buildings on Skomer, even tho' I offered to collect them myself? Jack says he is a mean brute, as he won't ever use them himself.

Ah well, maybe I should put corrugated iron on the house roof—if I was a bachelor hermit? But as you sat behind the house on your 'Mountain' your eyes would be offended by the said corr-iron? You see how much I need an artistic wife to save me from becoming an unaesthetic brute! Mind you, Corr. iron looks good when painted, it's all wavy and graceful, easy to fix, draught-proof and will not blow off like slates. Sorry. Of course slates are much nicer. I quite envied the Skomer roof, of small blue Precelly slate.

Feeling depressed because I found a chinchilla buck had fallen over a cliff in North Haven and killed himself, and partly because one or two others have not been seen since they were set free. I felt for a moment that I ought not to marry unless I could be sure of success with the chinchilla scheme. A market report I read in the *Western Mail* stated that the demand for rabbit fur had slumped lately. It is early days yet, we must expect ups and downs in our enterprise, we are bound to lose a proportion of our breeding stock, but in the end must win by sheer force of numbers bred up each year.

There are now 26 bucks set free, I can count up to 18 of them on my daily round. No real signs of fighting between wild and tame bucks yet. The few tufts of fur I pick up so far are all from the white bellies of wild does.

The gulls are now laying—nicely fresh eggs. They are very filling. Charles is enraptured, gastronomically—he has a vast appetite. Gulls eggs are lawful meat, but all other island birds are protected. We live much already on island produce—gulls' eggs, rabbit, the boys fishing on summer evenings. Soon, I hope, vegetables from the kitchen garden. Have you ever tried the wild sea-beet from which sugar beet and beetroot derive? It grows quite freely on slopes exposed near Long Nose and Mad Bay. Also a kind of purslane, or glasswort with fleshy brown leaves growing quite low down in Peters Bay. We shan't be short of native plants to keep scurvy away!

It's very hot and windless today. It's lighthouse relief tomorrow so I'll be able to post this letter by the Trinity House boat.

Love and kisses, R.

[Written 8.5.28 in the Wheelhouse]

Dear Do,

Here are some notes from my diary.

Swift, cuckoos, lots of Sand-martins and warblers daily, most frustrating that I've no time to dawdle and record them in this lovely warm dry weather. We hauled sand from North Haven with buckets, getting a good ton up to the house for cementing. The boys were exhausted next day, so they went fishing, and I took it easy writing letters, painting numbers on the rabbit hutches and recording the does and bucks quarters.

But I have a confession to make, however. I weakly succumbed to the Trinity House Captain's offer of a trip around all three Lighthouses being relieved that day. There was quite a party from Neyland. We had a quite perfect cruise, first up thro' Jack Sound and straight North across St Bride's Bay—to land on the steps of the South Bishop Rock, inspected the several buildings, and I climbed to the tower. The keeper said its flashing light attracted many migrating birds in misty weather, striking the lantern with fatal results, then we signed the visitors book—dated 1851 on its flyleaf. Many starlings and small birds were resting on the grassy ledges here and there, and a steady stream of hirundines passed by, flying out to sea in the direction of Ireland, in fact all the way to the Smalls. Here, as the *Eden* entered the strong tide race she pitched heavily, causing *mal-de-mer* among wives and maidens.

One day we will sail out there, to this very remarkable 125 ft tall tower of the Smalls. You have to land at low tide, for at high tide the sea covers over the solid basalt rock on which it was built in 1861 by Trinity House. At a cost of 50,125.0.0 pounds, replacing the first wooden-legged structure completed by private enterprises in 1776. (I was given an information leaflet by the principal keeper!) It also tells a fascinating tale of grim winter storms, of the building of the present stone structure, block by block, on the quay at Sölva, each block locked to the next with thick copper bolts. This ensures a certain elasticity in the tall column, so that it can move slightly without cracking. The P.K. told us that when they have to tend the lantern at the top in gale conditions, you can feel the sway, then it's a great relief to descend to the solid living quarters lower down. The entry door is very high above the tide-mark, solidly water-proof, accessible only by ladder stanchions embedded in the base structure. Some of the ladies funked ascending, even when coaxed by the promise of a cup of tea.

It was all an interesting revelation to me of our neighbours' life on the smallest island you can imagine.

At low tide seals come out to sun themselves on the weed-covered rocks. For amusement the keepers fish at low tide and catch pollack etc. They have two months on duty and one month ashore. Not many visitors otherwise; a few Breton Smacks from Camaret in the summer set their pots for crayfish and visit, in order to exchange shellfish for cigarettes and tins of bullybeef.

It came on quite hazy for our return, so that we could barely see Grassholm and its white crown of gannets. We kept well south to avoid the dangers of the shallows around the Hats and Barrels Reefs, shown up by a lower lantern at the Smalls, which has a little window sending a fixed red beam over them.

And so at last we saw the white tower of 'Skokham' lighthouse, (through a clerical mistake when the lighthouse was being built about 1913 it was entered in Trinity House records as SKOKHAM, instead of Skokholm! So all their stores are still consigned to Skokham!)

Presently the *Storm Petrel* came sailing out to pick me up off Crab Bay, the Eden heaving to, and its jolly crew of the Rouse brothers and family waving goodbye from this splendid old tub, half-tug and half-retired cargo steamer!

9 May, 1928

Dear Do,

My last but one letter has caused me much pain, remorse, and lying awake, thinking what a rotter I was to criticise when you have such troubles. I selfishly think we could get married at some lonely seaside church in Pembrokeshire and steal away in the *Storm Petrel*. But of course others have a claim, especially to honour YOU, the sweet and lovely girl whom everyone adores. By now you will have seen Mother in London, and have heard she is quite determined to be at the event. The Rector is meanwhile trying to find out which is my official ecclesiastical parish, or if I have one, from the legal advisers of the church of Wales. It seems they are scratching their reverend heads over my case, including the information I have provided about my bride—I told the Rector of St Bride's your family are Church of England—but I did not dissemble too much when I told him that personally I saw God manifest daily in the wonders of nature, etc. His eyes twinkled at that—he said he too loved the good peaceful country life, and showed me his very fine garden in the shelter of the trees behind the church.

Now I have quite decided, since no one else seems to be able to, to marry you at St Bride's Church. I could beach my boat on the pebbles of the Haven on July 12th, and after the ceremony we shall sail away on our honeymoon. As you know the church is only a stone's throw from the beach.

It does not really matter how much you spend on furnishing the house. After all we have to be civilised even on Skokholm, and we (or at least I) shall be much happier and more agreeable if we have a comfortable home to live in. I was a miserable miser to try and limit your spending to the barest necessities. I am a complete ignoramus when it comes to furniture; all I need is a desk to scribble on and a roomy bookshelf! Yes we need respectable beds—the two I have here are not the sort I would like to see us sleep in permanently. Perhaps I should build a handsome fourposter with a canopy—I believe I could, given time. A canopy would help to keep off the draughts on stormy nights. You will then appreciate, as I have, how snugly the little house lies, prospected under the Mountain*.

Enid writes that she is free to come and keep house for me for a few weeks before the wedding, if I ask her. With your agreement I shall do so. She is a very discerning and lovely sister, and will put the right womanly touches to the old farmhouse.

Maybe we now have enough for all the winter fodder—for humans and rabbits? With the greens you have planted at Tyr Bont we shall have the essentials for the months ahead. I can always import farm hay and roots from Marloes. So just now I feel well equipped, though far from complacent, to stand the siege of Old Winter, which I endured—but yet enjoyed—last year. I agree that what ever happens a living from the natural products of the Island is possible.

Last night I had a marvellous dream of you picking white bluebells in the very blue bluebell field above Boar's Bay. You were my darling wife, wearing a coloured shirt above dark blue breeches, bare feet, and a head crowned with your halo of curls. Curious how

* [Nowadays referred to as 'The Knoll'.]

I often dream in vivid colour. But the dream ended when I stole up on you to steal a kiss among the scented flowers!

As to news of progress on the house, never fear it will all be finished in time. It won't, not by a long chalk. We have made a ton of mortar with bagged lime and ashes carefully sifted from discarded ash-heaps, mostly from the lighthouse dump. This mixture makes a quick-setting, strong plaster for stone-work exteriorly; inside the walls we use a weaker mixture with clayey earth, of which there is plenty under the turbary at South Pond.

We are now advanced in stripping the roof, bit by bit in order to mend the top of exposed walls with hard mortar lest the earthy dust beneath blows away. Starting the south face first, where your little kitchen awaits a new roof. What a fine house we shall have—walls of stone, mud mortar, priceless oak beams and pine rafters from dear old *Alice Williams,* you must take it as you find it, and we rebuild it, leaning all ways. A lovable old relic when you get to understand how it came to be built! (in a whimsical manner!)

After a day with my new trowel I am covered from head to foot in old disintegrated mortar, and ready for a swim in South Haven—marvellously bracing during the recent hot weather.

The first rain for a month has greatly refreshed the garden, everything shooting up since. A sharp wind later on stripped the most forward peas; these should not be set before mid-May, Bulldog Edwards tells me. If we raise higher walls around this ancient plot I hope we can grow earlier crops, protected by hardy fruit trees such as currants and apples?* We shall experiment.

Love and double xx xx xx from your humble and repentant R.

10th—Have been to St Bride's again, the rector said he'd be delighted to officiate, and took down preliminary details about bride, bridegroom, banns etc . . .

* [Apples never did grow—stunted sycamore and elder only.]

Tyr Bont
6 May, 1928

My dear and only love,

There—how d'you like that? I have gathered a little bag of dandelion seed for you, but how does one entirely get rid of the fluff? I have puff-puffed it until I am breathless.

When hedge-parsley comes into seed, I'll collect that too.

Your lovely descriptions of the wild flowers make me home sick for the Island. So I'm going to try to make you home sick for something you haven't got—tall trees.

I've noticed the oak is far ahead of the ash again this spring. But I've come to the conclusion there is nothing in the old saying, it was just the same order of budding last year and if last summer was a splash, heaven save us from a soak!

The beeches are all out in their tenderest green, footpaths and lanes are carpeted with their moulded brown leaf-sheaths. The dawn chorus of our garden birds is quite deafening.

I'm afraid I'm no good at making you envious. I'm so cross at not being allowed or able to come at Whitsun, but apart from other reasons I don't think Papa wants particularly to take me. And Mama pleads she is unwell. Papa selfishly announces he is not taking rabbits or anything so smelly—very disobliging of him. It seems such a waste of time to keep two very good does unmated a month longer than necessary in this season, but I haven't an adult buck. Liddy's family are especially fine I think—no light coloured ones . . .

Wednesday morning

Just had more wordy warfare with Papa about rabbits and chickens. He grumbled about my little chickens put out on the garden lawn, so I just told him rudely that I could not put them out in the field until I had built another fox-proof fence for the rabbits, as they occupy a chicken-run.

I was sorry afterwards that I had said anything, as it only made him more irritable. Really, deep down, he's just upset, Mama says, at my impending departure, and the general upheaval of the proposed sale of this place which he loves so much.

Just had your letter. Oh, how I long to be with you! How long did the hoopoe stay? Or is it just on migration? So sorry about the chin. buck killing himself. Do rabbits often fall over the cliff—perhaps he was blown off?

I am *very very glad you decided* on St Bride's Church. *Of course I agree!* It sounds beautiful. Will I have to go and live there for a week before our wedding—isn't there some rule about that? I hope so, then I'll be near my true love!

Must fly now and get breakfast for M. and P. or they'll feel out of sorts.

Hoping you'll get this quickly if you come ashore tomorrow—with a letter for your true love.

Do.

Bulletin from the lower Island
11 May, 1928

Gulls eggs taste better fried in batter! I have found a number of white bluebells to stimulate my dreams of my Lady Love. Vernal Squill is a vernal thrill spilling over open ground—it loves the sun. Beatrice's brat is of feminine gender. The materials—1 ton of bagged lime, ½ ton of cement, windows, flooring, battens etc., were delivered yesterday when we boated across one load, and one today. A third will be boated tomorrow.

Letter duly received, also watch. Many thanks and xxxxx, let me have the bill. Unless you can think of a cheap kitchen range, shall leave the problem just now, perhaps until you come in July?

In due course I must know your size in wedding-rings. (*Note* that if you don't do so I shall buy an outsize one in order to be sure I can get it on at the crucial moment!)

All the old garden in front of the house is now full up with luscious growing vegetables, including rows of chicory, kohlrabi, sundry kales, white carrot etc, some for transplanting to the outer rabbit garden. The latter now fenced with wire-netting and dug over, but about half is left rough for the weeds to be hoed down later, before planting out.

There is a horrid fast growing weed I can't remember seeing at St Mellons—can it be *slender wart cress,* which, according to my Wild Flower book is 'widespread on disturbed ground near the sea in southern Britain.'

Tuesday afternoon, 15 May, 1928

Three weeks residence beforehand is the conventional period for marriage in any parish, so we have entered into a conspiracy with the nice rector to accept Doris Shellard as resident in absentia as necessary, and I am now adopting St Bride's as Skokholm's Official Church. Mother and Enid intend to be present on this auspicious July occasion, wherever it is held. Dad may take it into his head to appear, but probably not, if it is at St Bride's.

Just came ashore on the prowl for more building material. I hope your London visit will be a great success. It should be in this lovely weather. I shall picture you in a fashionable sunhat, wielding a parasol as you and your Mama stroll of a fine Sunday around Hyde Park. Make the most of it, sweetheart. But don't be persuaded by anyone to be wedded anywhere but St Bride's. Now the thought of a wedding anywhere else dismays me. I have fled the society of man for that of the birds and lonely islands; and I remind you of the truth I once told you—that you fell in love with an island rather than your Islandman (as you like to dub me).

Enough said; and now to the practical problems:

Sensible of you to ask about mattresses. I would like you to get whatever you consider we need, so long as it's within region of twenty pounds, which I am afraid is all I ought honestly to spend on such household items just now. Sorry to seem mean, but I believe we agreed to live as simply as possible. So I send you my cheque for that amount. I don't expect to find time to do any shopping if the house is to be in reasonable repair by July 12th, with at least a good rain and gale-proof roof, though chaos beneath. So expect me to drop hammer and saw, and run to marry as I am, in my breeches. I am quite serious, except that, weather permitting I shall *sail* to claim my bride. I don't really mean to be miserly, but needs must.

Here are certain measurements . . .

(But what on earth do we want curtains for—on an island where no one can spy on us?)

Sorry, aren't I a pig? Ain't this a rotten letter? But I'm a bit fed up; every time I come ashore to pick up material, it's hardly ever ready at Martynshaven.

Thank you for parcel, the dandelion seed is a marvellous idea. It's possible to collect very little from the few dandelions which grow here, away from hungry rabbits—on the tops of the walls, and inside the old limekiln, but you have now inspired me to collect these as they seed.

I love you very much, R.M.L.

Sundry Notes from Ronald's diary: 11-15 May, 1928

Another lovely Sunday, day of peace and leisure for my two happy boys, both happiest on the sea, a day fit for Grassholm, but Jack resisted my hint that we might sail there and went for a nap instead! We had made a brief raid on the Stack, and robbed four nests of the great black backs there—unpopular bullies and predators of puffins; they will lay again if the first clutch is taken early.

Only two months left before the happy day! But too much to do. Stumbled on a nest of an oystercatcher with three eggs on the rocky crest of Bread Rock in the meadow, the sly parents trying not to betray it by running away silently with their conspicuous scarlet bills held crouching. The pair of meadow pipits near the house have four eggs, the wagtails in the yard have six. Still a few migrant whitethroats and willow wrens to be seen feeding about the nettles and hemlock around the old buildings.

Wheelbarrowing away loads of fallen plaster, and the detritus of years of occupation of the old house by fishermen and rabbit-trappers, who had dumped rubbish in the unused, largely roofless side rooms.

The two white doves have flown back to their old home at Hook.

The garden needs rain badly now. Saw a fieldfare there.

16 May, 1928

Dearest Do,

We have stripped most of the bad roof off where the old slates are loose, and began retimbering with the wreck beams. When we pulled out the old half-burned lintel above the fireplace in the little kitchen it proved to be an oak beam almost a replica of the one I was using to replace it, from the cabin of the *Alice Williams*! Although the old lintel was almost burned through in the middle, the butt ends built into the stone jambs each side were in perfect condition, their edges moulded smoothly like the *A.W.* beam is. It's nice to think that old beam must be about four hundred years old, cut from a tree that first sprang from an acorn many centuries earlier; now replaced by the cabin beam seasoned after seventy years or so of travel aboard the *Alice Williams*—and still as hard as stone.

Recently consulted my bank overdraft and find that I ought not to give you a wedding present of more value than five pounds. Perhaps we should forego giving each other expensive gifts? I suggest we give each other suitable small presents *after* the wedding? I get furiously cross when people give presents, often when they can't afford them, as a *surprise,* which the recipient may not in the least want! When Enid asked me what I would like as a wedding present I told her for goodness sake I don't want anything from my family—besides they can't afford to give them.*

Talking of money, I am determined that I am not going to spend next winter ferrying rabbits across to the mainland and getting stuck ashore with a weeping wife on the Island. I shall start catching 1st October (when the shearwaters have left) three men (including self) catching, and a Marloes fisherboat contracted to ferry the rabbits for us. We shall skin all the eligible chinchillas, so if the boat fails to come during bad gales, the loss of the carcasses won't matter so much. The profit will be in the skins. By Christmas the catching should be finished, and we can have peace again until next October, anyway that's my present thinking. Jack, the good fellow, says he'd

* [To this day present-giving still bores him!]

be content to be with us next winter, especially if we reroof the room next door to the Wheelhouse.

I have more to say, but too much to do.

With love and kisses,
Your sweetheart, very much so. R.
Seven new chin. babies.

In the train to Paddington,
17 May, 1928

My dear islandman,

I've no intention of inviting anyone to the wedding but Mama, Papa, Vi and her family. It's your large family's fault that you have four sisters. But surely you must realise that if we get both families down to St Bride's to see us safely off their hands, we need to do something hospitable with them? Some sort of wedding breakfast for the guests afterwards? . . .

You can't be more scared than I am at the thought of the whole ceremonial performance—I'm worse off than you are for I've hardly ever been to a service in a church since I left school, and will be a forlorn pagan not knowing what to do, when to kneel or when to stand, or pretend to say the prayers. Mama still declares that we ought to be married at St Mellons, thus simplifying matters for her and your family . . . However she is now more reconciled to what she calls our idiosyncrasies or idiocies. I dread to hear what Mrs Lockley says.

We had another little bazaar and jumble sale in connection with the Women's Institute; I had a plant stall, quite small and mostly potted flowers and bedding plants, yet I made about 3 pounds. I nearly had a fit when the money was added up, to think that I had managed to swindle the public to that extent!

Your economical bride bought a beautiful pair of second-hand breeches, some tennis trousers and ladies tennis shorts for six bob. But Papa has appropriated the breeches, which are white whipcord with buckskin strapping. They belonged to the local squire—Papa fell in love with them when he found they fitted him. It is just as well you can't have them, as I could never keep them clean! At least I refused to part with them until Papa had paid me double what I bought them for!

So glad the storm petrels have arrived. Please do say they'll be there in July. I'm most frightfully sad that I'm not coming down at Whitsun; probably Papa may take Enid down with him, and since Butterfield—the carter—is laid up, I hope Papa will change his mind and take the last rabbits. Have you named all the young does in hutches yet? . . .

I see a kitchen range advertised for 5 pounds, with oven and boiler, and will let you know if its good enough when I get back home. Also mattresses for 37/6 each.

Excuse more, nearly there and I promised to write a post card to niece Mary . . .

Ever so much love,
from Do. x x x x

Memo on arriving in London:

Thanks for sending size of windows. So you don't approve of curtains on an Island. Permit me to disagree, dear man; our curtains are not for keeping peeping Toms from peeping, but because they will help to keep us warm in winter, keep out draughts and above all soften the bareness of windows and their frames, etc. I shall have fun in selecting colours . . .

20 May, 1928

Dearest Doris,

A miserable nor'easter making things cheerless about the house and garden. We did not get up until 10.00 hours, rather overdone it for two days boating slates etc. I finally decided on asbestos tiles being most practical. We made three trips, the last ending up at 11 pm so we were not in bed before midnight; but today is one of those not-so-nice ones, when you will be less of an island-lover than usual and I shall have to cheer you up, and you do likewise to me. One can nevertheless always avoid a rude wind by going to the leeward cliffs. South Haven is our special refuge in this nor'easter, sheltered, warm and smelling sweetly of flowers. I can imagine tomatoes and peaches growing there in summer, if one could somehow screen them from the southerly gales.

23 May, 1928

Thank you sweet bride, for your letter written in the train and sternly headed My dear Islandman. NO, I shall hate a St Mellons wedding; but if you and everyone insists—to save expense all round —then I suppose I shall reluctantly have to agree. Very reluctantly.

I am disappointed not to be the owner of buckskin breeches with the splendid strappings, and shall reserve comment until I see the eloper wearing them. You did jolly well, as you always do, with the bazaar stall—I can picture you and Muriel hard at work, decoying would-be customers with smirking smiles to buy your bargains.

No more rabbit families in the hutches just yet tho' some ladies look big. I doubt if Carmen is going to oblige this time. I have named the does from A to Z in my stock book when recording the number of their hutch: Ann, Beatrice, Carmen, . . . Could you supply names from T onwards? I have seven stock bucks in hutches, only two mature (i.e. with large testicles). I can see a problem arising in that so many are look-alikes that I think we must soon permanently mark all breeding stock, for which purpose we could use numbered aluminium tags pinned low on the ear. Can you find out where to get them?

Some of the missing chinchilla bucks have reappeared, having wandered further afield and 'gone native', probably found wild mates been driven out by wild bucks? From the Wheelhouse windows in the evening, some wild bucks are very aggressive now. Incidentally I have noticed that the big gulls are only vaguely interested in our rather tame chin. bucks, the birds will repulse a rabbit too close to their nests, and the chins have learned to respect this territorial safety distance. The big black-backs hang around burrows where newly emerging babies begin to graze in the evenings. It is comical to watch how an adult rabbit will drive away a marauding gull, but the gull is clever enough to hop away a short distance then remain still long enough for the adult rabbit to lose interest, then suddenly the gull pounces and with one stab has the squealing baby firmly in its bill. By the same process of ambushing the big gulls grab a puffin, first battering it to death, and then perhaps finishing its meal in the sea. Sometimes a pair of ravens or crows appear and try to grab the prey; when the gull protects itself from one sable enemy, the other rushes in and grabs the food!

There seems to be a limitless supply of the eggs of the three types of gull nesting all over the island and along the cliff-tops. I am filling the *Alice Williams* brass-bound pickle chest with them. Never fear, I have been testing them meticulously and throwing away any which float even slightly! The lightkeepers put down several thousand altogether.

What do you suggest for lining the house? I suggest match-boarding as it is light and easy to install. The big *Alice Williams* beams are going to look quite handsome, projecting like those of some medieval barn.

The asbestos-cement slates are not dark blue-grey as I thought, but are pale, almost white. They can be painted any colour we like, or just left to mellow as they will. We have begun replastering the interior walls but they won't be finished until you come—since you insist I do not complete everything! But we must fill the bad cracks, if only to prevent the dust of the interior-filling continuing to leak out, as it does now, and smother the hair and face of -
Your amateur workman and home-builder.

Love and kisses, R.

20 May, 1928

Dear Ronnie,

(In retaliation for last letter addressed Doris!)

I AM going to give you a Wedding Present. But perhaps I shan't tell you what. But you can be sure it will be practical and useful—to both of us. So have a guess? Answer in my next perhaps, perhaps not.

The window in the loft is quite tiny, I remember now. So I hope you'll put in a large skylight in the end where the window isn't. I find you can buy ready-made metal skylights at any good builders' merchants. Even a small one over the stairs to the loft will make an enormous difference. I like skylights—they give a good light for painting.

Papa now says that he is too busy at work to leave for Pembrokeshire until Sunday, if he comes at all! Probably if Sunday morning is fine he'll set off with Enid, who said she'd meet him in Cardiff. Maybe they can signal you from the Deer Park?

How your letter makes me long and long to come—and work with you on your happy home building. It gives me a constant pain to think of what I am missing.

Of course I never seriously thought of a St Mellons wedding. I am now dreaming of you coming over the sea on a blue and sunlit day to lovely St Bride's Haven, to meet me (and no one else), and we shall walk up to the church for the simplest of ceremonies, with just our parents and sisters as witness. But so far Mama does not see it that way: she wants to have a wedding breakfast here at Tyr Bont—if we still live here—where she can put up my aunts, who are clamouring to be present. I have told Mama flatly that I no longer wish to discuss the matter. By the way, how much is a marriage licence?

This subject is now closed. I'm sick of the argument with Mama, and Papa makes no comment at all; he's bored with it all too.

Papa still uncertain today in spite of good weather forecast, don't be surprised if he does not come. Enid has sensibly phoned to say she will go down by train the following weekend if Papa fails her—in which case I have told her I will not be able to resist the opportunity to go with her!

I called on Mrs Henry yesterday and she gave me a box to take to Charles.

Au revoir. I'm selfish enough to hope Papa doesn't go now!

A great big hug in anticipation,

from Do.

At Martynshaven
26 May, 1928

Dear Do,

Martynshaven is very quiet this evening, St Bride's Bay lit up by the warm colour of the sunset. With this haven and the Hut in shadow there are few birds about. Just the scavenging gulls on the beach, and the odd Spotted Flycatcher catching midges from perches in the gorse. They are slightly crepuscular and go to bed late, a much loved bird of my early schooldays near Cardiff. So I was pleased to find a steady passing migration of these seemingly frail birds on the Island . . . A lonely Jackdaw turned up midday on the 22nd, the first I have ever seen on Skokholm, tho' they are very common on the nearby mainland.

I went ashore on the 23rd to fetch the mason, as Jack said his uncle would show us how to re-slate the roof. However he failed to turn up and I was glad, as I felt I could do the job even more lovingly if not so well as that old rascal. I gladly returned that day, and have ever since been a roofing expert, using great care to square up the slates one by one on the battens overlaying the wreck purlins.

Lovely summery weather, the *S.P.* moored in the calm harbour, the boys go fishing in the evenings, and to vary the work, I have been transplanting cabbages into the rabbit-acre and watering everything; it's now very dry.

26th. Today as per your letter, went ashore to fetch Enid, and your Pa, but not a sign of anyone, not even a message! So had to kick my heels and stay ashore in the Hut. On Sunday still no sign—a great disappointment, for I've been lovesick ever since I knew you might be coming. Which is why I said you had better not come for just one day. I am getting a bit queer in the head lately with all that sun beating down on the white tiles. Perhaps you will straighten me out after a certain Day in July?

Sunday, 27 May

Still no news. Jack came down early—still no mason, thank goodness, so we are off back to the roofing. A fisherman is posting this in the village. From your thwarted sweetheart R.

Notes from Ronald's diary:

Friday, 1 June-Sunday, 3 June

I had a signal that Enid was coming by train to H'west on Friday so we hastened to go ashore and I raced up to catch the Marloes bus so as to meet her at the station, but luckily missed it. On opening my mail found that Enid and Mr S. were on their way down by car after all. So tinkered with the old Talbot until they arrived, thinking I must get it licensed and going again soon, when the whole gang arrived, six with the children Mary and Brian. But miser me, no Doris Shellard, no rabbits, only bundles of cabbage and other plants . . .

We adjourned for a luxurious tea of home-made Rhydygath buns and Welsh cakes. After their departure Mr S., Enid, Jack and I sailed with a cargo of slates and timber in the good old *Foxtrot*, arriving almost at dusk, to be greeted by Charles at the landing steps, and a thousand puffins on their evening parade. Mr S. was marvellous, he laid half the loft floorboards while I tried to cover him above, laying the slates. Enid cooked our meals and planted the garden.

3 June, 1928
Alone in the Hut

Dear Do,

By now you will have heard all the news. I was very sad you could not come, only comfortless cabbages!

Papa was not too keen to return on Sunday, and kept putting it off, taking a bathe with us in S. Haven, but at last we sailed on the 3 pm tide, just Mr S., Jack and self. Enid remained behind with Charles. Your Mama, Vi and the children were waving excitedly from the Deer Park as we came through Jack Sound. The rest of the slates and sawn timber arrive tomorrow, so we shall try and sail at noon.

We have had two visitors lately: one, the local blacksmith, on his arrival to shoe the poor old lighthouse donkey. The wily blacksmith makes a point of coming only when the gulls are laying! But he should come more often for the poor donkey's hooves grow so long, the poor patient beast can hardly walk by the time shoeing comes. I think it is very cruel; but it seems that for many a long year the blacksmith has enjoyed this paid contract to shoe the donkey every twelve months. On this annual visit he saws off each hoof, with the old shoe (hardly worn) all in one piece. He sells these pieces as 'donkey hoof door knockers!' I've seen them hanging in his forge at Marloes, a shed so thickly painted with an annual coating of tar it is a wonder it does not catch fire! I can't help liking this Fleming-faced fellow, always greets you with a smile and a leg-pull . . .

The other visitor who came in the fishing boat was Tommy Reynolds, sometime taxi driver and our 'hut' site owner. He came to gather gulls eggs, but also, he told me later, out of curiosity to see what was going on!

Thank you for all the plants you sent, much appreciated by man and rabbit. A little wild bunny has somehow squeezed into the garden, but was snared by Charles last night so peace and weeds now reign supreme.

You see I am superlatively lucky in the way my life is developing, better than I dreamed it would. I can't believe my good fortune in the choice of a future wife, helpful loving sister, the wreck and not forgetting my faithful, clever sea-mate Jack. I could not have managed without him.

Love and kisses,
your repentant R.

Turtle-doves here everyday, quite tame after their long migration; we throw them bread crumbs and grain and they usually fly away at dusk.

At Tyr Bont *all alone*
31 May, 1928

Dear *Ronnie*, (Because I am cross and jealous)

I gave up calling you Ronnie because you said you disliked it so much. You might give up calling me Doris, knowing how I hate that name. In future all letters addressed to Doris will not be answered because I hate the name.

Since you were so *very* pressing in your invitation to me to come down with the others to the island I am naturally remaining at home! I hate to think that you might *waste* your precious time on me, and to be truthful I think my time was too precious to waste on you . . .

I don't think I had better write to you today, I am in a frenzy of jealousy and feeling quite vicious to think of the others going down and not me.

Maybe I shall tear this letter up when my rage subsides. Meanwhile I've been re-reading your recent letters to discover the unanswered questions you complain about . . . I can't find any . . . My hens are not laying well at present, too many broodies. With all your skill perhaps my hens will behave better on the island. Perhaps we could feed them on pickled gulls eggs from the *A.W.* chest?

Sorry to report that I have only 16 chickens at present, 11 are late-hatched and two of these are undoubtedly cockerels.

Please do *not* buy any more furniture for the house. I have already lots of stuff here and people are giving us more, or promising to. I can't stop them, they only laugh when I say we are not having presents! A kitchen stove is the most important thing at the moment.

I hope Enid will not buy any things for the house? Please do not deprive me of the pleasure of getting what I, as your wife, consider absolutely necessary. Of course clothes are our personal affair, but may I remind you that you did promise that you would marry me if necessary in your old breeches—and if it were not for the probability that the rector would turn me out of the church if I wore mine I might do so too. Mama thinks I must be wed in a white hat! How ridiculous! I only have one hat! I must go and feed the fowls, bother them! I don't feel in the least like sending you love and kisses today.

Goodbye. Your ill-tempered D.

P.S. I'm sending you some young greens for planting out, but they are special varieties NOT to be planted in the big rabbit garden, please. They are supposed to be very hardy, and ought to last through winter when we may be reduced to living on seabeet and seaweed.

How I long to see all the thrift and bluebells and the squill!

Life is cruel—

Nevertheless, ever yours. D.E.S.

Tyr Bont, St Mellons
1 June, 1928

Dear old Ron,

I shouldn't have posted that beastly letter yesterday. Not only was I lonely for you, but I had time to reflect on how terribly selfish I was to burden you with a wife just at the start of your new career, bringing you worries and financial problems. But I do so want to come and share everything—good or bad—with you, and I will try to be most awfully economical. I had qualms earlier, but when you wrote about the old man who kept a wife and 9 children on eleven shillings a week I thought to myself—Hang it all, if he can do so, surely we can manage to scrape up eleven shillings a week living even more simply on island food—supposing the chinchillas are not a financial success?

I would not have minded having a corrugated roof, if you really found that more economical. A turf roof like the Scandinavians would be more in keeping, green and starred with wild flowers. We should experiment, cost nothing but the labour.

Saturday night

Nice surprise to have a letter this morning. I thought when none came yesterday you were either too cross with me or too busy to write, and I would have to wait for Mama and Papa to return. About a wedding ring, let me know if you prefer thin gold or thick gold, or silver. Our Cardiff jeweller tells me he can get a ring made from old gold or silver, mined in Wales.

I have collected more dandelion seed, and stored it in a cold frame.

Everyone is trying to push me into having ceremonies and wedding clothes, and I absolutely refuse. Such gladrags won't be an atom of use to me afterwards unless to pawn, if we run short of cash. However I am sure you will appreciate a large fruity wedding cake, with your notorious sweet tooth?

Midnight again, so sweet dreams to you and a gentle repentant x.

Personal

In bed early, I am tired, lonely, lazy and got the megrims or monthly vapours (polite term for what we ladies call the curse—familiar to you, you once told me, because you had four sisters suffering the unwelcome unmentionable monthly phenomenon.) I don't know quite why I mention the unmentionable, but I am in a low mood and you should remember that it was the jealous Lord God of genesis who put this curse on women to punish her because 'she ate from the Tree of Knowledge'.

Forgive this late night scribble, inspired as the result of eating my lone bread and cheese supper in bed with a large glass of sherry to cheer me up . . . What a Jealous, Callous Lord God He was, give me Buddha every time! And if I have to obey the Lord's Genesis (chap 3) decree I am to be subservient, ruled over by my husband! Take warning Sir, that I shall not utter the OBEY phrase in the present Prayer Book ritual. Like the whimsical house you are rebuilding on our Island, you must accept me with all my faults, and love me for them . . . Tonight I drink to our happiness despite all hazards. A second draught of sherry. Goodnight, or I'll be drunk . . . ?

Tyr Bont,
5 June, 1928

Dear Ronald,

The expedition arrived back home yesterday. Everyone says how fit you look. Work evidently agrees with you. Papa says the Island is exceptionally beautiful just now, with acres of wild flowers. And storm petrels are flighting about the house each night, and one pair trying to nest in the walls. How jealous I am of Enid being there.

I don't know why I am writing to you again, as I have absolutely nothing fresh to say, unless to congratulate you on the progress Papa reports. Wish now I had not posted that silly letter ending in lofty God talk! Do tear it up. I am feeling 100% now. Minnie and I went to the cinema last evening. I was determined to drown my futile sorrows in riotous enjoyment—we ate a whole box of chocolates between us. Extravagance!

We are all going to the theatre on Friday to see *The Devil's Disciple.* Do you know it—one of Shaw's more agreeable plays? By all, I mean Vi and Martin are here, with the children. Incidentally Mary told me you took her in the *S.P.* for a sail in Martynshaven which she did not altogether enjoy. Also she says, with a great air of importance, that I should not feed my rabbits crushed oats, as you give yours 'proper whole oats'! How does she know?

Today Mama took Vi and Mary shopping, leaving me with young Brian, who loves messing about in the garden and feeding rabbits and chickens, and made me walk to the river. The shoppers came back with some useful catalogues. I am sending you one about kitchen stoves. I have marked one for you—a 36in. stove which costs £5.19.6d, which is the cheapest . . .

Papa thinks we should have a side boiler with tap, a bit tricky if you forget to fill it—it may crack when it runs dry? RSVP about this, please. I am all for simplicity. I shan't mind having to fetch water by bucket from the well—a nice break from house-work and a chance to look at birds.

Papa says you have made Enid very comfortable in the little bedroom. He is hoping to come down any day soon, in order to finish off the loft floor. But I very much doubt that he will!

Mama says we must have hair mattresses, which never lose their shape in seaside places. Mama says to buy new ones to your measurements. Papa says he has found some old ones in the lumber room-workshop at his dentist rooms which might do for the cots in the Wheelhouse. But I've seen them and really they're quite mouldy, and hardly worth the trouble of removing!

Bad news! It looks as if there are going to be two extra people at the wedding. My first cousin Kathleen writes that she wants to come, if she can get away. She has music exams in July. She is like a sister to me so I simply could not say NO. Mama, of course, couldn't say NO to *her* sisters! What does one say to all these good people? I'm just as miserable as you are over the whole business.

Perhaps I should not have said the thought of being married makes me miserable, but it is true—and only the thought of the glorious afterwards gives me the nerve to endure the actual ceremony. How cowardly!

Ever so much love from Do.

Ronald's diary:

Tuesday, 5 June

Finished roof except for space for skylight. The blackbird, whose nest we had to remove from the roofless room when enlarging it to become one kitchen, sings from the peak of the house, his favourite perch at dawn and dusk. How sweet to hear a woodland bird on our naked Island! There are two pairs, the other in Boar's Bay; at least five pairs of dunnocks are scattered over the eastern side, each holding nesting and singing territory where there is some cover.

June 8th. Enid and I ashore early, caught bus to H'west and got hair cut and shopped for stores.

9th. Too stormy to cross so we went to see Miss Bland and her Dale Fort zoo. I bought two goats for 1 pound, and we walked back with a nanny in milk and her billy kid. We named him 'Rufus' for his colour.

12-16 June

Finished relaying the floor of Enid's little bedroom, using pine-deck planking from the *A.W.* Today started to concrete the kitchen floor with cement and North Haven sand tinted with Venetian red powder over a rough base of clinkers, coarse sand and cement. The clinkers and cinder ash came from the ancient farm midden in the fold behind the Wheelhouse, sifted to remove the relics of many island feasts: limpet and winkle shells, bones, crockery sherds, broken metal (chiefly rusted traps and hand-made nails) pebbles and stones. Fixing gateway to rabbit garden.

Enid and Charles spend much time planting out rabbit greens in the rabbit-garden. Still a few marauding rabbits nocturnally nibbling these from undiscovered hidy-holes, but we have now I hope stopped up the last of these.

Saturday, 16 June

Put beading around the edges of loft floor, and sundry other jobs, including a stock check on the breeding does and bucks, a brief bathe with Enid in South Haven. Weather recently deteriorated, cloudy with mist but not enough rain to save us watering gardens.

Many local fishermen lost more than half their lobster pots in the great storm last Sat (9th) according to the wireless news at the Lighthouse.

Sunday, 17 June

Got the boat down and tinkered with the engine, but in spite of the reconditioned magneto (cost £3.10.0d) it behaved erratically. After lunch we sailed grandly up to Martynshaven, and were delightfully surprised to see Mr and Mrs Shellard waving from the cliff, impatient to meet us. They had been down yesterday and tried to signal the Island with a mirror as a heliograph! But not enough sun for the purpose!

After tea in the Hut they drove back to Rhydygath, dropping Enid and I at St Bride's to see the rector and finalise marriage plans. Enid and I enjoyed a leisurely walk back to the Hut, calling to chat with the Codd folk at Hook.

18-22 June

Rainy, but enough wind to sail most of the way home in the

morning, carrying the skylight and a lawn mower—the latter to serve the double purpose of cutting the 'lawn' approach to the house and providing rabbit feed. Spent afternoon putting ridging on the house roof, now completely slated. Put in skylight. Patched up living room floor with old flotsam from wreck—this is a 'patch-on-patch' affair, as I do not intend to start afresh on this job.

Part 10

June 1928

Preparing for a wedding

Guillemots

Martynshaven
22 June, 1928

Dearest Bride,

A whole eleven days passed with only one visit ashore, the time flew like magic. I was so busy (or dreamy) I wrote July instead of June in my diary. I think all the time of July 12th!

I have been painting the Hut green and now its suddenly pouring rain, to ruin my lovely paint! What the result will be I'll tell you later. Just now Enid and I are imbibing tea, and I am reading to her selected bits from your letters. Thank you, make the next longer please! I love you more than ever—if that is possible.

I agree with all you say about living simply, and happily, on island and sea produce—if the chinchilla scheme fails by some marketing problem.

About the extra people who want to come to the wedding, I decided I must go at once to H'west and get measured at the tailors for a top hat and tails, if the wedding is to be so fashionable. You of course will look angelic in a flowered hat and snow white lace train and I shall look like a lump of burnt brick! Whose wedding is this anyway? Not strictly ours by the way it's heading!

No, dear lady, I don't want all your Aunts and Uncles please! You would hate to have all mine. Naturally my sisters are welcome, so please let us stick to St Bride's, it is all arranged now, no need for entertaining afterwards. No wedding breakfast or cakc, just you and me sailing away alone, straight from the church. Mother I know will be happy as long as it is in a church, and she can stay with friends at Milford.

Yes, the storm petrels will be in residence when you come. They are the latest to arrive—at the end of April, and stay as late as October. Their single egg is not laid until this month, so we have seen no chicks yet. I think I told you that at least two pairs were attempting to return to nest in the house-walls: regretfully we had to banish them in plastering up their nesting crannies.

The stove you sent particulars of seems suitable, as it is in one piece, thus saving trouble fitting it in place, I hope. But I am not an expert in the cooking department. At Trehill the culm fire had a large built-in firebox with a roomy oven for baking on the R.H.side, and a boiler holding about four gallons of water on the left side, with a tap. As I think I said, the fire is never allowed to go out. At night it is made up by raking down the ashes of the day's fuel, and building up again with balls of culm. The kitchen poker is then plunged down to the bottom grating, to create a draught hole which keeps a bluish flame burning all night; this is called 'stumming' and needs a practised hand. It is for you to decide. At present I use the Valour Perfection two-burner oil stove with its movable oven top. Enid says it is too flimsy as a permanent cooker, but at least I have learnt how to bake a few loaves on it.

There is plenty of anthracite in Pembrokeshire, mined along the banks of the tidal Cleddau River above Milford Haven. Jack says the *Alice Williams* may have been used to ferry cargoes of anthracite between Pembs. and Ireland, but whether *A.W.* coal could be mixed with the island clay to make culm is a matter of experiment —we might try next winter? This wreck coal burns very well, but unfortunately is very sooty.

At least we are really well off for fuel, what with coal, jetsam firewood, and possible peat.*

I am trying to finish this letter to post to you this morning, as we plan to return to the island early. But I have begun to be doubtful— a gale appears to be brewing.

The very last job on the house will be to finish plastering the interior wall of the living room, enlarged as per your request by removing the dilapidated wooden partition of the entry room. The floor rather defeats me at present, it's such a conglomeration of rotten timber, half-buried red flagstones and the small exuviae of centuries of previous inhabitants, possibly going back to its first Norman owners, whose vassals reaped for them the harvest of rabbits sea-birds and fish? You and I will one day work out that fascinating story, I hope.

Each morning when I wake I want to sing with happiness as, rested and ready for action, I count myself once more the luckiest man I know, so extraordinarily fortunate in realising my dream, our

* [Skokholm peat turned out to be of poor quality and gave little heat.]

dream, to do well together on the beautiful Island set in the silver sea.

I send all my love to you—you, the perfect Island mate for your sentiently, imperfect but faithful husband-to-be.

R.M.L.

Tyr Bont
19 June, 1928

Papa was disappointed not to get to Skokholm on Saturday. His fault for not sending a signal via the coastguard at St Anne's Head, instead of trying the heliograph! So much for his wanted ambition to get across to complete the carpentry he started. However, they were delighted to see you sailing into Martynshaven on Sunday, and with what splendid result! No more nonsense when Mama was told you were unshakably determined that we be married at St Bride's, she approves that charming Haven, and has arranged to have the banns called for us at St Mellons church as well as St Bride's on June 24, July 1 and 8 ! ! !

Hurrah! it seems we have each saved two guineas or so on registration fees, which will perhaps help towards paying the 10 pounds I have just spent on hair mattresses, to be precise £9.11.6d. The man in the Cardiff shop said we could have three for 10% less if we paid cash, so I did, just in time before Mama took out her cheque book! She has caught the wedding fever in a big way!

This is just to get a letter to you right away, with Mama champing at the bit to go shopping again. She now says that I have nothing to get married in, so beware!

You can't think how my heart has gone sky high and all my troubles are vanishing, now our dreams are coming true.

Ever so much love,

Do.

[Undated]

. . . I am feeling on top of the world . . . ecstatic . . . Here it is a marvellous night, still quite luminous although it must be all of eleven o'clock as I write. The sky is a great blue dome fading away to a greenish hue at the horizon below darker banks of cloud. How glorious it must be on the 'Mountain' just at this moment! And how I wish I was there with you, just you and me under the darkening sky and all around vast ocean, no sounds except the music of the birds and the surf. Sometimes the world can seem so beautiful that I just want to weep. I am never sure quite why—it must be pure sentimentality!

How I used to glory in being alone. Now I have someone - YOU—to share the glorious moments with me I feel that everything in future is going to be beautiful and that I will always be good and kind. But I know I should never keep such serenity and goodness up at such a pitch—even on a beautiful island. Something always brings me down from the clouds like a pricked balloon, and I remember the mean sort of creature I am, often catty and cross about something. I wonder why you ever came to propose marriage to such an ordinary woman like me—against all rhyme and reason!

Today I am brought to earth with a decided bump! I have an appointment with Papa, who says I must go to the dentist (not himself, but his partner!) to have a check before leaving civilization!

Later I had a bad tooth out, and was told casually that anyway I had too many teeth crowding my jaw—at my great age!

About the stove for the island kitchen. I hope you kept the leaflet I sent you. I find there is an agent in H'west who supplies Express ranges, and can deliver to Martynshaven.

Thank Enid for her cheerful, practical letter. She says Charles is a great cake maker, as well as eater. I am glad for I've made three sponge cakes lately all as flat as pancakes.

Enid says the rabbit garden looks nice now it is properly fenced, the chicory showing its handsome blue flowers. Difficult to associate Skokholm with wire-netting fences—doesn't seem to fit in somehow?

I must get this posted and tackle the garden weeds, as another prospective buyer is expected tomorrow,

Ever so much love from D.

P.S. I have only one worry—supposing storms prevent you crossing to St Bride's on July 12th?!

Skokholm
24 June, 1928

Dearest Lady,

It's another glorious Sunday, as most Sundays seem to be lately. We had a bathe, then freed the new billy, Rufus, keeping Matilda locked up to prevent her milk being suckled. Checked on the breeding does in the hutches. It was just right for a little excursion, so at 2.30, all of us, Enid and I, Jack and Charles, and two light-housemen, embarked on the last of the north stream on a faint breeze from the SW, sailed around the Stack and across to the Mewstone, tall and southernmost point of Skomer. There cormorants were nesting, with pockets of guillemots and razorbills. Then around the cliffs to enter the deep fiord of the Wick. It was a marvellous sight with myriads of kittiwakes on the lowest footholds, so low it's a wonder they are not washed away by the waves. Above them the ledges packed by groaning guillemots, razorbills here and there in separate niches, and gulls soaring above on the off-chance of snatching an unguarded egg or chick—I never tire of going there.

On the other side of this huge cleft, the cliff slopes gently, and in this fine weather you can jump ashore there at low tide and scramble along the rocks to a bouldery beach strewn with tons of accumulated driftwood, including useful-looking planks, and miscellaneous jetsam. Jack says it has been a never-failing hoard for repair work; since whatever is washed in is never washed out again, the shape of the beach under the overhanging cliff is protected from any winds blowing this jetsam back to sea. I can see we will never be short of planks and firewood in future . . . There was not a human soul in sight on this sloping height, only a couple of seals we surprised basking on the low-water reefs.

And so back direct to Mad Bay, on the favourable tide, through the curling South Stream under the lighthouse, and home to South Haven via the southern cliffs. It was a day of calm and happy exploration which I owed my hard working sister, soon to go home.

All my love,

Ronald.

Friday, 7 July, 1928

Dear Do,

Not much time to write. The week has flown, everyone busy in trying to get the house in something like habitable order. The *Storm Petrel* has been hauled to the winch, her bruises and bumps repaired by Jack, and smoothed over with two coats of new white paint in good time to dry for the 12th. Enid deserves our best thanks for her energy and skill in cleaning, washing and mending everything she can lay her hands on, between feeding us like fighting cocks.

The weather having become uncertain, we left Charles in charge and came ashore after tea yesterday, a brisk SW breeze blowing us easily to Martynshaven. We had had a signal from St Anne's coastguard that your goods would be at H'west station early today!

What huge excitement! I got Tommy Reynolds to take us to H'west to buy the wedding ring, stores and meet Mother off the London express. Sent her and Enid to Martynshaven by the Reynolds taxi. Having procured a lorry I then proceeded to load up all your goods and chattels, the chickens and the 12 chinchillas, and accompanied this precious cargo to Martynshaven, where all was duly and carefully unloaded, the articles marked by you KEEP DRY stored in the Hut, and the rest outside.

Thank you thoughtful bride, for the great care you have obviously taken with packing everything so well. And thank Papa for sending down his bicycle—it will be useful for riding up to the village.

Goodnight, dearest. It's twilight dark, too late to do more than eat late supper. Mother seems happy, but also very tired; she will sleep in one bunk, Enid in the other, and I on the floor! . . .

Shall post this last letter tomorrow, when Mother and Enid will go to Milford Haven to stay until after the wedding.

Ever and ever your R. x x x

Tyr Bont
30 June, 1928

Dear Ronald,

This may be the last letter. I've reams of questions to ask, and little time to reply:

1. Hope you aren't annoyed about the mattresses? They have just come and are jolly comfortable—so they ought to be, did I hear you groan? After all isn't it important that we be comfortable for the rest of our island nights?

2. I am cancelling the express stove we had reserved with the Cardiff firm, so you are free to obtain one like the Codds. Papa wants to pay for this, take note—another wedding present.

3. Do you know of a regular lorry that comes to Cardiff from H'west or Milford with stuff and could return with my goods and chattels?

4. How many chickens shall we need?

5. Mama and Papa have offered the wardrobe in my bedroom, but Papa has doubts about getting it up the steps to the loft. It can be taken apart in three sections. Anyway I shall send it down, as although it's not very handsome or an antique, I have grown fond of it . . .

I can't remember the other questions, so they can hardly be very urgent. But what is important is posting this letter to you now. I have been paraffining the poultry house perches, and the apple trees. The latter have woolly aphis badly, it's a horrid job because you have to hold the brush above your head to reach the top branches and the paraffin runs down your arms. The stink of it lingers, you can probably smell it on this letter—hardly the lavender scented love-letter?

I seem to be collecting an awful lot of presents. It is quite useless to protest because people just take no notice at all. Vi and Martin have given us a perfectly splendid dinner set, your Mother a canteen of silver, we have quilted eiderdowns for our beds. But are you really interested? I don't believe men really are. Mama is keeping a list of who is sending what, we shall have to write thankyou letters . . .

I have given much thought lately to the nuts and bolts of practical living at Skokholm, trying—as Vi told me—'not to over-romanticise the glamour!'

I spent 7 pounds on what nobody has thought about—a mangle, wash tub and washing dolly. You can't say I am not thoroughly practical, neither is it glamorous!

All is ferment here. Papa has found a house which he is going to buy on the sea-front at Penarth once Tyr Bont is sold. I have for ages been trying to get estimates for transport of our goods to Martynshaven.

I would like to bring something for Jack and Charles. Can you suggest something appropriate? Papa suggests a fishing rod for Charles and tobacco for Jack, but I'd like to give Jack something a bit more permanent.

Au revoir, I must rush this to catch the post,

For ever Do.

2 July, 1928

Dear Ronald,

I'm sending everything by rail after all! It is about half the cost of a lorry. You will have to engage transport to Martynshaven. But I do apologise for the delay, and trouble. They will arrive on Friday the 6th, by overnight goods train, reaching Haverfordwest by midday: the livestock an hour later by express passenger train. I will send a signal via St Anne's as I'm afraid this may mean you coming ashore at short notice, but it will do you good to rest a while after your prodigious house building!

Papa is restoring an old oak chest for us which he found in an old granary. Vi has given us a medicine chest!

Ronald's diary:

Tuesday, 19 June

Puffins are hatched. Razorbills and Guillemots also, their lively downy chicks making shrill calls from the ledges. The sprats and immature fishes which now swarm inshore at every flood tide are in great demand by all three auks, as well as kittiwakes, which don't nest here but seem to perch occasionally on the Stack—Patching living room floor. A fresh sou'wester blew up as I need to go to H'west, we left Charles in command and went ashore at 8pm and flew with the wind and tide to Martynshaven for the night.

22 June

Missed the bus. Got Tommy Reynolds to take Enid and I to H'west and Dale for 10s. Tried out clothes at the tailor's, and did some shopping for the house—ironmongery for doors and windows. Tommy collected us at 3 pm for Dale Fort, where Miss Bland had 13 chinchillas at 8s 6d each ready for me, fine well-grown pedigree ones and I am glad to have them. Settled down to letters and supper in the hut.

Saturday, 23 June

Good old Jack turned up at 8 and the three of us continued painting inside and outside the Hut, before rowing and sailing with the tide back to the beloved Island by noon. Carried on with the floor.

7 July

Took half the furniture and livestock in the *Foxtrot*. One hen suffocated and younger chickens very seedy from the long journey.

9 July

Painting woodwork and beams with solignum. Fetched another load of furniture—another headwind—sailing up and rowing back with bulky load.

10 July

Painting and carpentry. Jack whitewashed all outside walls. Skokholm settlement now all picked out in white as seen from the mainland. Weather uncertain—went ashore.

11 July

Fixing motor and finally got it going very well. All day I have been at fever pitch of excitement, and some nervousness. But that fire has died down, and I am relaxed, muscles tired but mind alert and far from sleep. The great adventure of sharing my life intimately with the woman I love deeply begins in another half day, and I feel quite shy and unready for this fusion of two souls—and two bodies?

Part 11
July 12th, 1928
To inlets and islands, together

'Tir Na n-Og'

Left to right: Mrs. S, Do, Ronald, Vicar, Mrs. L, Mr L. Seated: Vi, Mary, Enid, Kathleen, Mr. S.

Ronald's diary:

12 July, 1928—THURSDAY [underlined!]

A year ago Doris and I discovered our love for each other—a day of sunshine and happiness and heartache—the 12th of July 1927. We then agreed to marry on the 12th July 1928. It all came to pass today, when we were married at 12 noon in St Bride's church. There was sunshine and happiness, but no heartache today. Jack and I left Martynshaven at 11am and sailed and motored to St Bride's. The marriage ceremony was over by 1.30 pm. Mother, Dad and Enid were present of my people; on Do's side her parents, Vi, Mary and cousin Kathleen Carter. We dallied over a picnic lunch beside the limekiln in St Bride's Haven. Then Do and I sailed alone for Martynshaven, where we were met by the same guests who had laid on a wedding tea during our sail of an hour or more along the cliffs, seeing seals and sea-birds.

After tea we three (Do, Jack and I) sailed for the island as mist crept in. I had long promised Do we would have a honeymoon among the inlets and islands hereabouts . . .

13 July

Beautiful weather, Do and I walked round the island. Then set out alone for Milford Haven and had a glorious sail up to Castle Reach, where we slept in a wood and listened to a nightjar reeling.

14 July

Ran aground at Landshipping—left the boat on the mud and had bread and cheese at an inn. Cruised back to Skokholm by motor—pausing to admire a regatta at Pembroke Dock and get petrol.

Monday, 16 July

Northerly wind, decided to go to Grassholm—a good tide took us there in less than 2 hours. The gannetry was a marvellous sight, young birds in all stages from day old to half size and a few with darker neck feathers. A party had been there recently and ringed a number of nestlings. Saw kittiwakes, razorbills, blackbacks and herring gulls, one or two puffins and a pair of oystercatchers. The seals sang mournful sea shanties as the sea rose and washed them gradually from their resting places. Slept the night in the long grass on the eastern slopes- no petrels or shearwaters to disturb us!

17 July

Crossed over to Ramsey Island at high water so as to enter Ramsey Sound at slack tide. The farm is run by a Mrs Lewis and her son; she was most distressed because said son had gone ashore and had not returned. Later on we took her across the tide race to Porth Stinan and St Davids to find him. On our return at high water we had to fight against this remarkable tide sluice to get in to Ramsey North Haven. Slept in the heather.

18 July

Explored Ramsey thoroughly. Saw a golden eagle—which might be the one lost from Skomer two years ago? Buzzards, merlin, kestrels, nightjar—lots of land birds not breeding on Skokholm. No puffins or petrels. Many white rabbits.

19 July

Said goodbye to Mrs Lewis and her thriftless, shiftless son. Visited the Bishops far out in St Bride's Bay and were given a warm welcome and a meal at the South Bishop Lighthouse and in return took their mail to post. Home to Martynshaven in order to buy stores for our hard working Jack and Charles.

PART 12

Corollary

Shag

All through summer I love to walk in the quiet of evening, slowly and savouring the scented hushed air of that hour when the sea breeze usually dies and a gentle land wind invades the island. My lone stroll is through the old and new gardens to South Haven, to say good night to the boat and await the arrival of the first storm petrels. Such peace of mind and pleasure in walking through the rows of planted vegetables and small shrubs, to pull a weed, and always in the expectation of flushing some newly arrived migrant.

All is utterly calm, the *Storm Petrel* at ease on the mooring ropes. Maybe a day when we should have gone ashore, but we did not.

At dusk the storm petrels in their crannies have begun purring up and down the walls. The garrulous jumble song of the cock sedge warbler comes spasmodically but increasingly from the tall water-dropwort just below the wall, I have come to love listening to the varied repertoire of this our island nightingale. It bubbles forth at every other sound nearby. Presently the witch-like sound of incoming shearwaters will stir and then drown the piping of the oystercatchers in the home meadow. All these sounds around me just now, each has a significance, could we but interpret them right. Some inflexions of bird voices tell me plainly of their moods—of contentment, feeding and keeping in touch with companions, sharper notes of alarm and hostility, crooning and purring sounds as signs of love, and the continuous cackle of ecstasy of gulls during copulation.

I have woken very early, happy to walk over the whole island by starlight or the moon, the shearwaters less noisy on such clear nights. Indeed they cease calling and melt away almost without my noticing them.

I suppose I have been a loner most of my inner life, with a secret sustaining pleasure in studying nature, and recording my observations in notebooks and diaries, which I still hoard, going back ten years. I am apt to rush into adventures unprepared and untrained—like this chinchilla scheme.

Each visit to the mainland for me is a reality of returning—an abrupt waking—to a different world of commerce, money, worldly strife. But we hurry home to resume the dream. Life now is essentially the stuff that my boyhood dreams were built on, the mainland is an alien place, full of dull care, and the destructive folly of money-grabbing men . . . this dream island, Do shall paint, and we shall study together its manifold wildlife; there is so much to learn, how do birds navigate, how do puffin, shearwater and rabbit share their burrow systems? Just some of the mysteries we shall, I hope, solve between us in the years to come.

So preoccupied are my thoughts; suddenly I find the day birds in chorus, larks, curlews, lapwings, wheatears, and the gulls protesting and mobbing me as I cross the bog at sunrise. Presently the clang of *Alice Williams's* fog-bell, which summons us to meals.

Before I go to breakfast I enter the house, to open the new casement windows of the living room; these truly look out over the foam of perilous seas of fairy lands forlorn. On this glorious sunlit day there will be no need to shut them again, until my wife does so this evening!

R. M. L.

Afterword

How true were my uncle Ken's premonitions about the chinchilla rabbit trade, and the difficulty of breeding them on Skokholm. Trapping, ferreting and netting left a substantial minority of wild rabbits alive. In the 1930's depression the market for skins and rabbits slumped. Myxomatosis failed to reduce numbers due to the absence of the rabbit flea as vector. In the winter of 1938 the Universities Federation for Animal Welfare offered to make the island rabbit population a subject to demonstrate humane rabbit control, using calcium cyanide dust. It was almost completely successful, the vegetation grew luxuriantly the following summer, but a few rabbits remained in the cliffs and boulders where it was difficult to gas them, and war interrupted the programme. Today the rabbits are as numerous as ever.

By 1934 we were no longer spending all our winters on Skokholm, Father had started ringing birds and writing books and articles. More and more naturalists wanted to visit, as the island was becoming well known as a unique bird observatory. Although we only took ten or a dozen visitors at a time during the season, my mother had to provide food for their prodigious island appetites with the most primitive cooking facilities. Father revelled in sharing the island, and exchanging knowledge with other naturalists. I can picture him now, over breakfast in the wheelhouse, discussing the plans for the day from the head of the long refectory table! With maturity, and in retrospect, I know my mother was foolish not to insist on modernising her kitchen and getting more assistance, to take the drudgery out of catering on that scale. She would have much preferred to have the island to herself at any cost, being totally fearless of the sea, she was undaunted by winter sailing or the prospect of subsistance living. We did not return to live on Skokholm after the war, except to hand over the lease, to the Dyfed Wild Life Trust (formerly the West Wales Naturalist Trust) of which my father was the founder in 1938. Because the island had been commandeered by the War Office for the duration, we went farming in North Pembrokeshire (described in *Inland Farm* and *The Island Farmers*—Witherby).

In 1953 I emigrated to New Zealand, my mother followed in 1961, and her travels inspired her to take up painting again. She finally settled in a cottage close to the farm where I live with my husband. She died in 1989.

Meanwhile Father was frequently free to indulge his passion for island-going and writing books. Many moves later, in 1971, he came to live in Auckland with his third wife. From the windows of the house there is a grand view of the sea and the islands of the Hauraki Gulf. Beyond the garden there is a nature reserve Father was instrumental in establishing; it teems with birds feeding among the scrub and wetlands there, 'a unique wilderness in the city'. Recently, aged ninety, he has retired to a rest-home in rural Bay of Plenty.

Ann Mark

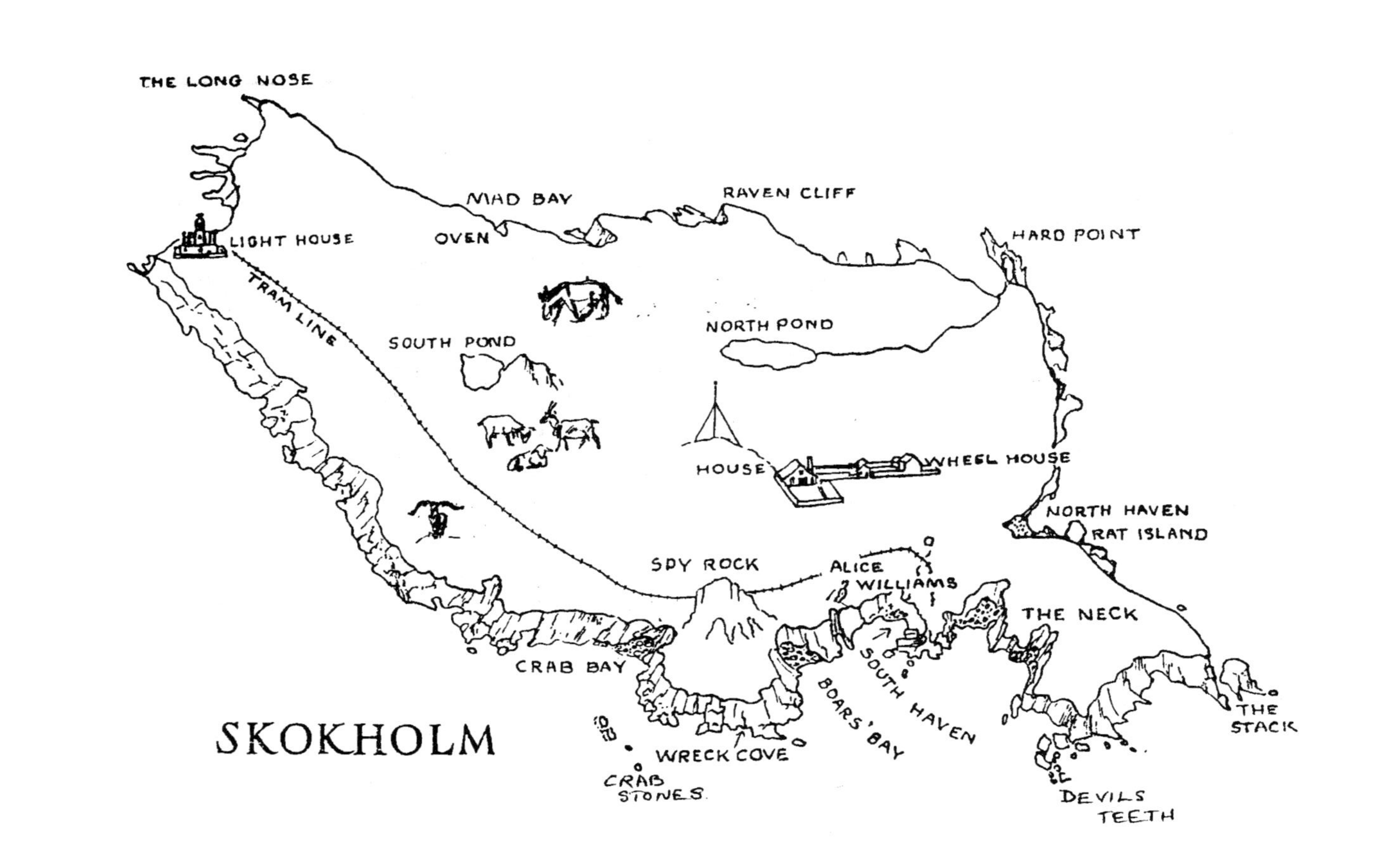
THE LONG NOSE
MAD BAY
RAVEN CLIFF
HARD POINT
LIGHT HOUSE
OVEN
TRAM LINE
NORTH POND
SOUTH POND
HOUSE
WHEEL HOUSE
NORTH HAVEN
RAT ISLAND
SPY ROCK
ALICE
WILLIAMS
THE NECK
CRAB BAY
SOUTH HAVEN
BOARS' BAY
THE
STACK
WRECK COVE
CRAB
STONES
DEVILS
TEETH

SKOKHOLM

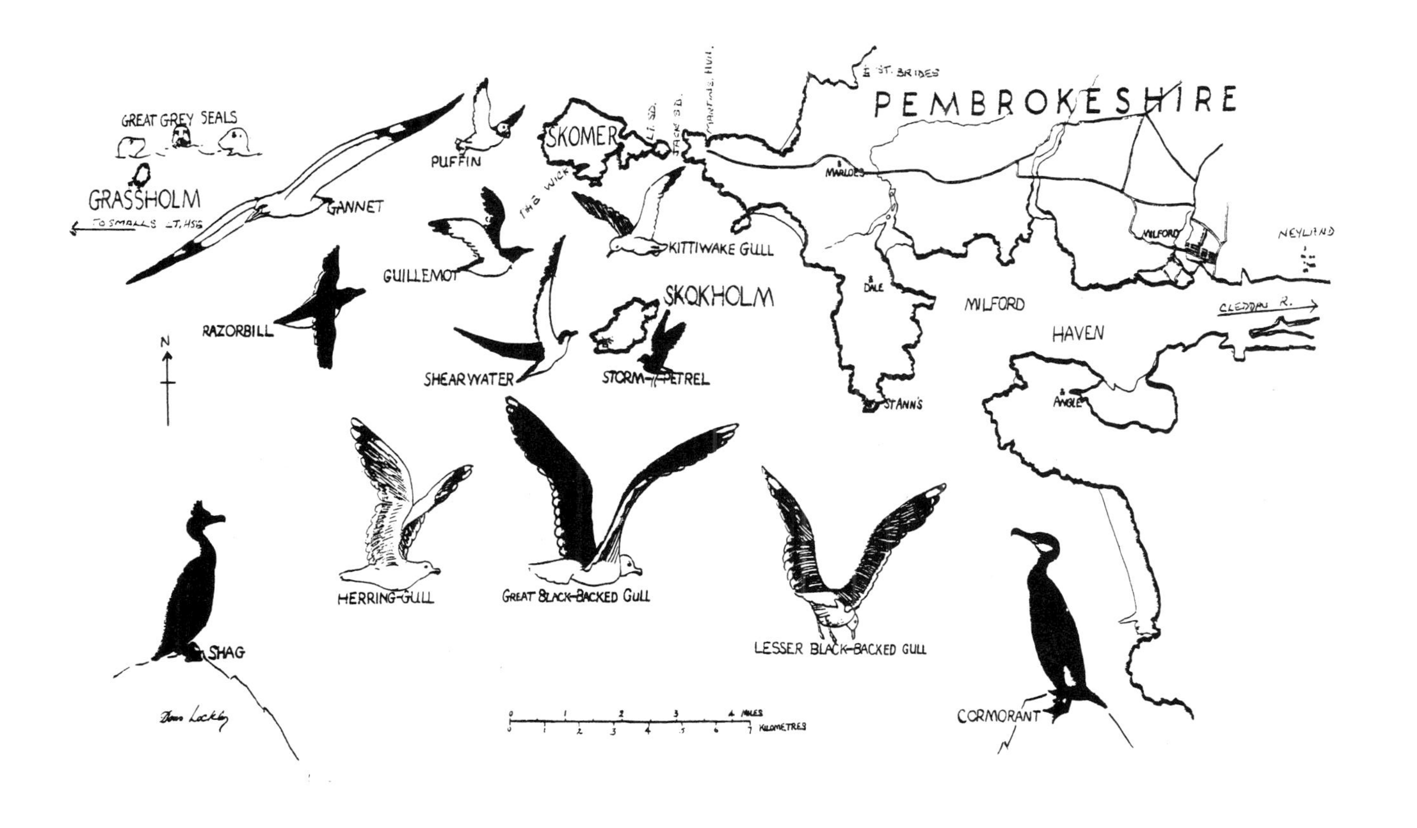
PEMBROKESHIRE
ST. BRIDES
GREAT GREY SEALS
GRASSHOLM
TO SMALLS LT. HSE
GANNET
PUFFIN
SKOMER
THE WICK
KITTIWAKE GULL
MARLOES
MILFORD
NEYLAND
CLEDDAU R.
GUILLEMOT
RAZORBILL
SKOKHOLM
DALE
MILFORD
HAVEN
ANGLE
ST ANN'S
SHEARWATER
STORM-PETREL
N
HERRING-GULL
GREAT BLACK-BACKED GULL
LESSER BLACK-BACKED GULL
SHAG
CORMORANT
0 1 2 3 4 MILES
0 1 2 3 4 5 6 7 KILOMETRES